WOMEN OF COLOR AND PHILOSOPHY

To present and future philosophers who are "women of color"

WOMEN OF COLOR AND PHILOSOPHY

A CRITICAL READER

EDITED BY
NAOMI ZACK

BLACKWELL
Publishers

Copyright © Blackwell Publishers Ltd 2000 except for chapter 1 (copyright © Joy James and University of Minnesota Press 1996); chapter 2 (copyright © Ofelia Schutte and Indiana University Press 1998); chapter 4 (copyright © Adrian M. S. Piper 2000); chapter 5 (copyright © Angela Y. Davis 1998); and chapter 10 (copyright © Linda Martín Alcoff 2000). Chapter 12 and editorial introduction copyright © Naomi Zack 2000.

First published 2000

2 4 6 8 10 9 7 5 3 1

Blackwell Publishers Inc.
350 Main Street
Malden, Massachusetts 02148
USA

Blackwell Publishers Ltd
108 Cowley Road
Oxford OX4 1JF
UK

Library of Congress Cataloging-in-Publication Data
Women of color and philosophy : a critical reader / edited by Naomi Zack.
    p. cm.
  Includes bibliographical references and index.
  ISBN 0–631–21865–3 (alk. paper) — ISBN 0–631–21866–1 (pbk. : alk. paper)
    1. Philosophy, Modern — 20th century. 2. Women philosophers — United States — 20th
    century. 3. Philosophers — United States — 20th century. I. Zack, Naomi, 1944–
B105.W6 W64 2000
191′.082—dc21

                                                                                99–056766

British Library Cataloguing in Publication Data
A CIP catalogue record for this book is available from the British Library.

Typeset in 10.5 on 13 pt Photina
by SetSystems Ltd, Saffron Walden, Essex
Printed in Great Britain by
MPG Books Ltd, Bodmin, Cornwall.

This book is printed on acid-free paper.

Contents

The Contributors

Linda Martín Alcoff is Professor of Philosophy, Political Science, and Women's Studies at Syracuse University. She is the author of *Real Knowing: New Versions of the Coherence Theory* (1966), the editor of *Epistemology: The Big Questions* (1998), and co-editor, with Elizabeth Potter, of *Feminist Epistemologies* (1993), and, with Eduardo Mendieta, of *Thinking from the Underside of History* (forthcoming).

Anita L. Allen joined the tenured faculty of the University of Pennsylvania Law School in 1998. Between 1987 and 1998, Allen was Professor of Law at Georgetown University Law Center, and in 1996 was made Associate Dean for Research and Scholarship. She was previously a member of the faculties of the University of Pittsburgh Law School (1985–7) and Carnegie-Mellon University (1978–81). She has been a member of the visiting faculty at the Harvard Law School (1990–1) and was the first Distinguished Reuschlein Professor at Villanova Law School (1998). She briefly practiced law with the New York firm, Cravath, Swaine and Moore (1984–5). Allen has published dozens of articles, many relating to privacy and private life. The most recent include: "Privacy and public life: talking about sex as a problem for democracy," *George Washington Law Review* (1999); "Lying to protect privacy," *Villanova Law Review* (1999); "Coercing privacy," *William and Mary Law Review* (1999); "The social contract in American case law," *University of Florida Law Review* (1999); and "Confronting moral theories: Gewirth in context," in *Gewirth: Critical Essays on Action, Rationality and Community*, edited by Michael Boylan, 1999). In addition, Allen has published three books: *Uneasy Access: Privacy for Women in a*

Free Society, 1988); *Privacy: Cases and Materials* (with R. Turkington, 1999), and *Debating Democracy's Discontent* (with M. Regan, 1998).

Yoko Arisaka is Assistant Professor of Philosophy at the University of San Francisco. She was born and raised in Japan and moved to the United States in 1982. She received her Ph.D. in philosophy from the University of California at Riverside in 1996. During the fall of 1997 she was a CNRS research associate at the École des Hautes Études en Sciences Sociales in Paris. Her research includes modern Japanese philosophy, nineteenth- and twentieth-century continental philosophy (emphasis in phenomenology), Asian philosophy, philosophy of mind, and political philosophy. She has published several articles on Heidegger and on Nishida, the founder of modern Japanese philosophy. She is a co-editor of *Nishida and the Question of Modernity* (forthcoming) and is currently working on her book, *Philosophy and Imperialism: Asian Modernism in Prewar Japan*.

Dasiea Cavers-Huff is Associate Professor of Philosophy, History, Humanities, and Ethnic Studies at Riverside Community College, in Riverside, California. She received her Ph.D. at the University of California, Riverside, in 1997. Prior to her studies at Riverside, she spent four years studying within the Cognitive Sciences Specialization at the University of Maryland, College Park. In addition to her research in the cognitive sciences, she is currently working on the interface between psychology and race.

V. F. Cordova has a BA in philosophy from Idaho State University and an MA and Ph.D. in Philosophy from the University of New Mexico. Cordova has taught at the University of New Mexico; the University of Alaska-Fairbanks; Oregon State University; and Idaho State University. She has been a visiting scholar at Colorado State University and a Rockefeller Fellowship recipient at Lakehead University, Ontario, Canada. Cordova presently holds an adjunct position at Idaho State University in Pocatello, Idaho.

Angela Y. Davis is an internationally renowned activist-scholar who is currently Professor of History of Consciousness at the University of California at Santa Cruz. She gained her BA in French Literature from Brandeis University, and her MA from the University of California at San Diego, where she also completed work for her Ph.D. in philosophy.

Davis also studied philosophy at the Sorbonne in Paris and at Johann Wolfgang von Goethe University in Frankfurt, Germany. In 1972 she received an honorary doctorate in philosophy from Lenin University. Davis's work has been published in numerous journals and anthologies, and her five books include: *Women, Race and Class, Blues Legacies and Black Feminism: Gertrude "Ma" Rainey, Bessie Smith and Billy Holiday*, and her autobiography. Davis has been the subject of numerous biographical sketches, scholarly essays and books, films and sound recordings. (This information on Angela Davis is taken from George Yancy's account, for which he thanked Stephanie Kelly: Ed.)

Barbara Hall is Assistant Professor of Philosophy at Georgia State University in Atlanta. She received her Ph.D. from the University of Arizona in 1997. She also holds a JD from DePaul University and a BA from the University of Illinois, Chicago. Her areas of philosophical specialization and interest include philosophy of law, African-American philosophy and reproductive rights.

Joy James is author of *Shadowboxing: Representations of Black Feminist Politics*; *Transcending the Talented Tenth: Black Leaders and American Intellectuals*; *Resisting State Violence: Radicalism, Gender, and Race in US Culture*. She is also editor of *The Angela Y. Davis Reader* and *States of Confinement: Policing, Detention and Prisons*. James is currently the Distinguished Visiting Scholar in African American Studies at Columbia University.

Adrian M. S. Piper is Professor of Philosophy at Wellesley College and a conceptual artist. The recipient of Mellon, NEH, Guggenheim, and Woodrow Wilson Research Fellowships, she is a Fellow of the New York Institute for the Humanities at New York University and recently a Distinguished Scholar at the Getty Research Institute. Educated at CCNY, the University of Heidelberg, and Harvard, her principle publications are in metaethics, Kant's metaphysics, and the history of ethics. She has taught at Georgetown, Harvard, Michigan, Stanford, and UCSD. The two-volume project from which her essay in this collection is excerpted, *Rationality and the Structure of the Self*, is nearing completion.

Anne Schulherr Waters is of Seminole, Choctaw, Chickasaw, Cherokee, and Jewish descent. She has four graduate degrees, including her JD from the University of New Mexico Law School, and a Ph.D. in philosophy from Purdue University. A philosopher and poet, she is published in the philosophy journal *Teaching Philosophy*, and in two anthologies, *Living the Spirit*, edited by Will Roscoe, and *The FLO Anthology*, edited by Julia Penelope and Sarah Hoagland. Waters is currently co-editing, with Leonard Harris and Scott Pratt, an *Anthology of American Philosophy* for Blackwell Publishers. She is also compiling a set of contemporary essays for a Blackwell *American Indian Philosophy Companion*. She is guest editing, with M. A. Jaimes-Guerrero, a special issue of *Hypatia, A Journal of Feminist Philosophy: American Indian Women and Feminism*, and is gathering together the first American Indian Philosophy section of the *American Philosophical Association Newsletter*, which will include her own paper, "American Indian Identity." Waters organized for the recently created American Indian Philosophy Association (and is current president of it), as well as the recently approved American Philosophical Association (APA) "Committee on American Indians in Philosophy", of which she is chair.

Ofelia Schutte is Professor of Women's Studies and Philosophy at the University of South Florida. Her areas of teaching and research are feminist theory, continental philosophy, philosophy of culture, and Latin American social thought. She is the author of *Beyond Nihilism: Nietzsche without Masks*, and *Cultural Identity and Social Liberation in Latin American Thought*, and numerous articles on feminist, Latin American, and continental philosophy. A former Fulbright scholar to Mexico, she serves on the board of the feminist journal *Hypatia*. Her current interests include poststructuralist, multi-cultural, and Latina feminisms.

George Yancy received his BA in philosophy from the University of Pittsburgh and his MA in philosophy from Yale University. He is editor of *African-American Philosophers, 17 Conversations* (1998). He has contributed articles and reviews to such scholarly journals as *Social Science Quarterly, The Western Journal of Black Studies, The Journal of Religious Thought, Hypatia: A Journal of Feminist Philosophy, Popular Music and Society*, and *The College Language Association Journal*. Yancy is currently editing *Cornel West: A Critical Reader* for Blackwell Publishers. He is presently McNulty Fellow in the Philosophy Department at Duquesne University.

Naomi Zack received her Ph.D. in philosophy from Columbia University in 1970 and then left academia for twenty years. Since her return she has written two books: *Race and Mixed Race* (1993) and *Bachelors of Science: Seventeenth Century Identity, Then and Now* (1996). She has also edited two anthologies, *American Mixed Race: The Culture of Microdiversity* (1995) and *Race/Sex; Their Sameness, Difference and Interplay* (1997), and has co-edited *Race, Class, Gender and Sexuality* (1998). Recent publications include the introductory textbook, *Thinking About Race* (1998). Zack is associate professor in the Philosophy Department at the University at Albany and is currently working on two new books, *The Philosophy of Science and Race* and *Descartes' Dreaming*.

Acknowledgments

I am grateful to the contributors for expanding my perspectives about the relevance of race, ethnicity, and gender to philosophy. I thank Lewis R. Gordon for suggesting people whom I might contact as potential contributors. I thank George Yancy for assistance in obtaining his interview with Angela Davis for this volume, and for a careful reading of the penultimate copy of my introduction.

The following essays are reprints or based on earlier publications; Blackwell Publishers and I are grateful to the sources for permissions.

Linda Martín Alcoff's "Epistemic Credibility: Are Social Identities Relevant?" was first commissioned for a forthcoming anthology, edited by Nancy Tuana.

Angela Y. Davis, "Interview with Angela Y. Davis," in George Yancy (ed.) *African American Philosophers: 17 Conversations* (New York: Routledge, 1998).

Joy James, "Discredited Knowledge in the Nonfiction of Toni Morrison," in Joy James, *Resisting State Violence: Radicalism, Gender, and Race in US Culture*, Minneapolis: University of Minnesota Press, 1996.

Ofelia Schutte, "Cultural Alterity: Cross-Cultural Communication and Feminist Theory in North–South Contexts," *Hypatia* 13/2 (Spring 1998) (published by Indiana University Press).

Kimberly Van Orman assisted me with the preparation of the pre-publication manuscript, through funding from the Faculty Research Award Program at the University at Albany. Once again, I thank Mary Dortch for expert trans-Atlantic desk editing. I am grateful to Steve Smith and other staff members at Blackwell in Malden, MA, for support of the project and I particularly want to thank Beth Remmes for her conscientious editorial management.

NZ, Albany, NY, August 1999

On the basis of the available documents, the existence or non-existence of an organized sect of witches in fifteenth- to seventeenth-century Europe seems to be indeterminate. It is a dilemma, however, which to my eyes at least has only relative importance.

Carlo Ginzburg, *The Night Battles: Witchcraft and Agrarian Cults
in the Sixteenth and Seventeenth Centuries,*
translated by John and Anne Tedeschi

There is no true word that is not at the same time a praxis. Thus, to speak a true word is to transform the world.

Paulo Freire, *Pedagogy of the Oppressed,*
translated by Myra Bergman Ramos

"Eventually it comes to you" observes Lorraine Hansberry, "the thing that makes you exceptional, if you are at all, is inevitably that which must also make you lonely."

Patricia Hill Collins, *Black Feminist Thought:
Knowledge, Consciousness and the Politics of Empowerment*

Introduction

NAOMI ZACK

About the Title

The title, *Women of Color and Philosophy*, is intended to signal a recognizable subject, or one that can at least be imagined, by all philosophers, regardless of their race or gender. However, I arrived at it through a process of compromise, which required that I relocate some of my own ideas into a broader perspective. The idea for the book sprang into my head (or out of it) all in one piece. It occurred to me in the fall of 1997 that the work of existing women philosophers who were not white and who did not work exclusively as feminists or as scholars of race or ethnicity, would be worth collecting as a professional document. I did not know how close to the center of the field were the main scholarly interests of members of this group. The women of color in philosophy with whose work I was already familiar could not be categorized as mainstream philosophers. I wondered about the ways in which women of color in philosophy believed that their work was related to philosophy as it is understood by those white male philosophers who appear to work in the center of the discipline.

I invited and solicited essays from African, African-American, Asian-American, Hispanic, Jewish-Arab, Native-American and, to count myself, Mixed-Race, women philosophers.[1] My original call for papers was titled, "Women of Color Do Philosophy." The word "Do" meant the action verb, and the syntax of the title was inspired by the book title *Men Doing Feminism*.[2] I read in the title *Men Doing Feminism* an intention to bring attention to the unlikely event of men working as feminists. It is of the same magnitude of unlikeliness for women of color to work as philosophers.

The title "Women of Color Do Philosophy" soon made me uncomfortable because I began to think that the label "of color" was overused and metaphorical. Also, when I told several white male philosophers about the project, they reacted playfully, as though visualizing a chorus line of "women of color" executing an erotic dance *meme*. I remembered that even now, some educated people still project stereotypical attributes of unrestrained sexuality and stupidity onto nonwhite women, in contexts where nonwhite women appear to have social roles more advantaged and privileged than roles tradition-ally assigned to them.[3]

I changed the title to "Nonwhite Women Do Philosophy." As a result of my work on race, I was more comfortable with "nonwhite" than "of color." I do not think that racial categories have the physical reality they are assumed to have in common sense. There are no general genes for race, there is greater variation within, than between, any of the three or four major racial groups, and racial categories change historically and geographically.[4] Racial categories are not only socially constructed in the ascription of psychological and cultural traits to biological difference, but the biological difference itself does not have the scientific foundation it is assumed to have at the folk level. It therefore seemed to me that "nonwhite" was an accurate, no-nonsense way of referring to all the ascribed categories of race, other than the white one, with a minimum of socially-constructed connota-tion. At any rate, simply listing all of the racial categories with which the contributors identified would have made too cumbersome a title.

However, one African-American woman who was a potential contributor to the anthology objected to the use of the term "non-white" in the title, on the grounds that it was a negative designation rather than a positive or affirmative one; it defined people in terms of what they were not. I thought that this was how many whites, including hard-nosed social scientists writing for the government, labeled blacks, Asians, Indians, and Hispanics, and that insofar as all of the racial categories were made up and ascribed, it was just as well to use the most official label, which was also an inclusive one. But I knew that not everyone presently doing philosophical work on race agreed with me about the extent to which all racial categories are ascriptive. One recurring objection to my emphasis of the biological emptiness of race in previous publications has been that this emphasis seems to neglect the social importance of race, and the value to blacks, Asians and Indians, of their phenomenological experience of their racial identities as physically real.[5] The phenomenological experience may be culturally constructed, and it has a history of being reactive to white racist ascriptions of the false biological notions. But, in conjunction with shared culture and group loyalty, the phenomenological physical reality of race is an important basis for ongoing liberatory activism and scholarship. I therefore did not have a satisfactory answer to the potential contributor who objected to the word "nonwhite" in the title, and I thought that her article was an important contribution to the anthology.

More problematic, several Latina potential contributors informed me that they could not include their work in a collection with the adjective "nonwhite" in the title, because they identified themselves as racially white. I responded that I had read their references to themselves as "women of color" in previous publications. Their response to me was that the terms "nonwhite" and "of color" were not synonymous, precisely because of the metaphorical connotations of the term "of color." I thought it ironic that some philosophers deliberately chose metaphor for the sake of precision, whereas I had disciplined myself to eschew metaphor. I did not think that a collection such as this would be complete without the views of Latina or Hispanic women philosophers.

I figured out that there is, in this case, more to the deliberate choice of metaphor than an avoidance of precision, so that what looked to be a metaphor might be a more comprehensive term. The label "metaphoric" for a racially white person's self-designation as a person "of color" is itself a metaphor. Not all people who are "of color" are "nonwhite" because the term "of color" can be informatively applied to a person who is racially white but does not share the culture of white people who belong to the dominant groups of national origin in American society. In broad parlance, "race" refers to biology and "ethnicity" refers to culture (leaving aside the frequent use of "ethnicity" as a euphemism for racial nonwhiteness). The term Hispanic is a deliberate social construction that refers to members of ethnic groups in the United States whose families are originally from Spain, South America, Central America, Puerto Rico, Mexico, and other places. Although it is recognized (demanded) on the census and other classifying forms that "Hispanics" identify as "white" or "nonwhite," the dominant British and European ethnic groups in the United States discriminate against all Hispanics in ways that closely resemble racial discrimination.[6]

My penultimate attempt at a title was "Of-Color Women Do Philosophy." It satisfied all the contributors. By making "of-color" an adjective, I hoped to avoid the overused metaphor. I also sometimes considered "Of-Color Women Do Philosophy Now," with an exclamation mark at the end. I knew that this would be a title with attitude. But a cooler head than mine pointed out that such a title might not be taken seriously by those potential readers who, in the hopes of parties to a book like this, will take it seriously. I imagined that the images of a chorus line would be replaced with images of a rap group. This daunted me. I thought that there might be quite a few working philosophers who would not be intellectually adverse to a book that evoked images of a chorus line, but who *would* be intellectually adverse to the juxtaposition of rap music with (academic) philosophy. Even many working philosophers too young to retain memories of chorus lines might be intellectually adverse to the juxtaposition of rap music with academic philosophy. Of course, some academic philosophers now write about rap music in cultural analyses of race, but I did not want the success of this project to depend on the acceptance of their work, as philosophy, by other academic philosophers.[7] I chose discretion, having by then read a sufficient number of completed contributions to trust in the valor of the contents.

Rationale for the Book

For philosophers, generally, there is something inappropriate and irrelevant about considering the race or gender of a philosopher, *as a philosophical issue*. For women of color who are philosophers, it may be embarrassing to bring attention to their race or gender in the context of their work as philosophers. The disciplinary constraints of philosophy are not merely matters of pride based on achievement but call upon the virtue of pride in a refusal to make requests for reasons of weakness, incompetence, or disadvantaged social status. Philosophers do not cry and they are not supposed to whine or complain.

We are philosophers. In spite of that fact, or because of it, the *intersection* of the categories of professional philosophers, women, and persons of color, merits inquiry in light of demographic facts, late twentieth-century social politics, the distribution of human talent and the nature of philosophy. These illuminating objects are the rationale for the present collection. I would be remiss if I did not explain how this were so, although many members of the contemporary intellectual community outside of philosophy would justly accuse me of telling them what they already know.

As I've already noted, being both a philosopher and a woman of color is an unlikely event. The current membership of the American Philosophical Association is approximately 10,000.[8] For several years, it has been estimated that African Americans comprise a little over 1 percent of that membership.[9] The number of women in academic philosophy is commonly believed to be less than 10 percent of the APA population, although the number of women awarded Ph.Ds in philosophy has been increasing in recent years. At the time of writing, I do not have figures for the numbers of Hispanics or Asian Americans in philosophy. Ann Waters, chair of the APA Committee on American Indians in Philosophy, claims that there are only three Native Americans, counting herself, who have Ph.Ds in philosophy. I know of only one self-identified mixed-race woman philosopher.

While pursuing leads for potential contributors, I worked with a list of twenty women of color presently employed in the field. My most liberal estimate of the number of women of color who are presently employed as philosophers would be thirty (out of 10,000). These figures are not what critics of affirmative action policies believe has been effected, in the profession of philosophy specifically, or in higher education generally.

Late twentieth-century social politics have, to a significant extent, been shaped by a battle between those who think that the differences in socioeconomic status associated with differences in race and gender are the result of individual character and natural endowments, and those who think that such differences are the result of widespread racism and male dominance. There is no evidence of an hereditary basis, linked either to false constructions of race, or biological sexual difference, for the kinds of talent, acquired intellectual skills, or reflective disposition that are associated with the practice of philosophy. The same can be said about those traits of character that conservative apologists credit with advantageous social or economic status, in general. I am simply going to assert these premises of biological neutrality, although I would advise skeptics holding out for a philosophy gene to consult Richard Lewontin's short book on human genetics, *Biology as Ideology.*[10]

The social politics have played out, in liberal arts and humanities areas of curricula and scholarship in higher education, in ways too complex to do more than allude to here. There is room to say, however, that what libertarians and conservatives interpret as excesses of feminism and multiculturalism are believed by them to constitute an intellectual hegemony in contemporary academic publication, as well as in teaching. But most observers, regardless of their political positions, would agree that although such an hegemony may exist in a number of departments of English and History in American universities, it has no presence or interdisciplinary influence in philosophy departments.

The philosophical canon is now splintered in comparison to what some remember or imagine as twentieth-century time periods dominated by pragmatism, Logical Positivism or ordinary language analysis.[11] At present, mainstream critics and cartographers of the field seem to share the consensus that the best philosophy is coextensive with the work of the (white male) giants of the twentieth century and their intellectual heirs: Frege, Russell, Moore, Wittgenstein, Austin, Quine, Chomsky, Davidson, Kripke, David Lewis and on political issues, Rawls and Robert Nozick.[12] The giant legacy anchors contemporary *analytic philosophy*, which is now focused on meaning and other aspects of language, and a number of (what often appear to be) formalized attempts to solve the mind–body problem.[13] There are no enthroned giants from the history of philosophy before the twentieth century. Analytic philosophers generally believe that continental philosophy is incomprehensible or else poorly done, and Heidegger, Sartre, Foucault, and Derrida, not to even mention Rorty, are consigned to the *margin(s)*.[14] The heirs to greatness in the margins are likely to begin their careers in obscurity and remain there – if they can get jobs in a market that since the early 1980s has had roughly double the number of candidates as jobs.[15] While continental philosophy, philosophy of science, feminism, Africana studies, ancient philosophy, and early modern philosophy are recognized areas for both research and teaching, they are often not considered to be real philosophy by the heirs of the giants in the center. Medical ethics, business ethics, and environmental ethics are viewed as even further from real philosophy, and they are further tainted by being "applied." Given the normativity of the centrality of contemporary philosophy of language and philosophy of mind, the failure to be aware of the work of the field's smallest nascent, intersected minority, cannot be singled out as deliberate discrimination against members of this group. As of now, there is no tradition or body of work that could be called the work of women of color in philosophy.

If there are at most thirty living women of color who are academic philosophers and if that number is only the result of post-1960s affirmative action policies, then perhaps their relative obscurity is as blameless as it is unsurprising.[16] One cannot get blood out of a stone. But it isn't a matter of blame. The point is that there is something intrinsically interesting about the demographics and given this, philosophers in other categories of race and gender might be – some would say *ought to be* – interested in what this nascent minority has to say about the field. Furthermore, the number of women of color who are philosophers appears to be growing and the present collection may be of interest or use to newcomers to the field who, on an individual basis, are curious about reference points or precedents.

There are not enough women of color in academic philosophy to speculate firmly about how issues of intersection affect them, but several questions do seem to present themselves. On the face of it, the categories of philosopher, woman, and person of color seem merely to combine in an additive way. However, research about other kinds of employment indicates that being a woman, and being black, for example, creates a new category of disadvantage because white women are preferred over black women and black men are preferred over black women.[17] Is the identity of being an academic philosopher sufficiently strong, either in itself, or through its association with white male intellectuals, to cancel out disadvantages due to female gender and nonwhite race? It seems unlikely, because white female philosophers and black male philosophers have in recent decades analyzed their own marginalization in the field.[18] The atypicality of a woman-of-color philosopher may result in initial failures of credibility with colleagues, as well as students. Being known as having doubly benefited from affirmative action hiring policies, and representing double evidence of departmental and institutional compliance with affirmative action guidelines for hiring, is more stigma than distinction. If one's scholarly interests are marginal in the field, there are further erosions of status. Overt or latent racism in departments and institutions, combined with requests for service on committees to vouchsafe diversity, are further sources of professional derogation and of stress on individual resources and personal well-being.

On the other hand, these adversities may bite less than they bark.

Because many of the negative stereotypes projected onto women-of-color philosophers have no sound foundation, they may be ultimately ineffectual. Philosophical ability is not determined by identity of race or gender and critical judgment over time may conclude that (some) scholarly work now located in the margins is of higher intellectual quality, as well as more interesting, than work done in the center. Jobs secured through affirmative action are nonetheless real jobs. Social aversion from whites based on race, and contempt by males due to gender (which includes sexual harassment), requires that women-of-color think carefully about what constitutes professionalism, a discipline that in the long run will benefit their own careers and raise professional standards overall. Being in high demand for service creates opportunities to choose those contexts of academic governance, minority representation, and curriculum development that merit an individual's participation. The uses of adversity can be sweet.

Some might inquire as to the philosophical import of the foregoing considerations. Demography, social politics, social psychology (or whatever field the distribution of human talent falls under), superficial external descriptions of philosophy, and descriptions and redescriptions of stressors on individual practitioners, are not philosophy. Therefore, if this book is about those considerations, it is not philosophy. Fortunately, or not, this book is not about those considerations. The essays herein are the philosophical work of academic philosophers interrogating what it is that they and their colleagues *do*, as philosophers. Such intradisciplinary interrogation is a time-honored philosophical subject. Nonetheless, we need to remember that philosophy is one of the few fields that has many practitioners who are certified, productively employed and well-regarded by colleagues both in the workplace and the profession, but who are considered not to be doing the proper or real work of the field, by other colleagues. That some could be philosophers in virtue of their employment and work, without that work being philosophy, is a situation that fortunately has no analogue in other exacting and humanly consequential vocations, such as brain surgery. Despite best efforts, I do not think that the work in this volume will be considered philosophy by those who have the highest status and influence in the field.

I do not know to what extent life experience influences the kind of work philosophers choose to do and I do not think that a general theory of such connections can be constructed, because there are too many individual variables. Still, it is sometimes interesting to know how individual philosophers believe that their lives are connected to their work. Having preselected the philosophers herein, on the basis of facts about their lives, I have asked them to indicate in their articles how they have experienced the connections between being women of color and philosophers.

Chapter Overview

There are three sections: Critique, Activism and Application, and New Directions. The articles were commissioned by author, rather than subject, and the ways in which they fulfilled the anthology proposal were left up to individual authors.[19] The section division is intended to delineate three critical strains: direct critique of traditional academic philosophy; the application of traditional philosophical methods to topics of social relevance that have not heretofore been considered by academic philosophers; the interpretation of traditional philosophy in ways that suggest new areas of study. This is not a precise division because critique inevitably suggests new directions, application develops applicanda in new directions, and new directions may in themselves constitute critique. Furthermore, the three section titles are by no means exhaustive of distinct themes or areas of study that women of color doing philosophy are engaged in or might develop. There were not sufficient potential contributors to divide the book into essays within recognized topics in the field, such as history of philosophy, Africana studies, philosophy of science, continental philosophy, and so forth. As well, I could not find anyone willing to write within philosophical topics central to the field. Of course, I hope that this anthology is only the beginning. I now turn to the contents.

The term critique, which derives from a contemporary understanding of *critical theory*, has an ideological dimension.[20] A critique of scholarly work or of institutional practice may describe its subject in ways that are not acceptable, or even recognizable, to actual participants. The motive for critique is often twofold: to accurately analyze a subject; to bring about change. Change ensues through agents who share a general value or goal with the critic, and accept the critical description of the subject in question, especially if the subject is their thought and action. For example, suppose that a critique of an institutional practice redescribes it as racially discriminatory when participants do not believe the practice is racially discriminatory. If participants recognize and accept the critique and share a belief that racial discrimination is morally wrong, an Aristotelean practical syllogism will result in nondiscriminatory institutional practice. In this example, the syllogism would be:

Racial discrimination is morally wrong.

This is a case of racial discrimination.

Therefore, —— (where —— is some action against the discrimination).

The success of the ideological aspect of critique is a hinged process that holds together only if certain conditions are met: participants recognize and accept the description as applicable to them; there is some shared goal or value between critic and participants concerning the topic of the critique; participants do act in the practical syllogism, the major premise of which has the shared value or goal as its subject.

The critiques of traditional philosophy developed by Joy James, Ofelia Schutte, V. S. Cordova and Adrian Piper, in Part 1, have existing philosophical activities or commitments to projects of speech, listening and writing, as their subjects. Each evokes values that the writer assumes are shared by philosophical readers. The actions at stake are different or changed philosophical activities or commitments to projects of speech, listening and writing.

In "Discredited Knowledge in the Nonfiction of Tony Morrison," James analyzes several critical issues raised by Morrison's work. While Morrison is deeply committed to the well-being of black people, her emphasis on the value and importance of community implies a commonality of interests between blacks and whites. James notes that the emphasis on service and community membership in African cultures predates both slavery and racism. Worldviews that preserve history through traditions of connection with ancestors are often distorted by racist mythologies about blacks, or by what Morrison calls "Africanisms." James claims that the psychic structure of community explored by Morrison is a type of knowledge that is discredited by academics, because the addition of multicultural subjects to curricula, without explanations of ongoing white supremacy, relegates the socially cohesive dimension of such knowledge to the realm of superstition.

In James's interpretation, Morrison seems to work with an idea of belonging to, and being claimed by a community, as an inescapable existential structure. In African tradition, which was at least partly retained through slavery, ancestors and others in one's community do not have to be alive or spatially present for individuals to fulfill obligations to them or enact the great dramas of human life and emotion with them. The relegation of such cultural traditions to superstition is a loss to contemporary white western scholars of culture, and at the same time it discredits traditional knowledge. For example, the western historical transformation of first the extended family and second, the nuclear family, to dispersed and attenuated personal groups, may not be catastrophes of social breakdown and alienation, as commonly assumed. Instead, for dominant groups these processes may result in new forms of a more fundamental psychic and social condition of belonging. Something similar, perhaps, might be said of the social need for "virtual" electronic communities at this time of maximum mobility and transplantation in the West, even though the mobility and transplantation appear to be due to the pursuit of self-enhancing opportunities, rather than forced diaspora.

In "Cultural Alterity," Ofelia Schutte is concerned with the ways in which global, postcolonial feminist theory can be negotiated between women in dominant western cultures and women in subaltern cultures in the South and East. However, her exploration of the way *alterity* can equalize asymmetrical incommensurabilities in communication would seem to have implications in any context of communication between those unequal in power or authority. The concept of alterity combines the notion of the other as different from the self with an acknowledgment of the self's decentering, as a result of the experience of difference. Different languages may be expressive of different standards for coherence and completeness and there may be a residue of untranslatability, because the stranger has a different sense of self and history.

Schutte's specific example is the ways in which members of dominant Anglo-American cultures render Latina women intellectuals invisible as producers of culture, because they are female and culture is presumed to be a category of the national, which is created by men. When Latinas are required to speak as experts on their own culture, their presentation is constrained and evaluated by the communication standards of the dominant Anglo-American culture. This results in frustration and missed opportunity because the Latina self is lost and thus unable to decenter dominant interlocuters.

In an intellectual memoir, "Exploring the Sources of Western Thought," V. F. Cordova relates her educational search for the *leitmotiv* that makes western philosophy distinct. Cordova contrasts what she learned about the roots of western philosophy with the Apache cultural beliefs her father taught her. Cordova notes that the ancient Greeks are often invoked as western sources but that the world of the Greeks and their view of human nature does not resemble the main themes of the West. The world of the Greeks was infinite, hylozoist, and organic. Man was a social being and open-minded about life after death. Time was cyclical and a mere measure of existence. Cordova pinpoints St Augustine as the transition thinker who created the western *leitmotiv*. There is one God, who created the world out of nothing and man exists in God's image with a divine soul and a corruptible material body. Time came into existence with the world. The role of man in the world is to master his passions, multiply, and subdue and name all things with the use of reason.

Cordova wryly notes that Augustine would be pleased with the contemporary map of knowledge which partitions the study of mind off from the study of material things, and posits existence and time as the result of an original "big bang." She suggests that the ideas her father taught her about the importance of community and attachment to the earth as Mother are closer to the worldview of the Greeks, than to the edifice wrought by Augustine. Few contemporary philosophers are directly concerned with religious issues, except perhaps to note Hume's criticism of rational proofs for the existence of God. Still, as Cordova points out, there are deep assumptions in western philosophy that are to this day the historical result of Christian theology. Primary examples are: acceptance of the mind–body partition in the foundation of the sciences; preference for individuals as the main unit of study in political and social philosophy; a human-centered, instrumental view of nature. Cordova concludes her essay with the suggestion that westerners develop a realization that their *leitmotiv* is neither absolute truth, nor the only intellectual approach to the world.

Adrian Piper, in "General Introduction to the Project: The Enterprise of Socratic Metaethics," offers an ethical critique of contemporary philosophical practice, in the context of an introductory exposition of Socratic metaethics, which is part of her two-volume work in progress, *Rationality and the Structure of the Self.* According to Piper, Socratic metaethics provides a method for unpacking the metaphysical presuppositions of normative ethical theories, by analyzing the different roles they assign to rationality in the self. Socratic metaethics grounds moral convictions and judgments in rational dialogue, as a way toward achieving moral truth. Piper reasons that the antirationalist view that something other than reason guides moral life leaves no way to formulate principles of action. Antirationalist or subjective metaethical theories posit the moral states of others as in principle inaccessible. Piper recognizes two branches of Socratic metaethics, Hume's and Kant's. Hume's insistence on desire as the sole cause of action diminishes the self as a rational agent. Piper therefore supports Kant's view, which entails that theoretical reason can effectively motivate action.

Piper motivates her position in metaethics by means of the philosophical virtue of rational discourse. She *transvalues* Nietzsche's devaluation of rationality as a character disposition of slave morality. Rationality is necessary when the freedom to act on one's impulses and desires is constrained by the impulses and desires of others. According to Piper, the valuation and cultivation of rationality is a weapon for the unempowered. Piper's project is of great interest in that she does not identify reason with oppression in the way not a few feminists in philosophy are presently wont to do. In this article, specifically, Piper emphasizes the cardinal virtue of rational discourse in traditional Anglo-American philosophy. Her model is the discourse of G. E. Moore, whereby philosophical expository standards of clarity, structure, and coherence constitute an appeal to the other's rationality. It is not necessary that a philosopher prevail in every encounter; ideals of personal civility are made possible by the control and sublimation of instinct, impulse, desire, and emotion. In a trenchant critique, Piper described failures of such intellectual virtue in vignettes of *Bulldozers, Bullies, Bulls,* and *Bullfinches* among contemporary philosophers. She attributes this breakdown in civility to the tight job market of recent decades, which makes it imprudent for upcoming philosophers to speak their minds to mentors and senior faculty, so that they can eventually do independent, creative work of their own. The result is now a "culture of genuflection" that "infantilizes" the unempowered. Piper believes that although philosophy may look outside itself for models of rationality – presently toward cognitive science – ultimately other fields will rely on philosophical standards of rationality, and within philosophy, existing exercises of civil rationality will only be countered by other exercises of civil rationality.

The section on Activism and Application contains an interview with Angela Davis and essays by Anne Waters, Barbara Hall, and Anita Allen. All of these pieces express intense concern with the well-being of individuals in ascribed communities, outside of academia. The attention to living community and the shared demand on the part of these writers that philosophy be socially relevant constitutes the "activism" in this section. However, what in other fields would be called "theory" is also well developed here, and this is the "applied" dimension in philosophical terms. Intellectuals who are primarily concerned with social change privilege actions undertaken in the world and construct scholarly accounts on the empirical base of historical events. The scholarly accounts are their "theory(ies)." Philosophers, on the other hand, work primarily in the domain of scholarship and they use empirical descriptions as evidence, to support their generalizations. The use of philosophical tools and scholarship to interpret, analyze, and make moral judgments about events in the world is therefore an "application" of philosophy. If activism and its accompanying theory(ies) are acknowledged to be part of philosophy then they become transmogrified into "applied philosophy."

It is clear in the interview with Angela Davis, conducted by George Yancy, that Davis views philosophy as a tool in the struggle for social justice concerning disadvantaged social class as well as racial and gender inequality. However, Davis does not think that identity or unity can be based on race or gender in themselves. Rather than concentrate on unifying black feminist theory, she would prefer to focus on "rehabilitating the role of the organizer." Unity needs to be produced politically in anti-capitalist regroupings (after the collapse of the Soviet Union). Davis's activism has taken the form of creating courses that focus on philosophical themes in black literature and the importance of gender analysis in black philosophy. She also works with organizations such as the Prison Activist Resource Center and the National Black Women's Health project. She describes her anti-racist activism and production of knowledge as motivated by a desire to heal.

Davis arrived in the field of philosophy through an undergraduate major in French literature which led her to Sartre. Sartre led her to Husserl and she studied with Theodore Adorno to learn how to use German idealism to develop a basis for a critical theory of society. Davis thus views philosophy, not as an abstract engagement with questions of human existence, but as part of a productive interaction with sociology, feminist theory, and African-American studies, to radically transform society.

In "That Alchemical Bering Strait Theory!, or Introducing America's Indigenous Sovereign Nations' Worldview to Informal Logic Courses," Ann Waters describes how she makes use of instruction in informal logic to engage the attention of Native American students and at the same time correct Euro-American distortions of indigenist history and experience. Waters first introduces her students to a number of fallacies in informal reasoning and she then teaches the rules for argument, using as content, common beliefs about Native Americans.

According to American Indian cultural traditions, they originated in the Americas. According to the standards of western science, American Indians have not proved this claim of indigenism. Waters argues that the acceptance of the Bering Strait theory, which asserts that the ancestors of American Indians migrated to this continent by crossing a land bridge from Asia, begs the question (because it assumes they did thus migrate) of whether Native Americans are indigenous. The existence of the Bering Strait land bridge could also support hypotheses of migrations from the Americas to Europe, as well as numerous migrations back and forth. There are further pertinent applications of other fallacies. Waters shows how it is a false claim that disease naturally caused a drop in Indian populations; it is false because some Indians were deliberately infected with smallpox through "gifts" of contaminated blankets. False definitions are used when sites of massacres are described on markers as places where Indians surrendered in battle. False dichotomies are created if it is assumed that individuals must be either American Indian or European, when some individuals are both, because they have mixed ancestry. Slippery slope reasoning is evident in Euro-American fears that the legal recognition and enforcement of treaties will lead to a take-over of all American land by Indians. Fallacies of authority have been consistently committed in granting greater credibility to Euro-Americans over Indians, in legal and anthropological studies of Native Americans. In all of these examples, and others, Waters's application of philosophy has the effect of persuasion. Her teaching creates a bridge between the traditional beliefs of Indian students and the beliefs of Euro-American students about Indians. Waters's essay about her pedagogical strategies in itself reads as a logical correction to received opinions about Native Americans.

In "The Libertarian Role Model and the Burden of Uplifting the Race," Barbara Hall addresses a difficult moral issue that swirls around positive valuations of tradition, and communitarianism, generally. What, if any, is the moral justification for claims made, within ascriptive groups where all membership is involuntary, by some group members on other members? Hall begins by noting that according to traditional liberal theory, individuals ought to be free so long as their actions do not directly harm others. Responsibility is usually assumed to flow from voluntary actions and it is likely to follow a situation of blame. Halls asks when a person can merit the blame of other group members for failing to meet special moral obligations that are entailed by group membership. She refers to H. L. A. Hart's analysis of responsibilities that come with roles, such as that of a sea captain who has obligations, not, in this case, to other sea captains, but to passengers and crew. Hall suggests that the obligations imposed on successful African Americans to function as role models that are appropriate for the young to emulate is a parallel instance of having obligations to others in virtue of a role. There is also a reputation or "ambassador" responsibility, which is placed on every member of the group as a result of the ways in which whites negatively stereotype African Americans.

Hall believes that the justification of these obligations is not a duty to uplift but a utilitarian obligation not to harm other members of the group. The imposition of role model status is justified because it will avoid negative influences on young members of the group. The assignment of ambassadorship is in itself a reaction to unjust external stereotyping, but given a status quo, such stereotyping can be countered only through direct, case-by-case disproof. Part of the identity shared by African Americans is a result of the deliberate external imposition of stereotypes on individuals, because they are members of the group. The obligations justified by Hall arise from this identity.

Anita Allen's general subject in "Interracial Marriage" is social issues that have been settled legally but which are still matters of moral controversy. While philosophers have paid adequate attention to topics such as abortion and capital punishment, which fall under this rubric, they have neglected racial intermarriage, a matter of deep moral controversy within the African-American community. Allen notes that although the US Supreme Court struck down all remaining laws against interracial marriage in *Loving* v. *Virginia*, 1967, black women in particular continue to be troubled by marriage between blacks and white. Positions against such intermarriage are based on beliefs that it violates obligations to respect and care for one's community of origin, as well as for one's family, friends, and self. These beliefs rest on a consensus that community members should design their lives to include kin, and that they should not put aside the human potential of the community in choosing a mate.

Allen argues that intermarriage can be reconciled with African-American community loyalties because it does not involve an intention to harm the community. Offspring are likely to identify as black, and black cultural identity does not depend on physical appearance. While intermarriage does present a moral challenge, it is not an insurmountable one and it may in individual cases be worth the effort. Allen concludes that different groups in American society have different ethical concerns and that the distance of ethics in academic philosophy from folk ethics is a loss of opportunity for American self-understanding. Were philosophy more inclusive in this sense, it might be more interesting to members of racial minority groups.

The third section of the book, New Directions, represents alternative interpretations of traditional philosophical subjects. The essays by Yoko Arisaka, Linda Alcoff, Dasiea Cavers-Huff, and myself, may be motivated by intellectual concerns arising from identities atypical in philosophy, but those concerns are more extrinsic to our writing than to some of the earlier essays. The results are still distant from the center, however, and readers should not allow their interpretations of how these essays are related to earlier themes of critique and application to be foreclosed by what in the end is the somewhat arbitrary division of the book.

Yoko Arisaka's subject is the philosophical location of Asian philosophy. She develops a comprehensive account of how the philosophical work of Asians generally have been excluded from western philosophy. At the same time, Arisaka's essay addresses the conceptual problems with the category of Asian itself and it is in that regard a work on Asian identity, particularly the problems that accompany the identity of Asian women in western contexts. Arisaka notes that the category of Asian is fragmented because it encompasses people from a variety of nations, languages, and cultures. But there is a commonality of personal and social values based on Confucianism: passivity, service, and harmony. The effect of these values in contexts of western discourse is that Asians are uncomfortable about speaking up and asserting themselves. This cultural predisposition is viewed by westerners as feminine, and it results in a double feminization of Asian women, first as Asians, and second as women.

Arisaka notes that Asian philosophy has not only been neglected in the West, but that even in Japan the study of philosophy is limited to European philosophy. A broad definition of academic philosophy would include inquiries into the good life and the nature of reality and these subjects have been extensively addressed, for many centuries, by thinkers in Asian countries. On the basis of Ariska's essay it is difficult to conclude that the exclusion of Asian philosophy from western canons is anything but the effect of Eurocentrism and orientalism. There is no intellectual justification for the lack of Asian views in traditional subjects that Asians as well as westerners have considered, especially insofar as western philosophers working in those subjects assume that their scholarship is universal.

Linda Alcoff, in "On Judging Epistemic Credibility," raises the question of whether social identities are relevant to the assessment of knowledge claims. Alcoff points out that most of our knowledge depends on testimony and that the social identity of the person making a claim or judgment is likely to effect their credibility. Whether social identities are ascribed or chosen, they have contexts of shared meanings based on group histories. Social identities influence perceptions and perceptions are part of knowledge: "Identities operate as horizons from which certain aspects or layers of reality can be made visible."

Alcoff draws on Foucault and Merleau-Ponty to broadly suggest how perception, as an important element in knowledge, is shaped by social identity. According to Foucault, perception is a learned process resulting from history and culture. Merleau-Ponty emphasized the bodily nature of perception and the ways in which our bodies are themselves constructed by history and culture.

This link between perception and social identity is addressed from another angle by Dasiea Cavers-Huff in "Cognitive Science and the Quest for a Theory of Properties." Cavers-Huff relates her studies in cognitive science and psychology to philosophical analyses of perception, which she argues require an adequate theory of properties. Such a theory is useful for accounting for similarities among objects, sorting objects, providing explanations, and specifying truth conditions for statements that refer to properties. Cavers-Huff rejects Platonism, Aristotelian realism and nominalism, on philosophical grounds. She then describes how cognitive science can be used to explain properties as relations among perceivers, objects, and their environment. These interactions have developed through natural selection, even though our phenomenological experience of the world is illusory relative to our biology and interests as members of a species.

Cavers-Huff claims that her experience as an African-American female in philosophy made her aware of the importance of adaptation, as well as of differences in perceptions of the world. The interactive and active nature of perception emphasized in her theory of properties seems to be an empirical, as well as a metaphysical, counterpart to Alcoff's claim that perception is influenced by social identity. Surely, attitudes and opinions and "perceptions" of social situations are influenced by identities. But Alcoff and Cavers-Huff both seem to be making the more radical claim that physical sensory perception is influenced by social identities in important ways. This seems to be a general empirical claim that would generate specific hypotheses that could be corroborated or falsified by experimental evidence in perceptual psychology.

In "Descartes' Realist Awake–Asleep Distinction and Naturalism," I present an interpretation of Descartes' awake–asleep distinction that relies more heavily on his realism than does the standard interpretation, which is based on the his Sixth Meditation epistemological references to the coherence of awake experience. Not only are some awake experiences incoherent and some dreaming experiences coherent, but Descartes explicitly says that when we are awake we are able to have accurate perceptions of the world, and when we are asleep we lack this ability. However, the realist distinction needs to be restricted to sensory experience only, because the first principles of philosophy, as well as mathematical truths, may be accurately experienced awake or asleep, and the fact that we are asleep "does not militate against them." I note the relevance to Descartes' realism of findings in contemporary neuroscience, which suggest suggest that the parts of the brain consistent with self-awareness, as well as abstract thought, are active in sleep. In his project to ground empirical science on certain knowledge, Descartes arrived at a concept of the self and the philosophical mind as something that is always capable of awareness and it looks as though that is how we in fact are.

My interest in Descartes is partly a matter of personal intellectual taste. I like his writing style and in this context, the fact that he is a realist about the external world . I am a realist myself because I think that much of contemporary criticism of human categories as socially constructed, rather than natural, presupposes that science can yield information about some things that are not socially constructed. However, realism about the existence of some objects of scientific study is not the same thing as a kind of realism that holds there is only one way of correctly perceiving everything in the world, extends to all realms of human experience and holds for all human perceivers. As well, it should go without saying that minimal and which relative scientific realism does not entail that everything is real that has been posited as real within unjust social contexts.

Notes

1 The two African women philosophers, one of whom lived in Cameroon, the other in the United States, were unable to submit essays within the editing schedule. The Jewish-Arab philosopher, who considered herself nonwhite, also had other demands on her time with which my editing schedule conflicted. There were two students, one Native American and one African American, whose work I would have been happy to include but they did not have time to revise or submit articles.

2 Tom Digby (ed.) *Men Doing Feminism* (New York: Routlege, 1998). Digby's book came out in the Thinking Gender series, edited by Linda Nicholson, a series in which I had also published an anthology, *Race/ Sex: Their Sameness, Difference and Interplay* (New York: Routledge, 1997).

3 See Naomi Zack, "The American Sexualization of Race," in Zack (ed.) *Race/Sex*.

4 See Naomi Zack, *Race and Mixed Race* (Philadelphia: Temple University Press, 1993); *Thinking About Race* (Belmont, CA: Wadsworth, 1998), ch. 3; "Race and Philosophic Meaning," in Zack (ed.) *Race/Sex*; "Philosophy and Racial Paradigms," forthcoming in *Journal of Value Inquiry*.

5 Frantz Fanon, "The Fact of Blackness," in Naomi Zack, Laurie Shrage and Crispin Sartwell (eds) *Race, Class, Gender and Sexuality: The Big Questions* (Cambridge, MA: Blackwell Publishers, 1998).

6 To be precise, the forms request that after respondents indicate their race, they indicate whether or not they are Hispanic. See David Theo Goldberg, "Made in the USA," in Naomi Zack (ed.) *American Mixed Race: The Culture of Microdiversity* (Lanham, MD: Rowman and Littlefield, 1995).

7 See: Tommy L. Lott, *The Invention of Race: Black Culture and the Politics of Representation* (Cambridge, MA: Blackwell Publishers, 1999), pp. 111–22; Crispin Sartwell, *Act Like You Know: African-American Autobiography and White Idenity* (Chicago: University of Chicago Press, 1998), ch. 5.

8 The exact figure as of May 1999 was 10,486 (*The American Philosophical Association Proceedings and Addresses*, 22/5 (May 1999), p. 83.

9 See Leonard Harris, "The Status of Blacks in Academic Philosophy," in Zack, Schrage and Sartwell (eds) *Race, Class, Gender and Sexuality*, pp. 48–9.

10 R. C. Lewontin, *Biology as Ideology: The Doctrine of DNA* (New York: HarperCollins, 1993).

11   See: Hilary Putnam, "A Half Century of Philosophy, Viewed From Within," in Thomas Bender and Carl E. Schorske (eds) *American Academic Culture in Transformation: Fifty Years, Four Disciplines* (Princeton: Princeton University Press, 1977), pp. 193–226 (Putnam pinpoints "analytic" on p. 220), and Alexander Nehamas "Trends in Recent American Philosophy," on pp. 271–307. For a broader list but one still lacking in either women or nonwhites, see Giovanna Borradori, *The American Philosopher: Conversations with Quine, Davidson, Putnam, Nozick, Danto, Rorty, Cavell, MacIntyre, and Kuhn,* trans. Rosanna Crocitto (Chicago: University of Chicago Press, 1991).

12   See Putnam, "Half Century of Philosophy," Nehamas, "Trends," and Borradori, *American Philisopher.*

13   For an overview of the half-century on these subjects, see Tyler Burge, "Philosophy of Language and Mind: 1950–1990," in *The Philosophical Review,* 101/1 (January 1992), pp. 3–51.

14   See Christopher Shea, "Leiter Fluid," about Brian Leiter's *The Philosophical Gourmet Report,* in *Linguafranca,* July–August, 1999, pp. 7–9.

15   See *The American Philosophical Association proceedings and Addresses,* 22/5 (May 1999), p. 98.

16   In 1996, Adrian Piper counted only three African-American women who were tenured academic philosophers. See "Adrian M. S. Piper," in George Yancy (ed.) *African American Philosophers: 17 Conversations* (New York: Routledge, 1998), p. 60.

17   Kimberle Crenshaw, "Demarginalizing the Intersection of Race and Sex: A Black Feminist Critique of Antidiscrimination Doctrine, Feminist Theory and Antiracist Politics," *University of Chicago Legal Forum* (1989), pp. 139–67.

18   On blacks and philosophy, see Lewis R. Gordon, *Bad Faith and Antiblack Racism* (Atlantic Highlands, NJ: Humanities Press, 1995), esp. parts II and III; John P. Pittman (ed.) *African-American Perspectives and Philosophical Traditions* (New York: Routledge, 1996). On philosophy and (white) female gender see Janet A. Kourany (ed.) *Philosophy in a Feminist Voice: Critiques and Reconstrutions* (Princeton: Princeton University Press, 1998); Mary Lyndon Shanley and Carol Pateman (eds) *Feminist Interpretations and Political Theory* (University Park, PA: Pennsylvania State University Press, 1991).

19   There is one exception. The reprinted article by Angela Davis was selected by the editor, after a number of other articles had been written, because of its specific relevance to the themes that were developing in the volume. The reprints by Linda Alcoff, Joy James, and Ofelia Schutte were selected by the authors, although they added introductions to key them into this collection.

20   On ideology and critical theory, see Zack, *Thinking About Race,* ch. 10.

PART 1
Critique

CHAPTER 1

"Discredited Knowledge" in the Nonfiction of Toni Morrison

JOY JAMES

This essay on Toni Morrison is a tribute to a thinker who is able to synthesize, while letting go of, preconceived notions of knowledge and experience and culture. Morrison is perhaps one of the most influential and provocative writers at the end of this era. Her work represents a fluidity and continuity in the "black" experience which filters into the "white" experience to help define humanity.

> *African American intellectuals and academic questions*
> The education of the next generation of black intellectuals is something that is terrifically important to me. But the questions black intellectuals put to themselves, and to African American students, are not limited and confined to our own community. For the major crises in politics, in government, in practically any social issue in this country the axis turns on issues of race. Is this country willing to sabotage its cities and school systems if they're occupied mostly by black people? It seems so. When we take on these issues and problems as black intellectuals, what we are doing is not merely the primary work of enlightening and producing a generation of young black intellectuals. Whatever the flash points are, they frequently have to do with amelioration, enhancement or identification of the problems of the entire country. So this is not parochial; it is not marginal; it is not even primarily self-interest. (Toni Morrison, "African American intellectual life at Princeton: a conversation," *Princeton Today*)

In her nonfiction essays, Toni Morrison's dissection of racist paradigms is framed by a worldview that testifies to African-American ancestral spirits, the centrality of transcendent community, and her faith in the abilities of African-American intellectuals to critique and civilize a racist society. Reading Morrison as a cultural observer and practitioner, I share a sensibility that privileges community and ancestors while confronting dehumanizing cultural representations and practices. I quote from Morrison's nonfiction to sketch a frame for viewing her observations on racist stereotypes and black resistance. Even in its incompleteness, a sketch reveals clues for deciphering how Morrison uncovers and recovers ground for "discredited knowledge" in which traditional and contemporary cultural beliefs held among African Americans are connected to political struggles.[1] The outline of a conceptual site or worldview is not an argument for black essentialism; recognizing the political place of African-American cultural views, which manifest and mutate through time and location, constructs these views neither as quintessential nor universal to everyone of African descent. Likewise, a passionate interest in African American intellectual and political resistance to anti-black racism is not synonymous with an indifference to non-African Americans or to accommodations to Eurocentrism and white supremacy.

Morrison explores the intellectual service of African-American educators in ways compatible with the role of the African philosopher, as development within and through service is described by Tsenay Serequeberhan:

> The calling of the African philosopher ... comes to us from a lived history whose endurance and sacrifice – against slavery and colonialism – has made our present and future existence in freedom possible. The reflective explorations of African philosophy are thus aimed at further enhancing and expanding this freedom.[2]

This call of the African philosopher or theorist, shared by the African-American intellectual, predates imperialism, enslavement, and racism. Morrison argues that the questions that African-American intellectuals raise for and among themselves reverberate beyond black communities. Therefore, exploring a worldview that presents service and community as indispensable, time and space as expansive, knowledge as intergenerational and responsive to the conditions of people, and community as a changing, transcendent but nevertheless shared and thorny tie, would frame responses to state violence and resistance to oppressive cultural practices.

Morrison's essays raise a number of questions about the possibilities for critiquing and developing curricular paradigms that acknowledge realities greater than those recognized by conventional academia. Worldviews contextualize educators' lives and shape how they develop curricula, pedagogy, and scholarship to talk about, or silence talk about, critical theory and racialized knowledge. Educators can challenge or reinforce academic relationships to the worldviews of alternative thinkers such as Morrison. For instance, teaching her writings without a critical discussion of racism and slavery is a perhaps not uncommon, appropriative act that reproduces racial dominance. In Morrison's work discussed below, one finds the demystification of racism tied to a deep commitment to the well-being of African Americans. Educators who unravel these ties depoliticize the radical nature of her writings, and, in effect, repoliticize the work as compatible with intellectual paradigms that are indifferent to the racist practices of American society.

In the classroom, expanding the intellectual canon to include Morrison and other Others – people of color, women, poor and working-class people, gay, lesbian, and bisexual people – for more inclusive and representative curricula does not subvert racialized hierarchies. Additive curricula do not inherently democratize education: in integrative reforms, the axis of the universe remains the same. For instance, bell hooks notes:

> A white woman professor teaching a novel by a black woman writer (Toni Morrison's *Sula*) who never acknowledges the "race" of the characters is not including works by "different" writers in a manner that challenges ways we have been traditionally taught as English majors to took at literature. The political standpoint of any professor engaged with the development of cultural studies will determine whether issues of difference and otherness will be discussed in new ways or in ways that reinforce domination.[3]

At best, additive curricula that offer no critique of the dominant worldview civilize racist practices; at worst, they function as decorative shields against critiques of Eurocentrism. Where analyses of whiteness as a metaparadigm are absent, critiques of racialized oppression are insufficient to create a learning environment in which teaching critical work maintains rather than dismantles communal ties and subversive insights. More accurate representation of the diversity of intellectual life and work of transgressive African-American intellectuals requires a context greater than the traditional academic paradigm. Perhaps the only way to attain greater accuracy and honesty is to stand on some terrain, within some worldview other than that legitimized by Eurocentric academe. Engaging in this "dangerous, solitary, radical work," we might finally confront the academic penchant for playing in the dark.[4]

Traditional worldviews
[In *Song of Solomon*] I could blend the acceptance of the supernatural and a profound rootedness in the real world at the same time with neither taking precedence over the other. It is indicative of the cosmology, the way in which Black people looked at the world. We are very practical people, very down-to-earth, even shrewd people, But within that practicality we also accepted what I suppose could be called superstition and magic, which is another way of knowing things. But to blend those two worlds together at the same time was enhancing, not limiting. And some of those things were "discredited knowledge" that Black people had discredited only because Black people were discredited therefore what they *knew* was "discredited." And also because the press toward upward social mobility would mean to get as far away from that kind of knowledge as possible. That kind of knowledge has a very strong place in my work. (Toni Morrison, "Rootedness")

Distinguishing worldview from superstition requires sketching the cosmology that grounds Morrison's work. Some black writers posit a non-hegemonic perspective in which (1) community or the collective is central rather than individual achievement or individualism; (2) the transcendent or spiritual is inseparable from the mundane or secular; (3) "nature" is a force essential to humanity; and (4) feminine and masculine are complementary rather than contradictory components of identity and culture. These beliefs (considered illogical in conventional US culture) are not exclusive to an "African-centered" viewpoint. There are similarities between traditional African cosmology and other cosmologies. For instance, in some traditional Native American worldviews, the concept of community also extends through time, for example, in Native American discussions of the seven generations.

What some call superstition or magic, John Mbiti describes as aspects of a cultural worldview in his book *Traditional African Religions and Philosophies*:

Most [traditional] peoples . . . believe that the spirits are what remains of human beings when they die physically. This then becomes the ultimate status . . . the point of change or development beyond which [one] cannot go apart from a few national heroes who might become deified. . . . Man [or Woman] does not, and need not, hope to become a spirit: [s]he is inevitably to become one, just as a child will automatically grow to become an adult.[5]

Mbiti notes that historically African worldviews have maintained nonlinear time in which the past, present, and future coexist and overlap. (This view is also held in other cultures and in some scientific communities.) Traditional African cosmology sees the nonduality of time and space. Rather than suggest a monolithic Africa, Mbiti's work describes the diversity of religions throughout the continent. Yet he maintains that various organizing principles are prevalent despite ethnic and societal differences. The cosmology he documents rejects the socially constructed dichotomies between sacred and secular, spiritual and political, the individual and community that are characteristic of western culture. This perspective reappears in African-American culture.

Worldviews or values are not deterministic. One may choose. In fact, Mbiti, an African theologian trained in European universities, selects Christianity, depicting it as superior to traditional African religions, which he notes share Christianity's monotheism. We may elect to reject the traditional worldviews that shape African cultures, as Mbiti does. Or we may reaffirm these values, as Morrison does. Stating that "discredited knowledge" has "a very strong place" in her work, Morrison refuses to distance herself from a traditional African and African American cultural worldview, despite the fact that academic or social assimilation and advancement "would mean to get as far away from that kind of knowledge as possible." Without considering the validity of this discredited knowledge or academically marginalized belief system, some may portray Morrison's work as romantic, ungrounded mysticism. Outside of a worldview that recognizes the values mirrored in her work, it is difficult to perceive of Morrison as anything other than exotic. Her fiction is not mere phantasm. As her nonfiction explains, she writes within the framework of African American cultural values and political and spiritual perspectives.

Morrison's work clearly relies on African-centered cultural paradigms that are documented by anthropologists, theologians, philosophers, and sociologists. For centuries, these paradigms have been derided by Eurocentric thought and dismissed as primitive superstition. The invalidation of these frameworks is traceable to European colonization on several continents for several centuries. Historically, European racial mythology determined whether people whose physiology and ancestry were strikingly different were capable of creating theory, philosophy, and cosmology or were merely able to ape superstition. Today, the rejection of discredited knowledge, held by not-fully-assimilated African Americans, branches from this disparagement of the African origins of these views. As Congolese philosopher K. Kia Bunseki Fu-Kiau notes in *The African Book without Title*:

> Africa was invaded . . . to civilize its people. . . . [Civilization] having "accomplished" her "noble" mission . . . African people are still known as people without logic, people without systems, people without concepts. . . . African wisdom hidden in proverbs, the old way of theorizing among people of oral literature [cannot be] seen and understood in the way [the] western world sees and understands [a proverb]. . . . For us . . . proverbs are principles, theories, warehouses of knowledge . . . they have "force de loi," [the] force of law.[6]

People whose traditional culture is supposedly known to be illogical, without complex belief systems, are generally received in racialized societies as dubious contributors to intellectual life or theory. Spoken and unspoken debates about their epistemic subculture range ideologically from reactionary conservatism to progressive radicalism.

Morrison's writings are radical precisely because they reject the Eurocentric labels of primitive for African cosmology and the epistemological aspects of African-American culture (all the while cognizant of the value of parts of European culture). Critiquing the racial stereotypes of white supremacy, she asserts the presence of traditional, communal culture as connected to black and African ancestors. Challenging hegemonic paradigms, Morrison delineates and deconstructs the European American muse's addiction to ethnic notions. She issues two complementary calls that politicize the spirit: to resist the racial mythology embodied in the white European American imagination and to reconnect with the values rooted in traditional African-American culture. Of these values, the one that provides the foundation for her work is that of African-American community: in her writings, Morrison draws down the spirit to house it in community.

The Centrality of Community

Perhaps one of the most debated concepts is the viability of an autonomous African American cultural community. Irrespective of the arguments that discredit this concept, Morrison expresses a personal sense of responsibility to community, making it a cornerstone in her work. The individual's salvation, her or his sanity, comes through relationship to others. This knowledge resonates in Morrison's work, and it inspires and informs her political risk-taking and daring. The community she explores is neither a global nor a nation-state one, yet she does not deny the existence or significance of either. The vibrant collection of people that engages her is the African-American community. And it is its synthesis of seeming polarities – maleness and femaleness, ugliness and beauty, good and evil, the spiritual and the mundane – that intrigues her.

In "Unspeakable Things Unspoken: The Afro-American Presence in American Literature," Morrison's analysis of her novels, particularly her comments on *Beloved* and *Song of Solomon*, illustrates her emphasis on community and the individual's relationship to it. In this essay, Morrison examines how language "activates" and is activated by outlining the context for the first sentences of each of her novels. She reminds us that this exploration into how she "practice[s] language" seeks and presents a "posture of vulnerability to those aspects of Afro-American culture" that shape her novels.[7]

Of those novels, *Beloved* is a striking example of her awareness of the destructive impact of unbalanced spiritual and political worlds on community. According to Morrison, *Beloved is* haunting because it works in part "to keep the reader preoccupied with the nature of the incredible spirit world while being supplied a controlled diet of the incredible political world."[8] An aspect of this incredible political world is this novel's inspiration in a specific historical tragedy, the story of an African-American woman, Margaret Garner, who tried to flee slavery with her children in the nineteenth century.[9] After she was captured in Cincinnati, Garner killed her daughter to save her from slavery and then attempted to take her own life. In a videotaped interview with the BBC, Morrison describes how her own haunting by Garner's life and death ended when she wrote *Beloved*. The context for community and the resistance to oppression is the groundwork for Garner's story of the "unnatural" mother who may or may not have demonstrated the incredible depths of maternal love and political resistance, as fictionalized in *Beloved*. In life and in death, individuals remain connected to and grow within the life of the community.

This is true as well in *Song of Solomon*, where the essence of community directs Morrison's discussion of freedom and grace, In her essay she describes the insurance agent whose suicide fulfills his promise to fly from (no-)Mercy Hospital:

> The agent's flight, like that of the Solomon in the title, although toward asylum (Canada, or freedom, or home, or the company of the welcoming dead), and although it carries the possibility of failure and the certainty of danger, is toward change, an alternative way, a cessation of things – as – they – are. It should not be understood as a simple desperate act . . . but as obedience to a deeper contract with his people.[10]

Morrison explains: "The insurance agent does not declare, announce, or threaten his act. He promises, as though a contract is being executed faithfully between himself and others. Promises broken, or kept; the difficulty of ferreting out loyalties and ties that bind or bruise wend their way throughout the action and the shifting relationships".[11] Dangerous but not desperate, the insurance agent embraces rather than flees his community. His notion of a contract is connected to a cultural understanding of community as transcendent; his flight transcends dualities that posit a divide between life and death. Morrison relates how his not-fully-comprehensible gift is acknowledged and received:

> It is his commitment to them, regardless of whether, in all its details, they understand it. There is, however, in their response to his action, a tenderness, some contrition and mounting respect ("They didn't know he had it in him.") and an awareness that the gesture enclosed rather than repudiated themselves. The note he leaves asks for forgiveness . . . an almost Christian declaration of love as well as humility of one who was not able to do more.[12]

Exploring the relationship between community and individual, Morrison suggests that her novels involve the reader and narrator in communal ties. In the worldview of her literature, knowledge emerges from connection to rather than alienation from other people. Wisdom arises within community, in spite of the flawed character of its constituents:

That egalitarianism which places us all (reader, the novel's population, the narrator's voice) on the same footing, reflected for me the force of flight and mercy, and the precious, imaginative yet realistic gaze of black people who (at one time, anyway) did not mythologize what or whom it mythologized. The "song" itself contains this unblinking evaluation of the miraculous and heroic flight of the legendary Solomon, an unblinking gaze which is lurking in the tender but amused choral-community response to the agent's flight.[13]

Morrison's own unblinking gaze fosters critical self-reflection in regard to African-American communities. It would be simple yet simplistic to idealize the African-American community as a haven of safety and harmony against dehumanizing racism. Nowhere do Morrison's essays argue for this perfected black bliss. Everywhere in her literature there exists the reality of the grim, bizarre, and determined struggle in community that embodies both the rotting and the purifying. Rather than succumb to romantic idealism, Morrison admits that her "vulnerability would lie in romanticizing blackness rather than demonizing it; vilifying whiteness rather than reifying it."[14] Her deconstruction of Eurocentrism and Africanisms coexists with a critique of the limitations of black community. Those limitations partly stem from African Americans' stunted group abilities and our refusal to recognize and honor the ancestors and each other. For example, Morrison details how in *Song of Solomon*, the ancestral figure represented by Solomon, who embodies the African ancestors' flight toward freedom, is not readily recognized by community members: "The African myth is also contaminated. Unprogressive, unreconstructed, self-born Pilate [the female protagonist] is unimpressed by Solomon's flight."[15]

Rejection, alienation, and violence toward self, others, or the ancestors, however, do not negate the reality of these ties. Relationships are determinant. One cannot erase community. One decides only how to relate to the community, which includes self, others, ancestors, and future born. Morrison's commentary on *Beloved* and *Song of Solomon* suggests that our ancestors are indispensable to community. Through them, the past sits in the present and future, guiding descendants. The writings suggest that to the extent that we recognize our ancestors, seeking their advice and spiritual power, we deepen our ability to grow in community with them.

The Role of African Ancestors

> When you kill the ancestor you kill yourself ... nice things don't
> always happen to the totally self-reliant. (Toni Morrison, "Rootedness")

For some worldviews, the greatest spiritual development is tied to service
to the community; in fact, in time through such work one will likely
evolve into an elder and later an ancestor. Ancestors are communal
members in these traditional worldviews.[16] The practice of honoring or
worshiping ancestors is prevalent worldwide. The symbols of European
American cultural icons are both physical and literary. For example,
the ancestral spirits of Confederate soldiers and slaveholders, in iconic
statues in Memphis, Jackson, or Birmingham parks, inspire devoted
visitors. The fervor of canonical reverence in universities belies the
disdain that many European-descended Americans feel for ancestral
worship. Popularized ancestors such as George Washington, Thomas
Jefferson, and Elvis evince complex relationships to and facile representations of white American freedom and civilization that are dependent
on enslaved or exploited African Americans. Increasingly, since the
civil rights movement, American culture has jumbled the contradictory
values embodied in ancestors who manifest oppositional worldviews:
holidays, coins, and postage stamps pay tribute to Washington and
Jefferson as well as Ida B. Wells and Martin Luther King Jr. (although
John Brown is rarely memorialized). All collectively comprise community. Extending through time and space to include our predecessors,
contemporaries, and future generations, community here is not bound
by physical or temporal limits; its relationships are transcendent. This
transcendence is marked by the presence of ancestors.

Morrison uses the term ancestor to refer to living elders and
ancestral spirits. (I reserve the term for historical figures.) Arguing
that "there is always an elder" in black literature, Morrison maintains
that a distinctive characteristic of African-American writing is its
focus on the ancestors: "These ancestors are not just parents, they are
sort of timeless people whose relationships to the characters are
benevolent, instructive, and protective, and they provide a certain
kind of wisdom."[17] For Morrison, studying how African-American
writers relate to the ancestor(s) is revealing:

> Some of them, such as Richard Wright, had great difficulty with that
> ancestor. Some of them, like James Baldwin, were confounded and

disturbed by the presence or absence of an ancestor. What struck me in looking at some contemporary fiction was that whether the novel took place in the city or in the country, the presence or absence of that figure determined the success or the happiness of the character. It was the absence of an ancestor that was frightening, that was threatening, and it caused huge destruction and disarray in the work itself. That the solace comes, not from the contemplation of serene nature as in a lot of mainstream white literature, nor from the regard in which the city was held as a kind of corrupt place to be. Whether the character was in Harlem or Arkansas, the point was there, this timelessness was there, this person who represented this ancestor.[18]

Speech about the ancestors not only enables critiques of historical oppression (such as the references to slavery made in *Beloved* and *Song of Solomon*), but it also establishes communal realities to support and reflect political-spiritual and secular-sacred traditions. Within this worldview, ancestors illuminate an avenue for liberation: listen, and you learn from them; acknowledge their contributions and legacies, and you share their power (which does not necessarily promise redemption). In their physical lives, our predecessors who attained the stature of elders helped others to develop as free human beings. As spiritual forces after death, they continue to guide human development. In this worldview, according to Congolese philosophy, knowledge is "the experience of that deepest reality found between the spiritualized ancestors and the physically living thinkers."[19]

As a living thinker, Toni Morrison is a mapper of recollection sites. Instructional and often inspirational calls to expansive community come from various locations of memory, which despite cultural variances point to unifying elements that are based on shared values. In my own recollection sites, I remember the values of family, peers, and teachers. I recall the political work in the 1980s of friends and activists countering apartheid and US imperialism in the Caribbean and Latin America, where Nicaraguans and El Salvadorans, fighting United States-funded contras and death squads, honored their dead by calling "Presente!" after their names were read in roll calls. I remember the teachings of activist elders and ancestors, the technique of seminary, and the spirit of African-based religious houses in Brooklyn and the Bronx. All these experiences politicized me and now remind me of the futility of traveling without faith or ancestral hope, and the liabilities of academic training that encourages ignorance of communal culture.

Morrison's writings present us with the knower who reaches

beyond the straitjacket of Africanisms into the past, which is the present and future, to pull out both the African presence and the European American imagining of that presence. Morrison is only one of many African Americans following liberating traditions that acknowledge the ancestors as part of a spiritual and political place and practice. Calls to the ancestral presence and the primacy of historical African-American figures appear in African American religion, politics, and art. This recognition is also in written (literary) and oral culture. For instance, the African American women's vocal group Sweet Honey in the Rock consistently honors the ancestors in song. Their "Ella's Song," dedicated to civil rights activist Ella Josephine Baker, uses excerpts from Baker's speeches: "We who believe in freedom cannot rest, until the killing of black men, black mothers' sons, is as important as the killing of white men, white mothers' sons."[20] In their introduction to the song "Fannie Lou Hamer," the group and its founder, Bernice Johnson Reagon, former Student Nonviolent Coordinating Committee activist and now director of African American culture at the Smithsonian, explicates their worldview:

> During the civil rights movement of the 1960s . . . Fannie Lou Hamer . . . became a symbol of the strength and power of resistance . . . We call her name today in the tradition of African libation. By pouring libation we honor those who provide the ground we stand on. We acknowledge that we are here today because of something someone did before we came.[21]

In the academic works of African-American intellectuals, the ancestral spirits also appear. Angela Davis speaks of the ancestors in *The Autobiography of Angela Davis* and *Women, Race and Class*.[22] Historian Vincent Harding pays tribute to the ancestors in *There Is a River: The Black Struggle for Freedom in America*.[23] Using "we" throughout his narrative history of African-American resistance to enslavement over centuries, Harding merges past, present, and future. With the pronoun "we" he includes himself in the historical telling of our liberation struggles. Finding the historical accounts of black radicalism in the United States to be limited by their abstractness, scope, and Eurocentrism, Harding's narrative both analyzes and celebrates the history of the African-American freedom struggles. Using the metaphor of a river and the imagery of a poem by Langston Hughes, he describes as mentacide the dehumanizing practices that turned Africans into slaves, arguing that to enslave a people, one must first destroy their belief systems, their knowledge in themselves, and their understandings of physical and metaphysical power.

Morrison's work is very familiar within this worldview, framing the vision of African-American artists and writers who assert that invoking the spirit honors the memories of ancestors. This act of conjuring also testifies to the prevailing wisdom that we, as a people, resist enslavement and genocide because of the spirits that politicize our lives. Reading as strangers in strange sites can politicize the spirit of our societies and instill some honest vigor in our intellectual and moral life. What prevents new, critical, and anti-racist readings are the racist stereotypes that have been imprinted on American literary and academic minds.

American Africanisms

My work requires me to think about how free I can be as an African-American woman writer in my genderized, sexualized, wholly racialized world. To think about (and wrestle with) the full implications of my situation leads me to consider what happens when other writers work in a highly and historically racialized society. (Toni Morrison, *Playing in the Dark*)

Writers working in a highly racialized society often express fascination with blackness that is both overt and covert. In *Playing in the Dark: Whiteness and the Literary Imagination*, Morrison maintains that Europeans and European Americans "choose to talk about themselves through and within a sometimes allegorical, sometimes metaphorical, but always choked representation of an Africanist presence."[24] She labels this practice and its arsenal "American Africanisms," which mirror European Africanisms. The term "Africanism" represents for Morrison

the denotative and connotative blackness that African peoples have come to signify, as well as the entire range of views, assumptions, readings, and misreadings that accompany Eurocentric learning about these people. . . . As a disabling virus within literary discourse, Africanism has become, in the Eurocentric tradition that American education favors, both a way of talking about and a way of policing matters of class, sexual license, and repression, formations and exercises of power, and meditations on ethics and accountability.[25]

As a literary and political tool, Africanism "provides a way of contemplating chaos and civilization, desire and fear, and a mechanism for testing the problems and blessings of freedom."[26] The distinctive difference of the New World, she writes, is that its claim to freedom coexisted with "the presence of the unfree within the heart of the democratic experiment."[27] It is arguably still the same. Morrison advises that we investigate "the Africanist character as surrogate and enabler" and the use of the "Africanist idiom"to mark difference or the "hip, sophisticated, ultra-urbane." Her own explorations inform us that within the "construction of blackness and enslavement" existed

> not only the not-free but also, with the dramatic polarity created by skin color, the projection of the not-me. The result was a playground for the imagination. What rose up out of collective needs to allay internal fears and to rationalize external exploitation was a [European] American Africanism – a fabricated brew of darkness, otherness, alarm, and desire that is uniquely American.[28]

Newly constructed beings and inhumanities, such as the white male as both exalted demigod and brutish enslaver, were sanctioned by literature. Morrison emphasizes the cultural aspects of dominance in order to critique the European American literary imagination: "Cultural identities are formed and informed by a nation's literature . . . what seemed to be on the 'mind' of the literature of the United States was the self-conscious but highly problematic construction of the American as a new white man."[29] In the formation of this new American identity, blackness as embodied in the African was indispensable to elevating whiteness. In this exaltation of whiteness, the Africanist other became the device for "thinking about body, mind, chaos, kindness, and love; [and] provided the occasion for exercises in the absence of restraint, the presence of restraint, the contemplation of freedom and of aggression."[30] Within this framework, the boundaries of the conventional literary imagination were set to ignore or rationalize enslavement and freedom that was based on enslavement. Transgressing such boundaries is rarely encouraged. Those determined to see themselves without mystification, however, do cross these borders. According to Morrison, an exceptional few and brave

European American writers attempted to free themselves of their entrapment in whiteness. She describes the courage in Herman Melville's tormented struggle to demystify whiteness in *Moby Dick*:

> To question the very notion of white progress, the very idea of racial superiority, of whiteness as privileged place in the evolutionary ladder of humankind, and to meditate on the fraudulent, self-destroying philosophy of that superiority, to "pluck it out from under the robes of Senators and judges," to drag the "judge himself to the bar," that was dangerous, solitary, radical work. Especially then. Especially now.[31]

Today, this "dangerous, solitary, radical work" is discouraged by claims that race or discussions of racism politicize and so pollute literary work:

> When matters of race are located and called attention to in American literature, critical response has tended to be on the order of a humanistic nostrum – or a dismissal mandated by the label "political." Excising the political from the life of the mind is a sacrifice that has proven costly. I think of this erasure as a kind of trembling hypochondria always curing itself with unnecessary surgery.[32]

This surgery is also selective, usually performed only on those deviating from the dominant ideologies. Literary works derive their meaning from worldviews that intend political consequences. Worldviews carry cultural values as well as political agendas. Only by replicating or naturalizing the dominant political ideologies – in effect, reproducing the racialized hegemony – can writers claim to be apolitical. Morrison clearly identifies her work as a practical art with a political focus, writing in "Rootedness: the ancestor as foundation":

> I am not interested in indulging myself in some private, closed exercise of my imagination that fulfills only the obligation of my personal dreams – which is to say, yes, the work must be political. It must have that as its thrust. That's a pejorative term in critical circles now: if a work of art has any political influence in it, somehow it's tainted. My feeling is just the opposite; if it has none, it is tainted.[33]

These writings enable discussions in a society guarded against analyses of white supremacy. Her critical thought, despite increasing calls for the irrelevance of race, is particularly important in a society that routinely rejects such commentary as politically uncivil. Racial discourse seems to be pulled by marionette strings that work to curtail anti-racist critiques. As Morrison notes in "Unspeakable things unspoken",

> For three hundred years black Americans insisted that "race" was no usefully distinguishing factor in human relationships. During those same three centuries every academic discipline, including theology, history and natural science, insisted "race" was *the* determining factor in human development. When blacks discovered they had shaped or become a culturally formed race, and that it had specific and revered difference, suddenly they were told there is no such thing as "race," biological or cultural, that matters and that genuinely intellectual exchange cannot accommodate it. In trying to come to some terms about "race" and writing, I am tempted to throw my hands up. It always seemed to me that the people who invented the hierarchy of "race" when it was convenient for them ought not to be the ones to explain it away, now that it does not suit their purposes for it to exist. But there is culture and both gender and "race" inform and are informed by it. Afro-American culture exists and though it is clear (and becoming clearer) how it has responded to Western culture, the instances where and means by which it has shaped Western culture are poorly recognized or understood.[34]

African-American culture exists within the worldviews that shape and inform it. This culture and its practices reappear in Morrison's work. For instance, typical of the African and African American call-and-response tradition, she receives the call to testify to worldviews that are greater than white myths and to demystify, and thereby resist, a Frankensteinian blackness. Politicized by and politicizing the spirit, she issues her own charge to intellectuals and educators. This spirit is one of black resistance to oppression, a resistance historically rooted in the African-American community, its elders, and its ancestors. This spirit fuels current social debates. The worldview that shapes her politics is rooted to traditional African culture. This worldview coexists with and influences other perspectives within the dominant culture.

Conclusion

The ability to distinguish between humane culture and dehumanizing, racialized. mythology presupposes critical thinking that is grounded someplace other than in the conventional academic mind. Because critical race thinking is rarely encouraged in racialized settings, we seldom ask how a people, manufacturing and depending on racist myths and ghosts in order to see their reflections in the world, lose more than they gain. It seems that hauntings cannot be restricted. Inevitably, the racially privileged caste and its entourage find themselves marked and demarcated, more obsessed and possessed than their demonized Africanist inferiors. Morrison's work clinically and coolly dissects this production and possession. It calls us to witness a literacy that predates and overcomes Africanism, individualism, and materialism. With this literacy, we read about spirit and power through time and space. This knowledge is made meaningful – or meaningless – by the worldviews we embrace, viewpoints that credit – or discredit – the questions raised by the nonfiction of Toni Morrison.

All educators reflect and articulate worldviews in which they reveal themselves as compromised or uncompromisable knowers, either reproducing or resisting dominance. (There seem to be at least three types of compromised knowers connected to academe: the unwittingly, the voluntarily, and the forcibly compromised.) Bernice Johnson Reagon maintains that the uncompromisable knower is the one who straddles, standing with a foot in both worlds, unsplit by dualities and unhampered by a toxic imagination.[35] As I straddle and sometimes seem to fall from places in which an African-American spirit world and European American racial mythology converge, I marvel at Morrison's grace, her ability to call out both the reactionary – the Africanisms of the racist mind – and the revolutionary – the African ancestors and communal commitments.

Whether it is reactionary, reformist, or revolutionary, movement for curricular change entails a spirit of political struggle. Three oppositional tendencies generally appear: advocacy for a romanticized past as intellectually civilized; acquiescence to hierarchical but relatively stable structures; and visionary projections toward the unknowable known as the promise and risk of future justice. Those of us who straddle walk between worlds, in a space where insight and agency arise from community. Between, in, and within these worlds, some intellectuals respond when called. Morrison is such a traditionalist, an uncompromisable knower, a straddler with deep communal ties. How else could she blend two worlds to stand, rooted as she is, politicized by and politicizing the spirit? In that rootedness she writes:

> There must have been a time when an artist could be genuinely representative of the tribe and in it; when an artist could have a tribal or racial sensibility and an individual expression of it. There were spaces and places in which a single person could enter and behave as an individual within the context of the community, A small remnant of that you can see sometimes in Black churches where people shout. It is a very personal grief and a personal statement done among people you trust. Done within the context of the community, therefore safe. And while the shouter is performing some rite that is extremely subjective, the other people are performing as a community in protecting that person.[36]

Because cultural remnants are markers for realities denied or suppressed in a racialized society, African-American subjective and communal rites reveal the immeasurable distance between African ancestors and European/American Africanisms. Through her essays, which are unique and representative, political and spirit-filled, Toni Morrison invites us to struggle with these distinctions and differences in a polarized world.

Notes

An earlier version of this chapter appeared in *Resisting State Violence: Radicalism, Gender, and Racial in US Culture*, Minneapolis: University of Minnesota Press, 1996.

1 Toni Morrison, "Rootedness: The Ancestor as Foundation," in *Black Women Writers*, ed. Mari Evans (New York: Doubleday, 1984), p. 342.

2 Tsenay Serequeberhan, *African Philosophy* (New York: Paragon House, 1991), p. xxii.

3 bell hooks, *Yearning: Race, Gender and Cultural Politics* (Boston: South End, 1990), p. 131.

4 Toni Morrison, "Unspeakable Things Unspoken: The Afro-American Presence in American Literature," *Michigan Quarterly Review* (Winter 1989), p. 18.

5 John Mbiti, *Traditional African Religions and Philosophies* (London: Heineman, 1969), p. 79.

6   K. Kia Bunseki Fu-Kiau, *The African Book without Title* (Cambridge, MA: Fu-Kiau, 1980), pp. 62, 63.
7   Morrison, "Unspeakable Things," p. 33.
8   Ibid., p. 32.
9   The Garner story appears in Angela Davis *(Women, Race, and Class*, New York: Random House, 1981, p. 21); she is quoting from Herbert Aptheker, "The Negro Woman," *Masses and Mainstream* II/2 (February 1948), pp. 11–12.
10 Morrison, "Unspeakable Things," p. 28.
11 Ibid.
12 Ibid.
13 Ibid., p. 29.
14 Morrison, *Playing in the Dark: Whiteness and the Literary Imagination,* (Cambridge, MA: Harvard University Press, 1992), p. xi.
15 Morrison, "Unspeakable Things," p. 29.
16 Morrison, "Rootedness," p. 343.
17 Ibid.
18 Ibid.
19 Fu-kiau, *The African Book*, p. 62.
20 Sweet Honey in the Rock, "Ella's Song" *B'lieve I'll Run On . . . See What the End's Gonna Be* (Ukiah, CA.: Redwood Records, 1977).
21 Sweet Honey in the Rock, "Fanny Lou Hamer," *B'lieve I'll Run On.*
22 Angela Davis, *Angela Davis: An Autobiography* (New York: Random House, 1974); Davis, *Women, Race and Class.*
23 Vincent Harding, *There Is a River: The Black Struggle for Freedom in America* (New York: Random House, 1983).
24 Morrison, *Playing in the Dark*, p. 17.
25 Ibid., pp. 6–7.
26 Ibid., p. 7.
27 Ibid., p. 48.
28 Ibid., p. 38.
29 Ibid., p. 39.
30 Ibid., pp. 47–8.
31 Morrison, "Unspeakable Things," p. 18.
32 Morrison, *Playing in the Dark*, p. 12.
33 Morrison, "Rootedness," pp. 344–5.
34 Morrison, "Unspeakable Things," p. 3.
35 Bernice Johnson Reagon, " 'Nobody Knows the Trouble I See', or 'By and By I'm Gonna Lay Down My Heavy Load,' " *Journal of American History* 78/1 (June 1991), pp. 111–19.
36 Morrison, "Rootedness," p. 339.

CHAPTER 2

Cultural Alterity: Cross-cultural Communication and Feminist Theory in North–South Contexts

OFELIA SCHUTTE

When I began writing about identity issues and Latin American culture, I had already finished my first book on a major European philosopher. It was a feminist work on Nietzsche. The very project of writing such a book had already taken me well beyond the usual construct of a philosopher in the United States, given that mine was the first feminist book, I think, to be published on Nietzsche in this country. In the course of writing this book, I remember one moment when I was retracing Nietzsche's steps and visiting the places he loved near the Swiss Alps, and where he was inspired to write, when I thought to myself: when I am done with this book, I am going to do some things differently. I am going to focus on philosophers who are alive (so if I have a question I can actually ask them), and I am going to write on subjects that relate to my *concrete condition*. This condition, as I depicted it to myself years ago, was, in the simplest terms: the fact that I am Latin American and the fact that I am a woman.

As a philosopher, my aim is to address philosophical issues from a concrete condition, from my lived experience. In my productive life, living and writing have been strongly interrelated. But why I thought about my cultural background and my gendered position in society as the specific parameters from which I could conceptualize my writing is something that still baffles me. It seemed to happen spontaneously, as a direct consequence of where I found myself socially situated. Perhaps it was the contrasting sense of being a Latin American, a Cuban, doing research in Europe on a German philosopher (whose own sense of identity evoked a kind of national/cultural displacement) as well as my sense of being a woman among so many men in philosophy that fostered this drive in me to think through these constantly perceived differences. For example, I felt I was surrounded by wealth as I travelled in the developed countries. I wondered why buildings were so beautiful, so freshly painted, so architecturally appealing. I wondered why even travelling on the subway seemed to be a luxury. At the same time that I saw the lovely promenades and rows of grand houses or public buildings before me, simultaneously I could see ("in my mind"), almost superimposed on these scenes of wealth, the Third World barrios, the unpaved streets, the barefooted children. It was like having a sense of double vision, except there was no name for this experience back then. The reality of the world of Nietzsche research did not seem wholly real, because my sociocultural reality was missing in it.

As much as I enjoy this world of research, I carry in myself another world that is far more real to me than that privileged one. I am marked by Latin America, its beauty and its pathos, for good or for bad, whether I like it or not. And perhaps because I am marked by it and because I do not see enough of it in the North, I want to mark my writing with it. As Latinas and Latinos in the North, we are all-too-invisible as producers of culture yet all-too-visible as immigrants, as excess populations who still carry an accent when we speak or carry a view of friendship or of family that simply does not fit into the northern expectations. I feel the tensions and the contradictions between different cultures in me; these tensions are becoming more central as topics of my current writing.

In this essay, I address differences in communication between what I call incommensurable speaking positions. It has been a first attempt for me to think the concept of alterity (otherness, difference) from a Latina feminist position.

Communication, Identity, and Difference

This essay will address the issue of understanding cultural differences in the context of cross-cultural communication and dialogue, particularly those cases in which such communication or attempted communication takes place between members of a dominant culture and a subaltern culture. From an examination of these issues we can perhaps draw on some ideas that will permit us to reach a fuller understanding of cross-cultural feminist exchanges and dialogues. The reason for focusing on the topic of cross-cultural communication is that recently, I have become increasingly aware of the levels of prejudice affecting the basic processes of communication between Anglo-American and Latina speakers, as well as the difficulties experienced by many Latin American immigrants to the United States. It seems to me that in these times of massive prejudices against immigrants and of extraordinary displacements of people from their communities of origin, the question of how to communicate with "the other" who is culturally different from oneself is one of the greatest challenges facing north–south relations and interaction. If the question before us is how to frame the conditions for the possibility of a global feminist ethics – or whether such an ethics is indeed possible – I see no better place to start than to examine the conditions of possibility for cross-cultural communication as such.

My methodology for understanding what is at stake in cross-cultural and intersubjective communication will depend largely on an existential-phenomenological concept of alterity. In this tradition, the breakthrough in constructing the concept of *the other* occurs when one combines the notion of the other as different from the self with the acknowledgment of the self's decentering that results from the experience of such differences.[1] Moreover, the breakthrough involves acknowledging the positive, potentially ethical dimensions of such a decentering for interpersonal relations (as in Levinas, Irigaray, and Kristeva), in contrast to simply taking the decentering one might experience in the light of the other's differences as a deficit in the individual's control over the environment.[2] According to this understanding, interpersonal and social interactions marked by cultural (as well as sexual, racial, and other kinds of difference) allow us to reach new ethical, aesthetic, and political ground.

In other words, the other is not the one who passively confirms what I am predisposed to think about her; she is not the one who acts as the mirror to my self or the one whose image justifies my existing ego boundaries. If this were the case, the other would only be a stand-in for the self's narcissism. Just the contrary; the other is that person or experience which makes it possible for the self to recognize its own limited horizons in the light of asymmetrically given relations marked by sexual, social, cultural, or other differences. The other, the foreigner, the stranger, is that person occupying the space of the subaltern in the culturally asymmetrical power relation, but also those elements or dimensions of the self that unsettle or decenter the ego's dominant, self-enclosed, territorialized identity.

In addition to these presuppositions regarding otherness and difference derived from the phenomenological-existential and poststructuralist tradition, I will take into account recent methodological developments regarding the concept of cultural difference as represented in postcolonial feminist theory. Working against the background of the West's history of colonial enterprises and its exploitation of other societies and cultures, postcolonial theory, in its various manifestations, pays special attention to issues of language, class, and racial, ethnic, sexual, and gender differences, and to the justification of narratives about the nation-state.[3] Postcolonial feminist theory, in turn, directs its attention to the lives of women and to the tensions affecting women whose voices appear in national narratives and accounts of diasporic migrations. At stake in these "post" theories is a certain loss of innocence with regard to narratives of identity because of a more critical awareness of the regulative power such narratives have in defining who we are, who we aren't, and who others are and aren't.[4] The regulative power of narratives of identity is something with respect to which we are, to some extent, complicit, but we are also able to examine these narratives from some distance. Postcolonial and feminist critics have therefore used psychoanalytic theory to investigate further and to elaborate aspects of the relation between self and other in the light of accepted narratives of cultural identity and difference. In particular, Kristeva has studied symbolic analogies between the foreign other and the Freudian concept of the uncanny in the self – what she has called the stranger within the self.[5] Postcolonial feminisms, problematizing the western concept of self, question the regulative use of gender in national and postnational narratives, but also the Enlightenment concept of individualism that fails to notice the complex, multi-layered, fragmented, contradictory aspects of the self.

Finally, and on a different note regarding issues of alterity and identity, one more presupposition guiding these reflections is the belief that what we hold to be the nature of knowledge is not culture-free but is determined by the methodologies and data legitimated by dominant cultures. In other words, the scientific practices of a dominant culture are what determine not only the limits of knowledge but who may legitimately participate in the language of science. In everyday practices, outside of university environments, women are seen as particularly illiterate when it comes to having scientific knowledge or being able to discuss scientific issues with experts in the field. One does not need to have read Foucault to realize how very interconnected is the relation of knowledge to power. My point is that cultural (not just scientific) knowledge involves a highly constraining form of power. This power involves constraints over oneself and constraints over others. The type of constraints I shall try to examine and deconstruct to some extent are those dealing with a dominant culture's understanding of cultural differences. In addition, my analysis tries to understand sociocultural differences without subjecting them to masculine-dominant, gender-normative categories and maxims.

There is a need to develop a model of ethical and philosophical understanding in which the meaning of sexual difference is not limited by a gender-normative bias regarding what constitutes "the female body" or the proper function of a woman's mental abilities. Similarly, there is a need to develop a model for the understanding of subaltern cultural differences. In other words, both the critique of gender-normative biases and the critique of cultural imperialism need to be taken into account. Nevertheless, given that quite a number of critiques of cultural imperialism are themselves based on masculinist (often highly authoritarian) models of liberation from imperialism, which in turn presuppose and reinforce the domination of men over women in liberation struggles, the critique of cultural imperialism should be tempered by some kind of pluricultural feminist perspective. All these considerations lead to a feminist postcolonial perspective that can balance the struggle against the legacy of colonial-imperial domination with the struggle for the creation of feminist and feminist-compatible societies.

The Disparity in Speaking Positions

These reflections begin with some of my personal impressions regarding the difficulties of cross-cultural communication when one culture circumstantially holds the upper hand over another. The culture with the upper hand will generate resistance in the group that fails to enjoy a similar cultural status, while the culture of the subaltern group will hardly be understood in its importance or complexity by those belonging to the culturally dominant group unless exceptional measures are taken to promote a good dialogue. Even so, it is my view that no two cultures or languages can be perfectly transparent to each other. There is always a residue of meaning that will not be reached in cross-cultural endeavors, a residue sufficiently important to point to what I shall refer to more abstractly as a principle of (cross-cultural) incommensurability.[6]

The most common way to point to this excess of meaning is to refer to the untranslatable aspects of a language vis-à-vis another language. In this case, one might think of incommensurability arithmetically as a kind of minus effect to cross-cultural communication: what I get from the differently situated speaker is the conveyable message minus the specific cultural difference that does not come across. Theorized in this manner, the way to maximize intercultural dialogue would be to devise a way to put as much meaning as possible into the plus side of the exchange, so that as little as possible remains on the minus side of it. But although creating more effective means of communication between disparate groups can help reduce social conflict and tension, I don't believe much is understood about cultural difference if incommensurability is thought of in this predominantly quantitative manner.

Another way to think of incommensurability, and one that is much more relevant and fruitful for our discussion, is to look at nodes in a linguistic interchange or a conversation in which the other's speech, or some aspect of it, resonates in me as a kind of strangeness, as a kind of displacement of the usual expectation. Cultural alterity requires that one not bypass these experiences or subsume them under an already familiar category. Even the category of cultural diversity is called into question when diversity is institutionalized so as to mask a more radical view of differences. Postmodern postcolonial discourse looks for the possibilities of using nontotalizing concepts of difference rather than "the consensual, ethnocentric notion of the pluralistic existence of cultural diversity."[7] In the establishment's view of diversity, the rules controlling the representation of diversity usually reflect the will of the winners in political and military struggles. As Lyotard's debate with Habermas makes clear, the rationality of consensus is only a few steps from the desire for one system, one truth – in sum, one rationality – to dominate human civilization. In its extreme, the will to one truth has yielded the totalitarian Reign of Terror.[8] The representation of the one system as "pluralist" and favorable to cultural diversity must be called into question because of the sweeping power exercised by the system to harness the many into the yoke of the one.[9] Even when the system is formulated as pluralist, the drawback is that only those differences are likely to enter the plural stage as are able to fit within the overall rationality that approves and controls the many as one.

Perhaps partly, though not exclusively, on account of this reason – because the new paradigm is born specifically out of the life experiences of many migrant and postcolonial peoples – some postcolonial critics have started to theorize the question of cultural difference in terms of what Homi Bhabha has called a "disjunctive temporality"[10] and Néstor García Canclini has labeled a "multitemporal heterogeneity."[11] These categories refer, in the first case, to the splitting, and in the second case, to the superimposition of temporalities marking off cultural differences, speaking positions, and narrative timeframes. Feminist readers in the West may note an affinity between such articulations of differentiated timeframes and the differentiated perceptions of time addressed by Kristeva in "Women's time." Kristeva notes how the construction of female subjectivity (and, indeed, of the women's movement) is affected both by the linear time of production and the cyclical repetitive time of reproduction, neither of which can be fully reduced to the other without misunderstanding the cultural construction of female subjectivity.[12] The dominant representations of time underlying a person's sense of self and a people's sense of history vary with culture and, within and across cultures, they also vary according to multiple factors depending on speakers' cultural locations. In Latin American societies, as García Canclini's work demonstrates, African, indigenous, Spanish colonial, modern, and global narrative timeframes may intersect, simultaneously or disjunctively, a speaker's discourse. Taking this thought further, I would note that when such culturally situated speakers enter diasporic locations – as happens when they migrate from their original societies to the United States – they will bring with them these forms of cultural difference and hybridity. It is not exceptional for many Latin Americans to become acculturated as a result of sociocultural influences crisscrossed by two or more incommensurable cultures, sometimes in literal juxtaposition. For example, in the Caribbean, because of the effects of colonization, some of the Yoruba deities gained counterparts in the Spanish Catholic roster of saints. We could say the Catholic and the Yoruba figures inhabit two very different kinds of temporalities: one linked historically to a Hispanic, the other to an African, past.

From the standpoint of the worshipers' experiences, in some cases one of the temporalities would be superimposed on the other, while in other cases the two would become distinct.

In *Borderlands/La Frontera*, Gloria Anzaldúa, speaking as a Chicana-Tejana-lesbian-feminist writer, juxtaposes the temporality of ancient indigenous myths with her postcolonial North American existence. The shifts from English to Spanish to Nahuatl in Anzaldúa are not just shifts in languages or "codes," as she calls them, but in temporalities of perception and consciousness.[13] These pluricultural temporalities create a disjunctive tension with the linear temporality of modernity governing the identities of producers and consumers in advanced capitalist societies. These multiple and disjunctive temporalities create a displacement in the relation between self and other, allowing the recognition of alterity both inside and outside the self. Their premise of selfhood begins with the acknowledging and appreciation of the nonidentical self. Anzaldúa's multi-hyphenated *mestiza* self reminds us of Kristeva's stranger within. More broadly, it exemplifies feminism's notion of the differences not only among but within women. These multiple layers within the self, responding to different perceptive fields and different, not necessarily commensurable temporalities, can predispose us psychologically to appreciate both the richness and the incommensurability of cultural differences. They lay the groundwork for cognitive, perceptual, and linguistically constituted relations between ourselves and others where the other's differences, even if not fully translatable into the terms of our own cultural horizons, can be acknowledged as sites of appreciation, desire, recognition, caring, and respect. I am speaking here of a psychological state in which the stranger is not abjected, derided, persecuted, shut out of view, or legalized out of existence, but – departing from the premise that the other is also human – neither is she subjected to the demand that she be the double, or mirror image, of ourselves.

The question arises of how the principle of incommensurability applies to feminist ethics when feminist ethics is engaged in making and executing normative judgments cross-culturally. Will the feminist ethical claim or the normative judgment be impaired by the principle of incommensurability, and if so, to what extent? How are feminist ethical terms negotiated cross-culturally? Should they be negotiated at all? My first task is to try to explain how the principle of incommensurability works at the concrete level of everyday experience. I will address this issue from an existential standpoint based in part on my personal experience.

The Culturally Different Other

What does it mean to be culturally different and to speak, at the level of culture, in a different voice? This question is generally answered by those with the power to mark others (or "the other") as different, rather than by those whose difference is in question in relation to the majority, or main members, of a given group. To be culturally different is not the same as being individually different or different by virtue of one's age or sex. If I am in a group among other women with roughly the same kind of education and occupational interests as myself and if we are roughly of the same age, what will mark me as culturally different is that I am, in today's terms, a Latina – a name that, while pointing to some aspects of my background, also erases important aspects of my individuality and the actual specificities of my cultural genealogy, which includes Caribbean, Latin American, and western European background.

"Latina" casts me in a recognizable category, through which the meaning of my difference is delimited according to whatever set of associations this term may evoke. "Latina" is not simply a descriptive term referring to someone with a Latin American or Iberian ancestry currently residing in the United States. It is a signifier that both masks and evokes a range of associations: hot blooded, temperamental, submissive, defiant, illegal or illicit, sexually repressed or sexually overactive, oppressed, exploited, and so on. But the thread that draws together all the stereotypical associations is one of invisibility as a producer of culture. One reason for this is that women in masculine-dominant societies, including Anglo-American society, are viewed primarily as transmitters rather than producers of culture. They are viewed principally as caregivers whose function in culture is to transmit and conserve, not question and create, cultural values.

Latinas in the United States are also invisible as producers of culture because the term "Latina" lacks a specific national reference and, in the mind of western modernity, nation and culture are still tightly interrelated. (For example, the great national museums of art and science exhibit those works that illustrate the cultural standards and the aesthetic and scientific power of various nations.) As a concept,

"Latina" exceeds the category of the national. Because as Latinas we are not tied to a specifiable national culture (in contrast to members of a culturally dominant group), to be culturally visible in the dominant culture we have to show that we know how to incorporate two or more cultures into our way of being. Furthermore, we must demonstrate that the way we bring such cultures together can benefit the Anglo-American public. In order to receive recognition as a cultural agent, I must show that I can be both a Latina and a North American; that I can alternate between these identities, so much so that in extremely "tight" cultural situations, I can perform, in my North American voice, a public erasure of my Latina voice, if need be. My white, Anglo-American counterpart is not called on to perform such a feat with respect to her own cultural background. She does not have to erase her Anglo-American cultural background to be legitimated as a member of North American society. If she comes from a working-class background, she may have to erase her class background to be fully accepted in some strata of society; and if she is a lesbian, she may have to erase her sexual orientation (keep it closeted) to be acceptable in some groups. But to gain recognition as a cultural agent she does not have to erase or dilute her Anglo-American background as such. Moreover, she does not need to combine her cultural background with, say, that of Middle Eastern, Asian, African, or Latin American people before being accepted as an important contributor to society and culture. If she is Jewish, she will face special problems the farther she is removed from assimilating fully into the Protestant, Anglo-American, Western European tradition.

Returning to the problem of the culturally successful Latina woman, an interesting phenomenon can be observed. Once I am able to perform the feat of representing my culture in some distinctive way in the context of the dominant Anglo-American culture, I am no longer considered only a culturally marked "other." To my favor, I am now recognized as an accomplished handler and knower of cultures. In this capacity, I earn a special place in the group. I have stepped out of the "immanent" place of the other. I have, to some extent, transcended the "Latina" object-position and claimed my position as a cultural agent in terms recognized by the dominant cultural group. But in order to do this, I need to be knowledgeable in the language and epistemic maneuvers of the dominant culture, the same culture that in its everyday practice marks me as culturally "other" than itself. From a cultural standpoint as well as a psychoanalytical one, I have become a split subject. When I act as "myself" (in my reflexive sense of self, the "me" that includes and grows out of my early Cuban upbringing), my Anglo-American sociocultural environment will often mark me as "other." When, alternatively, I discursively perform the speaking position expected of a subject of the dominant culture, I am recognized as a real agent in the real world.

Still, something fundamentally important is missing in this latter recognition (a misrecognition, actually). What my interlocutor fails to recognize is that delimiting my capacity to speak in my culturally differentiated voice will have an effect on what I say in response. When one feels rejected, one switches tracks, as it were, and enters the dominant discourse, not without realizing what is lost. What my interlocutor recognizes is not what I would have liked – an encouragement to communicate insights I offer from a standpoint of cultural difference – but only my ability to enter a standard Anglo-American speaking position, a position that exists in negotiated tension with my culturally differentiated, reflexive sense of self. In other words, the local master-narrative exists in tension with what the Latina knows and experiences, and the former shuts out the latter. This is why sometimes, when some interlocutor responds to me (say, at the office) in reference to the self I perform there as a speaking subject, I get the sense that this colleague is not speaking to me at all; that my interlocutor is missing something, because the "me" that is culturally different is ignored, shut off, or bypassed.

There is a sense of frustration but also of missed opportunity in these mishaps in cross-cultural communication. What remains to be understood in the statements of the culturally differentiated other – that is, the incommensurable something not subject to perfect cultural translation – may actually be the most important part of the message my Anglophone interlocutor needs to receive. As I perceive it, my interlocutor takes in a fragment of the message and discards the rest. But one suspects it is precisely because the discarded part of the message would require the radical decentering of the dominant Anglophone speaking subject that it fails to reach such a subject's ears. Who or what is the other for the dominant, enlightened subject?[14] It is the one he would like to speak with occasionally, preferably in a foreign or distant location; it is the one he defends abstractly in arguments for democracy or against oppression. But let not the other (as other) make any demands in his everyday world, for in this case he might have to change his way of being. He might have to acknowledge his own split subjectivity, change his fixed way of life, welcome the stranger within, and perhaps alter his views and relations with others in ways he had not foreseen.

Cultural alterity therefore points to an ethics and to ways of knowing far deeper than the type of thinking wherein dominant cultural speakers perceive themselves to be at the epistemic and moral center of the universe, spreading their influence outward toward other rational speakers. Cultural alterity demands that the other be heard in her difference and that the self give itself the time, the space, and the opportunity to appreciate the stranger without and within. As Kristeva poignantly observes, "How could one tolerate a foreigner if one did not know one was a stranger to oneself?"[15]

If I may extrapolate from the kind of personal experience mentioned above to the situation of communication and dialogue among women north and south of the border, one sees how difficult it is for groups that are deeply entrenched in their own values, and that have the power to ignore the values of other groups, to attain any adequate understanding of cultural alterity. The reason for this is that people of different cultures do not speak the same (cultural) language and do not share the same cultural imaginary order. The science of anthropology has had to deal with the issue of cultural incommensurability for a long time. Why is this sense of incommensurability so hard to grasp for philosophy? Philosophers are often taught that philosophical claims can be stated in a language that is essentially outside of culture. This move essentializes philosophy, requiring an arsenal of conceptual weapons to police its boundaries, much as governments hire border patrols to keep illegal aliens outside the border. But isn't the language used to put forward philosophical claims – even the most formal and abstract language – already part of a culture? Aren't our conceptions of ethics, reason, and philosophy part of culture? Perhaps the issue should be put another way. Philosophers may acknowledge that incommensurability exists among various cultural formations and that it will impede the mapping of various cultural discourses that tries to match them perfectly. The debate lies in whether such incommensurable elements should be assigned to what is irrelevant to philosophical meaning and knowledge, and thus irrelevant to the operations of reason; or whether, as I suggest, the incommensurable elements should be seen as inherent to the processes of reasoning itself.

In my view, cross-cultural (rational) discourse should be seen as limited by those elements of cultural difference that I have called incommensurable. That these elements of cultural difference cannot be fully apprehended in their "internal" intracultural meaning by outsiders, however, should not be taken as a sign that they are irrelevant to an understanding of cultural difference. Nor does it mean that acknowledging incommensurablity will weaken the possibility of cross-cultural dialogue. Quite the contrary. Communication, including cross-cultural communication, involves two aspects, the second of which is often neglected. First, one must understand what is being said. Second, one must relate what is being said to a complex set of signifiers, denoting or somehow pointing to what remains unsaid. It is because of this very important (open-ended) dialectic between the said and the unsaid that the principle of incommensurability in cross-cultural communication assumes considerable importance.

In cross-cultural communication, each speaker may "say" something that falls on the side of the "unsaid" for a culturally differentiated interlocutor. Such gaps in communication may cause one speaker's discourse to appear incoherent or insufficiently organized. To the culturally dominant speaker, the subaltern speaker's discourse may appear to be a string of fragmented observations rather than a unified whole. The actual problem may not be incoherence but the lack of cultural translatability of the signifiers for coherence from one set of cultural presuppositions to the other.[16] Alternatively, the dominant speaker, relating only to fragments in the other's narrative, may believe that the whole message was transmitted, when only part of it was. This asymmetrical, non-reciprocal gap in communication can be tested, for example, if a third party interrupts the conversation and the subaltern speaker tries to resume it after the interval. The dominant speaker, lacking the sense that some element in the communication was still missing and believing that he has already heard the whole statement, does not perceive that the interlocutor should have the space to complete what was left unsaid. The subaltern speaker, in turn, is at a loss to explain that she had saved the most important part of the message for the end. Now she realizes that the interlocutor wants to move away from the subject of cultural difference, not toward it.

The speaker from the dominant culture is basically saying: communicate with me entirely on the terms I expect; beyond this, I am not interested. The ethical principle of cultural alterity must point to the inadequacy of such a speaker to engage in cross-cultural as well as interpersonal dialogue and conversation. Yet by the conventional norms of his own culture, the dominant speaker may never understand that he is silencing the culturally differentiated other because it never occurred to him to think that cross-cultural communication contains important, yet incommensurable, elements. Alternatively, he may be conscious of such incommensurable elements, but pay special attention to them only when the contrast between cultures involves a strong polarity, as in the cases of Asian or African cultures in contrast to Anglo-American culture. In this case, too, the Latina's subaltern message will not be heard, because her closer proximity to the West will disqualify her from the neo-romanticized picture of the more culturally distant other.

It is incumbent on those speakers of the dominant cultural language not to foreclose the meaning of statements to only those meanings that are readily available to them. Assuming that one could map the statements of the culturally differentiated other according to three categories – readily understandable, difficult to understand, and truly incommensurable – one should never close the communication at the level of the first category, but should make the effort to let understanding reach into the other two domains. For example, if a Latina speaker alters the usual syntactical order normally used by English speakers, and if she also speaks with a heavy accent, these factors may make it harder for the native English speaker to understand what she is saying. With some effort, however, it is possible to figure out what is being said, if one is intent on paying attention and in engaging in follow-up questioning. Unfortunately, I have seen repeated cases of a Latina treated as if she were speaking nonsense, only because her accent, her sentence structure, and perhaps her vocabulary differ from that of ordinary English usage. Rather than taking the effort to listen to what the other is saying, the native speaker will treat the non-native speaker as if she were linguistically or intellectually incompetent. From the perception "I don't immediately understand what the other is saying," the dominant speaker will draw the invalid conclusion, "the other is speaking nonsense," "the other is incompetent," "the other does not belong here," and so on. The relegation of the culturally different "other" to a subordinate position, as this exemplary exercise shows, may itself be diagnosed as a lack of culture. Cultural prejudice of this sort is indeed a sign of a cultural deficit on the part of the dominant culture.

Furthermore, and with respect to the third category or level, placing a high stake on the incommensurable as that which requires recognition (rather than erasure or denigration in relation to a dominant culture) is fundamental to acquiring an understanding, even if only a partial understanding, of the culturally differentiated "other." If we hypothesize that incommensurability is largely manifested not only linguistically but in terms of disjunctive or heterogeneous temporalities, given the centrality of the concept of time in human existence, the very fabric of all social relationships will be affected by it. For example, intergenerational issues, productivity, leisure, and aging will not carry the same overall meaning for people of different cultural backgrounds.[17] Recognizing how culturally incommensurable clusters of meaning affect basic everyday interactions will bring culturally differentiated speakers one step closer to improved communication and understanding.

Woman as "Other" of Another Woman

Although in some of my examples I have been using the masculine pronoun to designate the culturally dominant speaker and the feminine to designate the subaltern, the relations of cultural dominance and subalternity can also obtain among speakers of the same gender or in the reverse combination. Basically, in coupled dualisms or binaries, the normative term "others" the non-normative one (that is, the normative term subjects the non-normative term to the subordinate position of "other"). This is one of the reasons why deconstructive feminist theory is so intent on moving beyond oppositional binaries and their corresponding forms of exclusion. For example, as de Beauvoir and others have shown, in the man–woman binary, *man* is taken as normative for the human species, while *woman* is cast in the position of "other" of the normative. But take other examples: if the lady of the house is considered normative with respect to domestic authority and values, the female domestic worker will be seen as "other"; if the white woman is considered normative with respect to social status, the *mulata* will be other, and so on. Conversely, in popular culture, if the barrio is considered normative, high culture will be considered "other." In North–South and West–East binaries, if North and West are considered normative in terms of cultural standards, then South and East will be considered "other."

In anti-imperialist politics, the terms are reversed. The northern and the western aggressors take on a lower cultural status while the southern and eastern cultures are hailed. When western feminist theory fails to take into account the issues of colonialism and imperialism, the dangerous outcome will be that women from eastern and southern cultures will see in feminism the mark of western colonization. Feminism in this instance will be tied symbolically to western (capitalist) modernity and will not be dissociated from its values. In contrast, if feminism is seen as a movement of women in different parts of the world getting together and joining forces to overcome social, political, economic, and gender oppression, then this movement of emancipation becomes normative and the "other" becomes the outsider to, or obstructor of, this movement.

Herein lies the point of vulnerability for western feminism, for if feminism is defined too narrowly, it will make an "other" of women whose path to emancipation it may fail to understand or recognize. In particular, it may relegate to the status of "other" many women in eastern and southern countries whose views do not fit squarely into western feminist categories. Moreover, if Western feminism defines itself too narrowly or in terms that women in eastern and southern countries may not quite understand or appreciate – given the factor of cultural incommensurability – women in these countries may reject western feminists as "other." This potential type of mutual exclusion takes us back to the impasse between feminism North and South, East and West. As Trinh Minh-ha notes in *Woman, Native, Other*, it is easy for conservative males in Third World countries to denounce feminism as a foreign, western influence. When western feminists try to denounce the conditions of women's oppression in Third World countries in "terms made to reflect or fit into Euro-American women's criteria of equality," this indirectly "serves the cause of tradition upholders and provides them with a pretext for muddling all issues of oppression raised by Third World women."[18]

Fortunately, thanks to the insistent voices of women from developing countries and ethnic minorities and to the growing sensitivities of western feminists when it comes to conveying feminist messages in the light of cross-cultural differences, these difficulties are better handled now by feminists engaged in worldwide activism and politics.[19] What is less clear to me is whether western feminists (as they pursue philosophy, for example) view themselves as one of many voices in the struggle for women's social, political, economic, and gender emancipation on a worldwide scale. It seems to me that western feminism still harbors the hope that its own views of emancipation are universally valid for all the world's women, if only because western thought generally does not mark itself as culturally specific. Instead, it engages in the discursive mode of a universal *logos*, which it takes to be applicable to all rational speakers. Here the issue of colonialism must be brought up, even if it is unpleasant and even if it interrupts the discussion about the criteria for recognizing rationally competent speakers across cultures. Without reference to the historic conditions of colonialism, it is impossible to understand fully the western mind's presumption of speaking from the privileged position of universality.

The western colonial enterprise and its impact on the Americas were such that there was no way to understand the disparity of western and non-western cultures in an ethically responsible, reciprocal way. The conquest of America offered no reciprocal way of accounting for the differences among western and non-western cultures and peoples. To those people who were judged "less developed" in Western European terms it brought the forces that colonized and enslaved them. While the racial composition of the Americas has changed since the conquest and colonization, the problem persists that the people who have not reached the West's level of material development are often considered inferior. The impoverished Mexican migrant to California and the Haitian migrant to South Florida become, more than five hundred years after the conquest, the targets of the combined historical effects of colonialist, racial, linguistic, class, and, where applicable, gender prejudices.

Is it possible for contemporary western feminism to disentangle itself from the historical forces of western colonialism and from the erasure of otherness that such forces entail? What are the points of contact today between feminists from developing countries and western feminism? Is there reason to place hope in a new way of looking at things, the recently developed approach of *postcolonial feminisms*?

Postcolonial Feminisms

Postcolonial feminisms are those feminisms that take the experience of western colonialism and its contemporary effects as a high priority in the process of setting up a speaking position from which to articulate a standpoint of cultural, national, regional, or social identity. With postcolonial feminisms, the process of critique is turned against the domination and exploitation of *culturally* differentiated others. Postcolonial feminisms differ from the classic critique of imperialism in that they try to stay away from rigid self–other binaries.[20] In addition, an intense criticism is directed at the gender stereotypes and symbolic constructs of the woman's body used to reinforce outdated masculinist notions of national identity.[21] Postcolonial feminisms call attention to the process of splitting of culturally dominant subject in terms of the demands placed on the dominant subject by culturally disadvantaged others. These feminisms hypothesize, at the psycho-subjective level, that the unity of self or mind felt by the dominant subject is a totally artificial one, and that the oneness of his or her subjectivity (covering the fragments that make up his or her personality) is made possible only by adherence to a philosophy of colonialism, whether the adherence is owned up to or only enacted indirectly. In other words, postcolonial feminisms propose the view that we are not born a unified self, that the sense of being "one," of being a self, is something derived from language (becoming a competent speaker in a language), and that language itself is part of culture and reflects certain arrangements of cultural constructs with respect to how to understand cultural differences.

When a child is given a name, for example, Caroline, she is not told that the culture giving her this name is one that had a history of colonizing other people and of imposing its values on them. The psychological process of decolonization involves the attempt to unhinge the genealogy of one's name, of one's identity, from the inherited colonial culture. One must learn that one could not be oneself without a relationship to the other and that such a relationship ideally must not be wrought with injustices. While one cannot make time go backward, annulling western culture's colonialist legacy, it is possible partially to deactivate this legacy by establishing alternative practices and values with the intent of reversing the effects of colonialism. A coordination of heterogeneous elements with a special emphasis on undermining colonialism's understanding of cultural difference becomes the alternative route to the construction of identity in what we would like to call a *postcolonial* perspective or context.

If the postcolonial perspective entails acknowledging the reality of colonialism (or the fight against it) in the construction of cultural values and personal identities, what does a postcolonial feminism entail regarding the problem of cross-cultural communication? Postcolonial identities put in question the belief in the neutrality of the sign and the separation of the subject and object of knowledge, as accepted by the Enlightenment. They point out that these semiotic and epistemic assumptions will ultimately have repercussions on women's bodies and on women's affective well-being. As literary critic Nelly Richard observes from Chile, feminist (postcolonial) criticism should be able to uncover the concerted interests of the dominant culture hidden behind "the supposed neutral transparency of signs and the model of mimetic reproduction propitiated by the market through a passive consumption."[22]

Moreover, as Gayatri Spivak aptly illustrates by allusion to the status of indebted families in India, the interests of transnational global capital hiding behind the purported neutrality of global consumption are not gender-neutral.

> In modern "India," there *is* a "society" of bonded labor, where the only means of repaying a loan at extortionate rates of interest is hereditary bond-slavery ... [Below family life at the level of survival] there is bonded prostitution, where the girls and women abducted from bonded labor or *kamiya* households are thrust together as bodies for absolute sexual and economic exploitation.[23]

The deceptive transparency of signs, the growing expansion of passive consumption, the recourse to loans as the concrete mechanism for maintaining consumption, the exorbitant rates of interest imposed on already subaltern populations, and the woman's body as "the last instance in a [global] system whose general regulator is still the loan"[24] are interconnected forms of exploitation that only postcolonial feminisms can fully address at this time. Whether in Chile, in India, or much closer to home, postcolonial feminisms alert us to the voices of split subjects deconstructing the logic of the totality in the light of cultural alterity.

Feminist Agency and the Restructuring of the Imaginary-symbolic Order

These comments on bonded labor illustrate a final and nevertheless familiar point for feminists: namely, that the ultimate oppression a human being can experience is to be bereft of any meaningful agency.

African American feminist bell hooks has described oppression as the lack of choices.[25] I take this to mean that oppression involves conditions in which persons are deprived of agency, or that their options are limited to those that effectively fail to promote their own good.

If we look at the conditions that would empower women around the world to promote their own good, we see powerful interests set against women. There are powerful religious fundamentalisms all over the world and in various cultures that seek to define for women in categorical and absolutist terms what their own good is and to constrain women to act accordingly. These fundamentalisms also define the meaning of "nation" and "family" in categorical terms, promoting self-sacrifice and often war, while impeding those who are influenced by these ideologies from acting on their own desires for personal fulfillment and happiness. Some government and private institutions, moreover, derive enormous material benefits from women's cheap labor and from women's traditional family caregiving roles. There are forces in society that benefit from women ending up in prostitution, remaining illiterate, or being confined to economic and social conditions which, from girlhood on, subject them to recurrent violence and abuse. It seems that nothing could be more ethical than a universal feminist ethics designed to identify and correct such problems. How this is done, however, requires careful rethinking of how to employ the concepts of gender, identity, and oppression.

In my view, feminist ethical thinking needs to be "negotiated" cross-culturally. Such negotiation can be conducted on a case-by-case basis by individuals, or collectively by groups. The presence of so many mixed unions among people of different cultures offers some hope that effective cross-cultural communication in matters that pertain to intimate details of peoples' lives is not some sort of utopian fantasy. But people in mixed unions that are based on parity, as compared to the practices of dominant cultures with regard to subaltern cultures, are very strongly motivated to understand each other, as well as to communicate with each other so as to deepen and strengthen their understanding. Such individuals commit themselves to lifestyles in which giving of one's time to reach out to the other, as well as making space for the other's differences, are part of the very fabric of daily existence, neither a forced nor an occasional happening. People in mixed unions have also presumably experienced the positive benefits of their association to the extent that they would rather affirm what remains incommensurable in their distinct cultural horizons than shut the other out of their intimate life and feelings. No doubt, individuals who either work or live successfully with culturally differentiated others are highly skilled communicators, making optimum use of opportunities for cross-cultural, interactive engagements. The postcolonial feminist perspective highlights these interactive realities, deconstructing the traditional binarism of self–other paradigms, in which each side lays claim to either mutually exclusive or equal but separate realities.

Collectively, feminists can do much to promote cross-cultural understanding. Whether these groups are all-women groups or whether they include female and male feminists, perhaps their basic contribution is building and strengthening networks of solidarity. Although *solidarity* is an old term, long familiar to activists, the present circumstances at the turn of the century demand that we rethink and reawaken its meanings. Feminists from dominant global cultures and better-off economic sectors need to connect more closely with projects involving women and feminists from the periphery. We need to lobby actively for the inclusion of voices from the periphery so as to shake off the weight of colonialism and other oppressions that still mark the center's discourses. This is not to say that the voices from the periphery are not marked by the effects of colonialism, racism, and other oppressions, but that when such voices attempt to address these oppressions or engage in avant-garde cultural criticism, there is a common bond between us, despite our differences. It is up to us to recognize the centrality that this (other) bond represents and to help it assume its long overdue and legitimate place in the West's symbolic order and cultural imaginary. There is no other recourse but to destabilize and displace the subject of modernity from its conceptual throne and to sponsor alternative ways of relating and knowing that no longer shut out from "home" the realities of Latino, Asian, African, and other culturally marginalized peoples.

I believe that western feminism cannot reach a point of maturity in this age of global, transnational, and diasporic ventures unless it openly adopts a postcolonial perspective. If it does, we will switch our identities away from subjects of a totalized notion of culture and will come to view ourselves as subjects of cultural difference. The West needs to learn how to step out of its colonial boots and start experiencing the reality of its subaltern environment and the cultures of the peoples it has disenfranchized and continues to disenfranchize. A challenging but not impossible task lies ahead. This is why the struggle continues.

Notes

1   Although Sartre, Merleau-Ponty, de Beauvoir, Heidegger, and Lacan function as key background figures for the concepts of the other and alterity, it is Levinas who is remembered primarily for formulating an ethics of alterity. See Emmanuel Levinas, *Totality and Infinity: An Essay on Exteriority*, trans. Alfonso Lingis (Boston: Martinus Nijhoff, 1979). With the advent of poststructuralism, important new perspectives have been offered by Irigaray's feminist ethics of sexual difference and Kristeva's psychoanalytic-semiotic studies.

2   See n.1; see also Luce Irigaray, *An Ethics of Sexual Difference*, trans. Carolyn Burke and Gillian C. Gill (Ithaca, NY: Cornell University Press, 1993); Julia Kristeva, *Strangers to Ourselves*, trans. Leon S. Roudiez (New York: Columbia University Press, 1991); Kristeva, "Women's Time," in Toril Moi (ed.) *The Kristeva Reader* (New York: Columbia University Press, 1986).

3   For a concise overview of postcolonial theory see Aparajita Sagar, "Postcolonial Studies," in Michael Payne (ed.) *A Dictionary of Cultural and Critical Theory* (Cambridge, MA.: Blackwell Publishers, 1996). For classics from the Caribbean region see Frantz Fanon, *Black Skins, White Masks* (New York: Grove, 1963) and Roberto Fernández Retamar, *Caliban and Other Essays* (Minneapolis: University of Minnesota Press, 1989). For contemporary poststructuralist postcolonial criticism see Gayatri Spivak, *The Post-Colonial Critic*, ed. Sarah Harasym (New York: Routledge, 1990) and *Outside in the Teaching Machine* (New York: Routledge, 1993); see also Homi K. Bhabha, *The Location of Culture* (New York: Routledge, 1994). For postcolonialism and Latin American literary criticism (in Spanish) see the special issue on Latin American cultural criticism and literary theory of *Revista Iberoamericana* 62, no. 176–7 (1996); for postmodern studies in Latin America see John Beverley et al. (eds) *The Postmodernism Debate in Latin America* (Durham: Duke University Press, 1995) and the special issue "Postmodernism: Center and Periphery," of *South Atlantic Quarterly* 92/3 (1993).

4   This point is made by Sagar with specific reference to the work of Spivak, but it applies generally to deconstructive and poststructuralist feminisms (Sagar, "Postcolonial Studies," p. 427).

5   Kristeva, *Strangers to Ourselves*, pp. 181–92 and *passim*.

6   I will not be using the term *incommensurability* in the Kuhnian sense of

two incommensurable scientific theories that explain the same phenomena. By this term I try to designate the lack of complete translatability of various expressions or blocks of meaning between two or more linguistic-cultural symbolic systems. It may also refer to incommensurable ways of thinking insofar as the differences are culturally determined.

7   Bhabha, *Location of Culture*, p. 177.

8   "We have paid a high enough price for the nostalgia of the whole and the one, for the reconciliation . . . of the transparent and the communicable experience" (Jean François Lyotard, *The Postmodern Condition*, trans. Geoff Bennington and Brian Massumi (Minneapolis: University of Minnesota Press, 1984), pp. 81–2).

9   Cf. Bhabha, *Location of Culture*, pp. 152–5, 162–4.

10   Ibid., p. 177.

11   Néstor García Canclini, *Hybrid Cultures: Strategies for Entering and Leaving Modernity* (Minneapolis: University of Minnesota Press, 1995), pp. 46–7. Using Latin America's elites as a reference point, García Canclini describes "multitemporal heterogeneity" as a feature of modern culture resulting from modernity's inability to superimpose itself completely on Latin America's indigenous and colonial heritages. I am using the term somewhat differently because my primary references are neither to the perspective of modernity nor to that of the elites. My primary reference point is the existential-phenomenological sense of two or more experienced temporalities as manifested in the lived experiences of members of the population, including the economically disadvantaged, the popular sectors, the racial minorities, and, yes, extending to the middle and upper classes, where relevant.

12   Kristeva, "Women's Time," in Moi, *The Kristeva Reader*, pp. 188–95.

13   Gloria Anzaldúa, *Borderlands/La Frontera: The New Mestiza* (San Francisco: Aunt Lute Books, 1987), preface, p. viii.

14   I refer to the dominant enlightened subject in the masculine gender here because this account is based primarily on my concrete experience; in a later section, I address women's assumption of this voice.

15   Kristeva, *Strangers to Ourselves*, p. 182.

16   It would help to be acquainted with the underrepresented culture in order to appreciate this point. For example, feminists know that all too often, the patterns of gender socialization and the power one gender (the masculine) holds in the overall legal-ethical system of thought over the feminine will make it appear that a woman's reasoning is fragmentary or insufficiently coherent in comparison to the reasoning of successfully socialized males. Asymmetrically given cultural differences can have a similar effect. A Latina feminist must communicate with her Anglo audience not only as a feminist but as a Latina, because she is already marked as such by the dominant culture. If she draws too heavily on

her own cultural imaginary to explain her views, an account that is perfectly coherent to her may simply not carry over as such to her audience. The audience might complain that at times it could not follow the speaker or that the speaker was not sufficiently organized. This is not a matter of agreeing or disagreeing with the content of the speaker's message but of failing to connect the various aspects of the message into a fully coherent account. In my view, this could mean (though it does not necessarily have to mean) that the grounds for the speaker's reasoning are not readily available to speakers located in the dominant culture. Again, this could show how asymmetrical relations of power are reinforced between culturally differentiated speakers when one of the cultures is fully dominant over the other. Many different examples could be given of this phenomenon, not all of them similar. For especially racist dimensions of such asymmetry, consider Frantz Fanon's charge that a characteristic of the racism he encountered in France was the expectation that as a black person from the Caribbean, he could not speak French coherently (Fanon, *Black Skin*, pp. 35–6). Compare also Homi Bhabha's example of the Turk in Germany who feels he is being looked down on as an animal when he tries to use the first few words he has learned in the German language (Bhabha, *Location of Culture*, p. 165).

17 Obviously, there may be some overlap among people of different cultures regarding certain values, just as there may be differences in values among people of roughly the same cultural background. For example, political values can vary significantly among people of similar cultural backgrounds. Strong variations and disagreements can occur even among members of the same family just as, where such opportunities exist, a person can develop an affinity with the values of people from distant cultures. Agreement or disagreement on such *values* is a separate issue from the argument I am making about the principle of incommensurability as a factor to be reckoned with in cross-cultural communication between speakers from dominant and subaltern cultures.

18 Trinh T. Minh-ha, *Woman, Native, Other* (Bloomington: Indiana University Press, 1989), p. 106.

19 Since the opening conference in Mexico City sponsored by the United Nations' Decade on Women (1975–85), western feminists have learned that women from other parts of the world, including the West's own minority populations, have views of their own that require specific attention. These views cannot be assimilated into those of the western feminisms, because the way a woman looks at her condition in the world will depend on many factors, including her cultural and economic location. Theoretically, a helpful orientation toward greater acknowledgment of diversity came with the wave of "feminisms of difference" in the

1980s. See Raquel Olea, "Feminism: Modern or Postmodern?," in John Beverley et al. (ed.) *The Postmodern Debate in Latin America* (Durham: Duke University Press, 1995).

20   I offer a broad characterization of postcolonial feminisms so as to include different kinds of feminist critiques and my own voice in these debates. Racial, ethnic, class, and other differences are often incorporated, along with cultural and gender differences, into postcolonial feminist work. For some differences of opinion on the use of "postcolonial" as a category, see Sagar, "Postcolonial studies." I read Anzaldúa's *Borderlands/La Frontera* as postcolonial, though it is not clear she would accept this term, given the Chicana practice of not subsuming this identification under others. But the fit is quite clear: she talks about the land of ancestors that has been taken over by several different countries, as well as the different cultural formations emerging there over time. Moreover, she states, "I grew up between two cultures, the Mexican (with a heavy Indian influence) and the Anglo (as a member of a colonized people in our own territory)" (*Borderlands*, preface, p. vii).

21   This point is in Inderpal Grewal and Caren Kaplan (eds) *Scattered Hegemonies* (Minneapolis: University of Minnesota Press, 1994); see also Anzaldúa, *Borderlands*, and Spivak, *Outside in the Teaching Machine*, pp. 77–95.

22   Nelly Richard, "Feminismo, Experiencia y Representación," *Revista Iberoamericana* 62, no. 176–7 (1996), p. 744 (my translation).

23   Gayatri Spivak, *Outside in the Teaching Machine*, p. 82.

24   Ibid.

25   "Being oppressed is the absence of choices" (bell hooks, *Feminist Theory: From Margin to Center* (Boston: South End, 1984), p. 5).

CHAPTER 3

Exploring the Sources of Western Thought

V. F. CORDOVA

An examination of western thought is not an easy task. It is a task, however, which I have assigned myself in order to better understand "the man who owns the world." The following comments on western thought are a summary of my personal research project, which I present here without the usual scholarly footnotes. In the interest of those who pursue a similar course, I have included a list of suggested readings at the end of the essay to encourage further research into, currently, seldom explored ideas.

From within the western context, the task of exploring the sources of basic western concepts is seen as near impossible. "How," I have been challenged, "can you presume to generalize about a tradition that has produced such diverse thinkers as Kant and Descartes?" The argument that western thought is too diverse, or too complex, to lend itself to generalization is not a very good one. It is commonly under-stood that there are certain themes and concepts that prevail in western thought, which serve to identify such themes as uniquely "western." Indeed, if there were no such themes one could not speak of "the western tradition" or of "western thought," as of course we do.

Aside from the argument that diversity and complexity block the making of general statements about western thought, there is one other objection for anyone wishing to make such an attempt. No other people, some claim, have so thoroughly and exhaustively partic-ipated in self-examination as has western man: if there were some-thing to be said, it would have already been said. This statement ignores a fact about cultural milieus that has come into play only recently. This is the recognition that there are conceptual frameworks

consisting of a very few basic ideas that serve as foundational definitions or descriptions that permeate all discourse within specific cultural milieus. Each conceptual framework provides a description of
the world, of human beings, and of the role of human beings which is
consistent with the description of the world.

The belief that there are ideas and concepts that persist throughout
the ages in particular societies is usually applied only to cultures other
than those of the West. One can read or hear about "the Chinese
concept of man," for example, or speak of "Hindu metaphysics." Talk
of a "western concept of man," or of "western metaphysics," is likely
to be met with snorts of derision. Even so, there is a recognized
"source" of western thought that is acknowledged by westerners: the
ancient Greeks and Romans figure very prominently in the justification for the intellectual endeavors of many academic disciplines. The
phrase, "In the beginning . . .," has not only a biblical purpose but a
secular one as well. Whether the course of study be physics, biology,
history, philosophy, or literature, the introductions to such courses
pay homage to the early strivings of the Greeks in those fields; the
evocation of the names of Thales, Anaximander, Plato, Aristotle,
Thucydides, or Sophocles lend an aura of legitimacy to the task about
to be undertaken by the incipient scholar. One believes oneself to be
participating in a long honored and uninterrupted tradition of the
"western" world. This belief does not, however, correctly indicate the
sources of western thought and endeavors. Contemporary western
man and the ancient Greeks occupy different worlds, and their
conceptual frameworks cannot be the same.

If, then, the world of the West is not Greek, where could the source
of homogeneity of the western tradition lie – if, that is, there truly is a
homogeneity which allows for ready identification?

José Ortega y Gasset, in the 1930s, produced a small masterpiece
entitled, *The Revolt of the Masses*. Ortega set himself the task of
analyzing the western, or European, character for a clue to the
dilemma he saw facing the West during his lifetime. He, too, had to
account for the homogeneity of the European character. In his
chapter, "Who rules in the world?," Ortega addresses the homogeneity
that allows the discussion to take place of the singularity called
"western man," in the following manner:

> In each new generation the souls of men grew more and more alike. To
> speak with more exactitude and caution, we might put it this way: the

souls of French and English and Spanish are, and will be, as different as you like, but they possess the same psychological architecture; and, above all, they are gradually becoming similar in content. Religion, science, law, art, social and sentimental values are being shared alike. Now these are the spiritual things by which man lives. The homogeneity, then, becomes greater than if the souls themselves were all cast in identical mould. If we were to take an inventory of our mental stock today – opinions, standards, desires, assumptions – we should discover that the greater part of it does not come to the Frenchman from France, nor to the Spaniard from Spain, but from the common European stock. Today, in fact, we are more influenced by what is European in us than by what is special to us as Frenchmen, Spaniards, and so on. If we were to make in imagination the experiment of limiting ourselves to living by what is "national" in us, and if in fancy we could deprive the average Frenchman of all that he uses, thinks, feels, by reason of the influence of other sections of the Continent, he would be terror-stricken at the result. He would see that it was not possible to live merely on his own; that four-fifths of his spiritual wealth is the common property of Europe.

Ortega does not mention the American in this passage but he recognizes that "America has been formed from the overflow of Europe." All share in the "common European stock"; all that is "used, thought, and felt" derivates from a shared "psychological architecture." Ortega does not identify the source of the homogeneity, but at the end of his essay he encourages the seeking out and "unfolding" of a *leitmotiv* that may be "interwoven, insinuated, whispered" at the root of his major question: "What are the radical defects from which modern Europe suffers?" "It is evident," he goes on to say, "that in the long run the form of humanity dominant at the present day has its origin in these defects."

My own research into the sources of western thought is driven not so much by a search for its "defects" but rather in order to seek out the *leitmotiv* that makes it so uniquely "western." Where, in other words, is the source for the common "psychological architecture"?

I am no stranger to the exploration of ideas, not even to the notion that ideas are culturally based. I grew up in a home with parents of Apache and European ancestry. My father was culturally an Apache, my mother, "Hispanic"; she spoke Spanish and was a Catholic. Whenever there was a clash of values or a difference in the explanations of the world, my relatives would say that "they," meaning

Anglo-Saxon Americans, "had a *different idea* about that. It was noted, also, that Indians and Hispanics had "different ideas" about many issues; this point was taken for granted in my household. A comparison and contrast of ideas and questions about how such differing ideas might have developed was a normal, natural, family pastime. No value judgments were made over the ideas; they were declared neither right nor wrong, but simply *different*. It was assumed, also, in my family, that these "ideas" lay behind and justified the actions taken by their various adherents. It did not occur to me that Anglo-Saxon Americans would share the same worldviews that I saw in my family. We were, in fact, acutely aware that there was a difference between our worlds and theirs.

As my curiousity about these "worlds" developed, I enrolled as a philosophy student at a local university. I quickly discovered that my questions about origins of deeply held notions were met, not with the usual (in my household) excitement of intellectual dialogue, but with hostility. My questions seemed always to be "irrelevant" or "more appropriate" to some other academic discipline. The questions that I raised were about the "accepted" issues addressed in introductory philosophy courses. When the issue of God's existence came up, my question was why that issue was relevant; as well, I thought, spend time contemplating the existence or nonexistence of Santa Claus and Peter Pan. When the topic of "mind" or "soul" came up, my questions were on the origin of the ideas of "mind," "soul," and "body." The dilemma of "free will" versus "determinism" intrigued me in its insolubility given the parameters in which the dilemma was framed. Any talk about Earth, or as I had been taught by my father, "the mother," was not a topic that I could bring up without being referred to a course on "ecology." What I learned in these few courses was that I was an "atheist," a "non-dualist," a "sceptic," and most of all, a "pagan." What I was left with was a feeling that if I were to make any headway into exploring the origin of western ideas, I would have to do it on my own. I began with the acknowledged "forefathers" of western thought, the ancient Greeks.

The *Leitmotiv*

To approach a project without a goal is to go to an alien place without a map. I approached the ancient Greeks with a list of topics that I thought important for understanding the thought of any people. I wanted to know what their description of the world was, how they defined human beings, and their expectations of a human being in the world as they defined it. I also had with me the topics that seemed important in western thought as they differed from those of my Apache father, who it seemed, and my mother claimed, "had won the battles for our children's brains."

I was going to find the origin of the following ideas that I thought were uniquely western: among these were human dualism, monotheism, the dilemma of freedom and determinism, individualism, idealism, and the concept of the Earth as mere "matter." Along the way, I picked up other topics: there was the idea of the supposed superiority of humans to other earthly beings; the concept of "progress;" and the uniqueness of the European character over what Ortega called "the vegetative existence" of other peoples. All of these topics reduced to the *leitmotiv* which revolved around my three basic issues: (1) a description of the world; (2) a description of human nature; and (3) the role of human beings in the described world.

The Greek World

The world of the Greeks was that of an infinite and dynamic universe. The world and its order (*cosmos*) existed before the appearance of the gods. The model of the universe was that of an organism that lives, grows, flowers, and decays. The term hylozoist best fitted this world model: it was organic, alive, and in motion. The Greeks looked backward to a previous Golden Age that was now in the process of decay. The things of the universe were perishable and temporary; the universe, itself, was self-perpetuating. Even Plato, who postulates a type of creator for the things of the universe in his *Timaeus*, did not have this creator, or "demiurge," create *ex nihilo*, as did the Christian God: the demiurge created order out of something which existed in a chaotic state. Aristotle postulated a "first cause" but could not eradicate matter, because "substance," or the "stuff" out of which things came into existence, had to, thought Aristotle, co-exist infinitely with the "prime mover" or "first cause." Long before Aristotle, when the early thinkers were trying for better explanations of the world that those provided by Homer, there existed, for the Greeks, a very basic assumption about the universe: *there was something*. What that *some-*

thing might be was a topic of great concern: Thales thought it might be water; Heraclitus opted for fire; and Anaximander refused to name it at all. Anaximander called it the *undifferentiated*, the *unlimited*, which was infinite and indestructible.

The Greeks had a unique explanation of time. Time, for the ancients, was a *measure* (Aristotle), or the *number* (Plato), of motion, which was determined through measurement of the relative motion of astral bodies. On the basis of their organic model of the universe, they held a *cyclical* view of time: everything that was would return to its essential source and then a new cycle would begin. The universe was not, despite Plato's postulated demiurge who creates order out of chaos, generally seen as chaotic. The motion of the universe was random, like the pattern in wood: there is always a pattern, but what that pattern will be cannot be fully determined beforehand. One is only certain that there is a pattern; that the universe moves in a balanced and harmonious manner; and that, despite fluctuations in the motion, some sort of stability of motion is always maintained.

The fact that the universe moved in a particular fashion lent an aura of fatalism for human beings. This is the true source of the famous Greek dramatic tragedies. Someone once said that with the advent of Christianity there can be no true tragedy. Everything will be made right in the end by a caring God. The Greek tragedy is tragic precisely because it is "written in the stars" and susceptible to no one's ministrations or escape; even the Greek gods, meddlesome though they might be in the affairs of humans, were subject to the motion, and course, of the universe. The tragedy of Oedipus is tragic because what he does is done without his knowledge: he does not know that the man he slays is his father, nor that the woman he marries is his mother. He does not know that the Oracle has foretold his doom as a future slayer of his own father. There is no god that can forgive him his sins, no god that will give him a better life in some future world.

Man, in the Greek world is, as Aristotle says, a social being, or as he puts it in his *Politics*, "A man alone is either a god or a beast." Alone, he would not be human. Man shares this social type of existence with ants and bees. He has a responsibility toward his fellow men, as well as to his city or "hive." The origin of human beings is not as important to the Greek as it is for the Christian that will follow. Anaximander thought humans might have evolved from another form; the prolonged childhood of humans, he decided, would not have allowed man's survival into adulthood. Humans might have grown from the teeth of Titans, sown by the victors of the wars among the immortal gods. Man might have originally been a round being having both male and female characteristics, which upon separation, seeks always to find the rest of itself for union. The postulated "origins" were as various as were the thinkers who pondered such things. It was also possible, for the Greeks, that humans had always existed.

A human being might or might not have an immortal soul that contains memory and knowledge after death. Plato, often, presents the views of Socrates and other thinkers as "likely stories"; it is just as likely that death brings nothing more than a "dreamless sleep," as Socrates says in the *Apology*. Both Plato and Aristotle opted for a tripartite soul though each defined the triad differently: Plato thought humans to be made up of three souls: reason, appetite, and passion (or 'spirit'); Aristotle thought of the three souls as vegetative, animal, and rational. A male had all three, a slave and a female only the first two.

The Stoics defined humans as subject to the course of the universe: they were free to choose some actions and determined in the performance of others. Wisdom consisted of knowing the difference between the two sorts. "Evil" in the Greek universe was either the natural course of things or actions undertaken by humans out of ignorance. Religion, for the Greeks, consisted of paying homage to many gods, who represented many natural forces and human needs. Their rituals coincided with the seasonal courses of the Earth. The Earth, sun, moon, and stars, according to Plato in his *Timaeus*, were themselves immortal and divine.

The more I learned of the Greeks the less "western" they appeared. I learned to become suspicious of translations: what "god" does Plato refer to when the term is capitalized as is the Christian "God"? Plato does at various times refer to Zeus, Apollo, Aphrodite, and the sun. Sometimes his references are to "divinity" itself. Was Aristotle's "prime mover" the same as the Christian God? Would it have made a difference to western readers to refer to his famous work on *De Anima* as a work on the animas or psyche?

There were two exalted figures in the western tradition, Jesus and Socrates. They had both given their lives to a cause greater than themselves but the causes' resemblance ended there. Christ came, it is believed, to create new laws by which people should conduct their lives. Socrates died to uphold the laws of Athens. Shortly before his death, Socrates is reported by Crito to have postulated a confrontation and conversation between himself and the personified "laws" and the state. If men have failed him, say the laws, it is the fault of men and not of the laws. The laws have provided Socrates with the legitimacy of birth, with an education, with a social existence, with a fair trial. "You could have left at any time," he is told, and except for war, he chose not to do so. A city without laws, Socrates is convinced through his conversation, a *society* without laws, could furnish no social existence at all for anyone, and man is, above all, a social being.

Jesus Christ dies for a different cause. "The traditions of your fathers," says Christ, "will not save you." "You have neither father nor mother," he says to his followers, and, "my kingdom is not of this world." Christ came not to uphold the law, or even the present social order, but to create something new.

The Western World

I found no line of continuity between the Greek and Roman worlds and the contemporary European world. I did, however, discover the Church Fathers.

In the history books of my childhood I was always fascinated by "the gap"; this was the era then referred to as the "Dark Ages." Nothing, I was led to believe, had happened that was of any significance. I was to learn that that long thousand year gap was the silent pregnant pause that was to give birth to the contemporary West. While the Islamic world pored over the works of the Greek philosophers, Europe languished under the direction of the Holy Roman Church. I learned that the Greeks were "re-discovered" through the Islamic thinkers of the Mediterranean. Thomas Aquinas did not suddenly decide to read Aristotle one day. He was introduced to the work through the influence of Islamic thinkers. I learned that the Greeks were not always included in the histories of the West. I discovered the period of the Renaissance, and most important, the work of Michel de Montaigne. Here is a westerner offering to his fellow Europeans and fellow Christians new mentors for their course through history. Unfortunately, the works of the Greek and Roman thinkers appeared in the West only through the filter of Christian thought. We know the Greeks through the Christianized thinkers: we ignore the polytheism of the Greeks as a mere quirk; we imagine that Plato is a monotheist in the making; that Aristotle is introducing us to the "natural" world of the Christian God. The Renaissance period, even if I extended it back to Aquinas' time in the thirteenth century, was too late for my purposes. By the time that Aquinas grappled with Aristotle, the conceptual framework of the West had been set. The "new" Greek notions about the universe and human beings have had, without doubt, a tremendous influence over the course of western thought but there remained a very un-Greek cast to this post-Renaissance thought. And then I discovered St Augustine.

The World According to Augustine

Augustine is an interesting transition figure between the pagan world of Hellenic Europe and the Christian one that followed it. Augustine is the child of a Christian mother but he is also educated in the pagan philosophies. He is not only aware of the numerous sects, both pagan and Christian, that surround him, but actually joins a sect (Manicheism) at the same time that he is hired to become a teacher of rhetoric. There are still non-Christian thinkers during his lifetime (AD 354–430). Augustine is not an original thinker in the sense that he invents new ideas; rather, he is a synthesizer of various strains of thought. His goal is to firm up Christian beliefs in the face of much competition among Christian factions and pagan philosophies.

Augustine creates, out of pre-existing Christian and pagan notions, the psychological architecture that becomes the "common mental stock" of the European. His "inventions" are those against which all subsequent "scientific" discoveries must be weighed and measured. In his *Confessions*, he outlines the essential differences between the worldview he adopts from Christianity and that of the pagan world.

Augustine's work is guided by some assumptions about the world that come with his Christian beliefs. First of all, there is only one God: he created the world out of nothing, and he has a plan for this world. Second, human beings are creations of a God who makes them "in his own image," and they are superior to all other creatures. Third, regardless of his being in the image of God, a human being, because of his "materiality," is a vile and filthy creature doomed to live on a hostile and stingy planet. Fourth, God's plan includes a better world for those who obey his demands. These essential Christian ideas about the world will be reworked by Augustine so that he might defend the ideas from pagan onslaughts and Christian heretics.

Worlds are created through words. Augustine is well aware of the power of human beings to define and redefine the world. In his *Confessions*, he implores God to inform him of how it is that God creates through the uttering of a word. He is troubled by the phrase, "In the beginning You made heaven and earth." "For so Moses wrote," says Augustine, "wrote and went his way. . . ." Were Moses present, thinks Augustine, he could inquire of him what those words meant, but Moses is inaccessible. Augustine begs God to enlighten him, "But how do you create them? How, O God, did you create heaven and earth . . .? You spoke and heaven and earth were created; in Your word You created them."

The word of God and the words of Moses demand explanation, not because Augustine doubts their truth, but because the non-Christians with whom Augustine must contend demand such explanations. "What was God doing before He made heaven and earth?," ask the pagan thinkers, for a creation from "nothing" seems a strange postulation to pagans living in what they believe is a dynamic and infinite universe and who believe that "from nothing one can only get nothing." Augustine continues to address their odious questions in Book 11 of his *Confessions*: "If, they say, He was at rest and doing nothing, why did He not continue to do nothing for ever after as for ever before?" And, another question, "Now if something arose in the substance of God which was not there before, that substance could not rightly be called eternal; but if God's will that creatures should be is from eternity, why are creatures not from eternity?"

These were clever pagans, who plagued Christians over the inconsistencies of their new world definition. Augustine will answer them, if not to their satisfaction at least to his own. "I come now," he says, "to answer the man who says, 'What was God doing before He made heaven and earth?' Augustine, too, can be clever but he insists that he will not be: "I do not give the jesting answer – said to have been given by one who sought to evade the force of the question – 'He was getting Hell ready for people who pry too deep.' To poke fun at a questioner is not to see the answer."

Augustine has a better answer: since God exists in eternity in which there is no change and therefore no time, thinks Augustine, there simply was no such thing as 'before' before God created anything. Time comes into existence with the creation of the world. "Let no man tell me," says Augustine, "that the movement of the heavenly bodies is time." "Why should not time rather be," he asks, "the movement of all bodies?" Augustine can provide no other answer, given that he is committed to the "truth" as set forth in the biblical accounts of creation. He is committed to uphold the story of the battle of Jericho: "At the prayer of a man the sun stood still that he might complete his victory in battle, the sun stood still but time moved on." How is it, Augustine wonders, that time could continue if a day was, indeed, only a measure of the sun's movement through the heavens?

The similarity here to the more modern explanation of the universe by western physicists would be uncanny if it were not that Augustine had already provided the grounds upon which the contemporary explanation is based: What was there, we ask of the physicist, *before* the vacuum that exploded into a universe? There was, we are told, no "before" before the vacuum, for time came into existence with the "big bang." Time, in this case, is like that of Augustine, "the movement of all bodies." Time, according to Augustine, is something "extended" and it can, itself, be measured. Time is not, as the Greeks and Romans thought, itself, a mere measure.

For the West, a major philosophical, and perhaps scientific, question is "Why is there something rather than nothing?" The question assumes the pre-eminence of "nothing." The major assumption about the universe for the Greeks was, "There is *something*." Different words; different worlds; different questions.

Augustine, through his attempts to justify his newfound definition of the universe, sets out a definition of the world that will survive, almost unchallenged, for 1,600 years. He offers a new definition of the planet also. In the *Timaeus*, Plato describes the Earth as a divine being and a "nurse" for human beings. The major religious festivals, before Christianity, revolved around the celebrations of the changing of the seasons; these survive today as Christian rituals that have nothing to do with the planet's changing modes. Easter is celebrated in the spring, but a pagan spring ritual that once celebrated the renewal of the planet becomes the celebration of a resurrection of a God. Christmas is celebrated during the winter of the planet when she prepares for a well-earned sleep and her pagan residents celebrate what she has provided through the year; the Christian celebrates the birth of a god. The sacred groves of the ancient Greeks become, under Christian influence, shrines to the appearance of revered Christian personages. The Earth is transformed under Christianity; she becomes mere matter, a substance of lesser stuff; the *real* world is "not of this world."

Augustine and Christianity offer a new definition of the world, as well as a new definition of human beings. For the ancient Hebrews, man is a social being. The Hebrew god communicates with a group, a very specific group, of people. They are his chosen people. They have only one major command, to obey the dictates of their god. The promises of this god are not to individuals for the salvation of one individual but to the group, as a whole. Christianity offers a god who picks out individuals from the group for personal salvation. "The traditons of your fathers" are not, as they were for the Hebrews of the Old Testament, a means of maintaining a group identity that is necessary for their god's purpose. "You have neither father nor mother," says Jesus Christ, and so saying frees individuals from the ties so important to the Hebrews. The Christian god demands a new religious covenant: a covenant, not between himself and a group, as a distinctive group, but between himself and an individual who chooses to follow the dictates of the god.

The ancient Hebrews believed in the promise of their god to lead them out of diaspora after their first parents were expelled from their proper home (Eden), but their new home would be on this planet. The "new kingdom" would not be some other "world." God would simply provide another place on *this* planet.

Aside from redefining humans as individuals rather than as social beings (as in a flock or a herd), Christianity and Augustine posit humans as consisting of a dual nature: man has an immaterial and immortal soul, as well as a foul and treacherous body. Augustine's argument here is a clever one: all that God makes is good, but since God is the only reality and his creations are made from "nothing," that "nothingness" makes his creations distinct from God, regardless of whether humans are made in the image of God. How, then, are humans in the image of God? Through their immortal souls, says Augustine. This soul can communicate with God; it can choose to be led astray from the communications and dictates of God by the treacherous desires of an earthly body, but it can also choose not to be led astray. Augustine bestows upon his descendants the problem of "freedom and determinism" in his *Free Choice of the Will*.

Augustine needs an immortal soul as a characteristic of the human being. How else is a human to be rewarded for living a good life when the rewards do not come in the present life? In Augustine's era,

Christians had given up on the promise of Jesus Christ to return, physically, to the planet during the lifetime of his contemporaries. The soul, as an immortal thing, can look forward to the fulfillment of this promise even though the body may die and rot. All Christian humans will be rewarded for denying themselves the pleasures of the body and the world. All humans who fail to deny themselves these pleasures will be punished; an immortal soul will suffer what an embodied soul failed to suffer. Evil, which makes its appearance in Christianity as a sort of virus, cannot be blamed on God, for God is, by definition, a good God. Evil is the product of human choice, a result of the "free will" which can either choose to follow God's dictates or ignore them.

Through the granting of a free will to human beings, Augustine sets the stage for a philosophical dilemma that will plague his descendants for scores of generations. God, according to Christianity, has a purpose for man – a plan, a *telos*. God becomes a sort of playwright who has written a play in which the actors are unaware that they are following a script. God, being all-knowing, knows the outcome of the play; the actors do not. He sees the entirety of the play from beginning to end as one would view a cinematic film strip with all of its frames stretched out for his viewing. The actors are aware of only that frame in which they exist at the moment. Their lack of awareness of the future "frames" of the film (or "play") allows them to act as though they were making "free" choices over their actions. The problem here is that "freedom" can only be an illusory freedom. On the other hand, if humans are truly free then they can affect the outcome of God's script and that, under Christianity, is not possible. In order for God's plan for humans and the world to unfold, the universe must be determined; but if it is determined, then man is not free; and if he is not free then he cannot be held responsible for his actions. Augustine, therefore, offers us the dilemma of "free will" and "determinism." Humans are "free" because they cannot know, in full, the part they play in the overall scheme of things; they can, therefore, be held responsible for their actions. They are also determined because, regardless of what choices they make, their choices and actions are already known by God.

The problem of freedom and determinism is also important today. If the universe is not determined then we could have no certainty in our scientific endeavors; there would be no justification for seeking "truth." And if a person is not free than a form of fatalism would set in that would undermine any action at all on his or her part.

Augustine bestows upon his descendants a sort of bifurcated existence: man is both mortal and immortal, both free and determined.
This brings us to the third of my inquiry's focus: what is the role of
man in the universe as it is defined by Augustine and as he has
defined man? Christian man exists in a dilemma: he is essentially an
immortal being trapped in a mortal body. He is trapped also by the
concept of original sin, which he inherits from the act of disobedience
against God by Adam and Eve. Another trap for this potentially
ethereal being is the world in which he resides: man, having been
expelled from his proper home, is driven to subsist on a ground which
has been cursed and made stingy. Man must make his living by the
"sweat of his brow."

Man escapes his dilemma through only one course of action:
he, as an individual, has been promised a rescue – in the *future*. In
the meantime, he must prove his worthiness to be included in the
rescue. He does this through learning to master the desires (or
"passions") which the body inflicts upon the purer soul. He must
spread the word of the impending rescue; he must reach as many
individuals as possible. He has other commands from the god: he must
multiply his numbers; subdue and hold dominion over the rest of the
world; and, in the tradition of the commandment to Adam, "name all
things."

There is another role for man in the legacy from Augustine: an
attempt must be made to understand through the use of reason, but
"reason" must be of a special sort, that which has been enlightened
by the will of God. There is "truth" to be had in the universe and it is
absolute; it is *the* truth. In the "image of God," man sets forth to
participate in the creative activity in which God, himself, engages: he
will re-create himself and his world to, he hopes, the greater liking of
God.

The Age of Science

The contemporary western world is the product of many rebellions.
They are rebellions against the authority of the Church to declare
what "truth" will or will not be, and how that "truth" will be
adjudicated, and by whom. Perhaps the rebellions begin with Thomas
Aquinas' attempt to bring Aristotle into the Christian fold in the
thirteenth century. We tend to forget that the works of this holy

father of present-day Catholicism were placed on the list of banned material, that he was charged with engaging in "Averroistic" philosophy (after the Islamic thinker, Averroes). The Catholic Church's *Condemnation* of 1277 lists the Greek ideas found to be offensive to official doctrine. Among those banned ideas with which Aquinas might have infected believers were the following (the numbers prefacing the propositions correspond to the actual numbers in the Condemnation; there is a total of 219):

4   That one should not hold anything unless it is self-evident or can be manifested from self-evident principles.

8   That our intellect by its own natural power can attain to knowledge of the first cause. This does not sound well and is erroneous if what is meant is immediate knowledge.

39   That all the separated substances are coeternal with the first principle.

79   That if the heaven stood still, fire would not burn, because God would not exist.

80   That the reasoning of the Philosopher (Aristotle) proving that the motion of the heaven is eternal is not sophistic, and that it is surprising that profound men do not perceive this.

91   That there has already been an infinite number of revolutions of the heaven, which it is impossible for the created intellect but not for the first cause to comprehend.

92   That with all the heavenly bodies coming back to the same point after a period of thirty-six thousand years, the same effects as now exist will reappear.

99   That there is more than one prime mover.

133   That the soul is inseparable from the body, and that the soul is corrupted when the harmony of the body is corrupted.

138   That there was no first man, nor will there be a last; indeed, the generation of man from man always was and always will be.

154   That our will is subject to the power of the heavenly bodies.

168   That a man acting from passion acts by compulsion.

172   That happiness is had in this life and not in another.

180   That the Christian law impedes learning.

183   That the teachings of the theologian are based on fables.

168   That it is not true that something comes from nothing or was made in a first creation.[1]

The banned ideas read as a list of ancient Greek notions about man, the universe, and man's role in the world. They read, also, as notions that are today contrary to general beliefs in the West about man and the universe.

The bans against the work of Aquinas were lifted by the Church upon his canonization as a saint in the year 1325. The ideas, themselves, however, are still anathema to most Christian or western minds. The long Dark Ages, when no ideas were expressed except those approved by the Church, had so firmly entrenched some very essential ideas about the world and man, into the West, that any new idea could scarcely be comprehended. Furthermore, they were dangerous to the authority of the Church as the final arbiter of truth and falsehood.

There were other rebellions against the power of the Church over men's minds. What began with Aquinas continued in the Renaissance and in the Reformation: in the use of local languages instead of Latin for writing about ideas; in the Copernican idea which displaced geocentrism; the Newtonian notion of a "clockwork" universe; the discovery, by geologists, of the antiquity of the Earth. And then there were Darwin and Einstein.

If, I have been asked, I am aware of all of the changes which the western world has undergone through the various rebellions, how could I dare to claim a homogeneity of thought in the West? We now live in a "scientific" and "technological" age, I am reminded. Nevertheless, Ortega, writing in the first half of this century, found homogeneity. He credited this to a sharing of "spiritual wealth." It is the source of this spiritual wealth that I seek. It cannot be denied that the West, until recently, experienced one singular influence which is unique to itself: Christianity. It is also true that all of the ideas about man and the world held by the ancient Greeks and Romans are not the "paradigms" that operate in the western world today. When the Roman empire became the Holy Roman Empire there was more than a mere exchange of ruling parties; there was a change of worldviews, of conceptual frameworks.

After the conversion of the Emperor Constantine to Christianity in 325 and up until the rediscovery of the works of Aristotle in the thirteenth century, the western mind, as distinct from the Hellenic mind, became the "true" and "real" interpreter of what there was. This, according to Christianity, was the way the world was, "In the Beginning. . . ."

In the "modern" and "scientific" age we have come to reject the Christian origins of western thought. Like the *nouveau riche,* the *parvenu* who becomes ashamed of his humble beginnings, the West under an aura of "enlightenment" rejected its beginnings and sought new ancestors. Western man was no longer under the thrall of the Church fathers; he was following in the footsteps of the ancient and noble Greeks. All that he now knows and understands, he has taught himself to believe, is the end result of a process of inquiry that exists unbroken from the time of Heraclitus to that of Albert Einstein and Stephen Hawking.

In the process of seeking out the sources of western thought I have collected favorites among the western thinkers who would challenge established thought: Aquinas, who wanted to add the existential and "materialistic" thinking of Aristotle to the Christianized version of Plato offered by Augustine; Montaigne, who holds up the Greeks and Romans as models to those in the sixteenth century who would reject the stodgy Church fathers; Benedict de Spinoza, who suggests a new explanation of the world; Thomas Hobbes, who presents up a version of man and the state that is divorced from the Church; David Hume, who questions the search for certainty which the Church bequeaths to its followers; Ludwig Wittgenstein, who questions the very act of questioning. There are some ideas, Wittgenstein says, that are "shunted" as to an "unused siding" that lie beyond question. Wittgenstein sets himself the goal of "showing the fly the way out of the bottle." First, I maintain, one must convince the fly that there is a bottle!

The Bottle

The contemporary western world would appear to have no resemblance to the medieval world ruled by the Catholic Church. Supersonic jet planes whisk us off to any part of the world that takes our fancy. Computers allow us to communicate with anyone else on the planet who has a computer. Television allows me to see the events happening throughout the world. I can enjoy, for my breakfast, a cup of coffee or cocoa from beans grown some place other than within my country boundaries. I can sit at my window wearing garments produced by the willing hands of persons throughout the Third World. I sit on a chair that is made from the exotic wood of ancient forests in far off lands. Medicines have been developed that forestall the diseases that remain the only biological prey on humankind. I live in the modern, scientific, technological age created by those made "in the image" of a god.

Nevertheless, were Augustine to be thrown into our midst today he would not find it difficult to get his bearings. In an academic department of physics, he could hold discourse with Stephen Hawking over "knowing the mind of God" and finding the final proofs for the Big Bang. It is not for originality that Hawking was awarded a medal by the Pope. Creation from nothing allows for the maintenance of a belief in a creator-God who creates *ex nihilo*. Augustine would reject, as do many physicists, those who would claim that the Big Bang never happened.

Augustine would be pleased that there were no sacred groves dedicated to pagan gods and that our festivals did not revolve around the glories provided by the planet. Earth would be still that same *material stuff* which exists only for the purposes of man. He would be pleased that our populations had grown to such immense numbers. He could applaud those politicians who forbid abortion and birth control information as a necessary requirement for foreign aid to other countries.

In a psychology department, Augustine could converse for days with the resident practitioners. Here would be those exploring the very essence of a 'soul'; it would matter little to him that talk had changed from "soul" to "self-consciousness" or "cognition." He would applaud the attempts to "biologize" the human body and the disciplinary separation between those who explore the psyche and those who explore the body.

The criminal justice departments would strike a chord with Augustine's demand for accountability for individual behavior. He would disapprove of the view that a man acting from passion acts by compulsion. The rise of American prisons, greater in number it seems than in all of China, would please Augustine. Genetic research that strives to prove that man's actions are preordained through biological causes would, Augustine might say, allow one to imprison those whom God has doomed, without enduring their actions in our midst.

In our political science and economics departments, Augustine would applaud the movement toward "globalization." He would realize that if a non-western nation accepts McDonald's, a church would soon follow, and on the heels of that, the establishment of "proper" authority, both governmental and clerical.

He would be astounded at the extent to which naming has been carried; a common toad in the wilds of the farthest reaches of the planet would have a Latin name.

Augustine might be shaken by the open sexuality and violence in the venues of entertainment but not surprised, because this is, after all, despite the "progress," not the City of God. Human beings would always be prey to the passions of the body; there would always be those who failed to exercise their God-given free will to make the proper choices over their behavior. This is to be expected, given "man's nature" after the Fall of Adam and Eve. It would matter little to Augustine that the traits of man were now credited to instincts rather than to original sin.

Here is the "bottle" of which Wittgenstein speaks: it is a matrix of explanations that have survived despite the many changes brought by the centuries. There is a definition of the world that undergirds all of western man's actions towards it. The world is "stuff," mere matter. The definition of a human being still upholds his "superiority" over all the rest of creation. Man is different. If not "ensouled," he is at least endowed with self-consciousness, which separates him from the rest of creation. Rescue of man and his perilous condition is still forecast to occur some time in the future. All present actions are predicated on the time to come and "progress" made towards that goal is carefully calculated. There is still abiding belief in the West that if the ceaseless action called "progress" should slow or halt, then all would fall back into the original "nothingness" from whence it came. The role of man, in the Augustinian *leitmotiv*, is still to prove his worthiness to the "generations to come" so that he might also, perhaps, astound the gods.

There are numerous other segments of the *leitmotiv* to be explored that space does not allow in a short essay. Making the "fly" aware that there is a "bottle," a matrix of explanations that hold the fly imprisoned, is not an easy task but it is an important one. Present explorations into the matrix have begun in what goes by the name of "postmodern criticism." The search, however, is similar to that of the man who looks for a lost item in the wrong room simply because "the light is better there." The "room" which holds the "original questions" to which all of the present unquestioned givens are "answers" is not in the halls of the Greeks and Romans but in the cloistered study of the Bishop of Hippo.

Conclusion

The world that I live in is not the world of my father. The Earth is not Mother. She is not the producer and sustainer of all things. I am not ensconced in the warm egg that floats shell-less in a vast and infinite universe which springs out of the Milky Way and the infinite darkness that represents, not emptiness, but potentiality. I am, at most, a nerve-end of the universe, and, at the very least, an oxygen-absorber. I have been told that I am but a fluff of cosmic dust afloat in an empty universe or that I am a sinful and flawed creature awaiting salvation. My father would have said that I was, as long as I existed, a factor in the course of the universe, and that my every action had a conse-quence on the whole. I was like a pebble dropped into a pond making ripples far beyond my immediate entry. I was not, however, a mere and singular pebble but a handful of pebbles: I was everyone that had ever existed in my genetic group. Most of all, I was what the Mother meant me to be.

As a *human* being, I have a greater responsibility toward the Mother than all other beings. I alone have a greater memory, and a language, and these allow me to remember the consequences of my actions. The memory of those consequences force me to be aware of my actions. None of my acts are meaningless. I am a factor in the universe. I am accountable for my actions.

As a *human* being, I am not alone. I exist in a group of like persons. My group exists in a larger group of beings also existing in groups of their own kin. The groups over the hill or across the river are different from me and mine: they have their own creation stories, their own truth, their own validity. I can learn from them as they can learn from me.

But I do not live in my father's world. I live in a strange world ruled by strange beings that take little account of my existence. I am a living fossil, doomed, by the progressive tide that carries the superior man into the glorious future, to solidify into stone. I can, at most, try to understand who he is, where he comes from.

Our world is a shared world, a single planet. It is beset by too many people and too few resources. The lifestyle created by science and technology is expensive for our planet to maintain. Three-fourths of the world's people live in lessened circumstances not of their choosing, in order to supply goods necessary for the "masters of the universe." The average African in the depths of the Congo does not need the precious metals he mines for the "developed" world; the Central American native would live a better life if more land was available to him instead of serving as a plantation for the developed world's culinary tastes. The rainforests, the lungs of the Mother, are not cut down to better the lives of the rainforest residents. The jet planes that fly us high and fast to every portion of the planet enlarge the ozone hole that penetrates the Mother's unshelled boundary.

We have a right, we who live on the margins of a world that no longer welcomes us as her indigenous and natural residents, to ask, "Who is this man who owns the world?", "What are the ideas that drive him?" I have always known that when it came to definitions of the world, of human beings, of the role of human beings in that world, *they*, the rulers of the world, had a *different idea* from my own. I have learned only recently that I am dealing with the ideas of the children of Augustine.

I know now, why it is that "that man" can disregard his actions towards the planet; it is mere "stuff," comprised of nothing. I know, also, the source of alienation that fosters the western notion of man as an isolated but superior being: this is not his real home; it is a simple waystation, a holding-pen, that he must occupy on his way home. I have learned why it is that he can disregard the alternative existences of human beings unlike himself; he alone is made in the image of the god, the chosen. The rest is chaff, of the sort that their Lord speaks of when he says, "Go, therefore, into the Land of Canaan . . . and slay every man, woman and child . . . and of those who remain . . . make them your slave."

Western man is undeniably diverse and extremely "complex," but he has also a homogenous strain that allows him to be identified – if one only looks in the correct room.

Suggested readings

In the course of my research I have found that philosophers writing in the first decades of the twentieth century were exploring ideas that today we take for granted. Francis M. Cornford, in his *From Religion to Philosophy*, does an excellent job of outlining the ancient Greek ideas about the world and man. J. B. Bury, in *The Idea of Progress*, traces the origins of an idea that we no longer question. José Ortega y Gasset, in *The Revolt of the Masses*, outlines some very basic western ideas about "modern" man that are little different from those prevalent today. A nearer contemporary, Ludwig Wittgenstein, in several of his later works, *Philosophical Investigations*, *On Certainty*, and his "Notes on Frazer's *Golden Bough*," questions the formation of modern paradigms of thought. Benjamin Lee Whorf, in the essays gathered in his *Language, Thought, and Reality*, offers some insights into the comparison of western and non-western thought. I would place Stephen Toulmin's *The Discovery of Time* in the same category of importance as J. B. Bury's exploration of the concept of progress.

Another fruitful area of research is in "transition" figures, i.e., those thinkers writing during the transition of one era to another. St Augustine is a transition figure between the Roman world and Christian. Thomas Aquinas reformulates Greek thought when he encounters the thought of Aristotle, and, in effect, ushers in the "modern" world. Michel de Montaigne, during the Renaissance, offers a comparison of Hellenic thought and those of his contemporaries. David Hume's work should be required reading for anyone wishing to understand the accomplishments of Immanuel Kant: what Hume calls into question, Kant re-establishes.

The history of philosophy is not, currently, a "hot topic" in philosophical circles, yet it is important for understanding current trends. A comparison of non-western thought with western is also of importance: one cannot make such statements as, "All humans . . . [etc.]," without being aware of the variety of ways that humans define themselves. I am indebted not only to those thinkers who question and explore what is taken for granted by others, but to my mentor, Dr Fred Sturm of the University of New Mexico, for granting justification to the comparative studies which I, quixotically, chose to undertake.

Note

1   Arthur Hyman and James J. Walsh, *Philosophy in the Middle Ages* (Indianapolis: Hackett Publishing, 1984).

CHAPTER 4

General Introduction to the Project: The Enterprise of Socratic Metaethics

ADRIAN M. S. PIPER

Rationality and Power

That human beings have the potential for rationality and the ability to cultivate it is a fact of human nature. But to value rationality and its subsidiary character dispositions – impartiality, intellectual discrimination, foresight, deliberation, prudence, self-reflection, self-control – is another matter entirely. According to Nietzsche, this fact of human nature becomes a value when it is valorized by a "slave morality" that assigns highest priority to the character dispositions of rationality and the spirit at the expense of natural human instincts. Like a good *Untertan*, I intend to do exactly that in this project. I am going to take it as a given that if a person's freedom to act on her impulses and gratify her desires is constrained by the existence of others' equal, or more powerful, conflicting impulses and desires, then she will need the character dispositions of rationality to survive. The more circumscribed one's freedom and power, the more essential to survival and flourishing the character dispositions of rationality and the spirit may become.

And I am going to presuppose as well that if such a person's power to achieve her ends is limited by a distribution of scarce social or material resources often less than fair or favorable to herself, then she may well find the character dispositions of rationality and the spirit to be a needed source of strength and solace. On these assumptions, the valorization of the character dispositions of rationality and the spirit that typify a "slave morality" does not express mere sour grapes, as Nietzsche sometimes suggests in his more contemptuous moments.

Nor does it merely make a virtue of necessity, although it does at least do that. It expresses the recognition of an intrinsic good whose value may be less evident to those for whom it is less necessary as an instrument of survival:

> How long will you wait to think yourself worthy of the highest and transgress in nothing the clear pronouncement of reason? . . . Therefore resolve before it is too late to live as one who is mature and proficient, and let all that seems best to you be a law that you cannot transgress. . . . This was how Socrates attained perfection, attending to nothing but reason in all that he encountered. And if you are not yet Socrates, yet you ought to live as one who would wish to be a Socrates.[1]

Think of these injunctions as conjointly constitutive of the Socratic ideal. As the product of biographical fact, Epictetus' loyalty to the Socratic ideal – and in particular his injunctions to "transgress in nothing the clear pronouncement of reason," and to "atten[d] to nothing but reason in all that [we] encounte[r]" are an expression of wisdom born of the personal experience of enslavement. They attest to the valuation and cultivation of rationality as the weapon of choice for the unempowered to use on their own behalf. They both underwrite Nietzsche's analysis of reason and the spirit as central values of a "slave morality," and demonstrate how that "slave morality" may have a kind of dignity that *übermenschlichen* views lack.

For if a person's freedom and power to act on his impulses is greater, then he may well find the indulgence of emotion, spontaneity, instinct, and the manipulation of power more attractive; and development of the character dispositions of rationality correspondingly less necessary, interesting, or valuable. After all, such individuals have at hand other reserves – of wealth, status, influence and coercion – on which to draw to achieve their ends. The ends which the character dispositions of rationality and the spirit may themselves inspire therefore may be accorded correspondingly less importance, if they are noticed in the first place. For such individuals, the Socratic ideal is no ideal at all.

Philosophy as an intellectual discipline is fundamentally defined and distinguished from other intellectual disciplines by its loyalty to the character dispositions of rationality, and so to the Socratic ideal. Anglo-American analytic philosophy is committed to these values with a particularly high degree of self-consciousness. Whatever the content of the philosophical view in question, the norms of theoretical rationality define its standards of philosophical exposition: clarity, structure, coherence, consistency, fineness of intellectual discrimination. And as a professional and pedagogical practice, philosophy is ideally defined by its adherence to the norms of rational discourse and criticism. In philosophy the appeal is to the other's rationality, with the purpose of convincing her of the veracity of one's own point of view. It is presumed that this purpose has been achieved if the other's subsequent behavior changes accordingly.

This presumption is fueled by philosophy's unsupervised influence in the political sphere – of Rousseau on the French Revolution, Locke on the American Revolution, Marx on Communism, Nietzsche on the Second World War, Rawls's Difference Principle on Reaganomics. In the private and social sphere, rational analysis and dialogue may just as easily give way to unsupervised imbalances in power and freedom, paternalistic or coercive relationships, or exploitative transactions. But even here philosophy may have its influence: in turning another aside from an unethical or imprudent course of action, or requiring him to revise his views in light of certain objections, or altering his attitudes toward oneself, or influencing others to accommodate the importance of certain philosophical considerations through compromise, tolerance, or mutual agreement.

In both spheres, then, the attempt rationally to persuade and to conduct oneself rationally toward others is an expression of respect, not only for their rationality, but thereby for the alternative resources of power – coercion, bribery, retaliation, influence – they are perceived as free to use in its stead. Toward one who is perceived to lack these alternative resources, no such respect need be shown, and raw power may be displayed and exercised more freely. For, as Hobbes reminds us,

> [h]onourable is whatsoever possession, action, or quality, is an argument or sign of power. . . . And therefore to be honoured, loved, or feared of many, is honourable; as arguments of power. . . . To speak to another with consideration, to appear before him with decency, and humility, is to honour him; as signs of fear to offend. To speak to him rashly, to do any thing before him obscenely, slovenly, impudently, is to dishonour.[2]

Hobbes is wrong to think that treating another with respect is nothing but an expression of fear of the other's power. But he is surely right to think that it is at least that. On Nietzsche's refinement of Hobbes's analysis, the appeal to reason expresses respect for another's rational autonomy to just and only that extent to which it simultaneously expresses fear of the alternative, nonrational ways in which that autonomy may be exercised. On Nietzsche's analysis of rational conduct, Hobbes and Kant may both be right.

So philosophy's traditional commitment to the Socratic ideal is one quintessential expression of a "slave morality" that acknowledges the danger of unrestrained instinct and the use of power in its service; by varying degrees it constrains and sublimates instinct, impulse, and the manipulation of power into a rational exercise of intellect and will that brings its own fulfillments:

> The ignorant man's position and character is this: he never looks to himself for benefit or harm, but to the world outside him. The philosopher's position and character is that he always looks to himself for benefit and harm. The signs of one who is making progress are: he blames none, praises none, complains of none, accuses none, never speaks of himself as if he were somebody, or as if he knew anything. When he is hindered, he blames himself. . . . He has got rid of desire, and his aversion is directed no longer to what is beyond our power [i.e. the body, property, reputation, office, and, in a word, everything that is not our own doing] but only to what is in our power [i.e. thought, impulse, desire, aversion, and, in a word, everything that is our own doing] and contrary to nature. In all things he exercises his will temperately.[3]

The philosopher, according to Epictetus, foregoes the gratification of desire and acquisition of external goods and power for the sake of cultivating the character dispositions of rationality. Seeing that these two alternative frequently conflict, she "atten[ds] to nothing but reason in all that [she] encounter[s]." The centrality and universality of the character dispositions of rationality to the discipline of philosophy, enduring over eighteen centuries, may explain why almost all philosophers, regardless of their express philosophical views on the value of rationality, try to muster the resources of rational argumentation, analysis, and criticism to defend those views. The consistency and sincerity with which they try to live up to the Socratic ideal bespeaks the seriousness of their intent to avoid the dormant alternatives.

Rationality as Philosophical Virtue

The priority accorded to the character dispositions of rationality in the practice of philosophy receives a more contemporary formulation in the following Anglo-American analytic version of the Socratic ideal:[4]

> [G. E.] Moore . . . invented and propagated a style of philosophical talking which has become one of the most useful and attractive models of rationality that we have, and which is still a prop to liberal values, having penetrated far beyond philosophical circles and far beyond Bloomsbury circles; it is also a source of continuing enjoyment, once one has acquired the habit among friends who have a passion for slow argument on both abstract and personal topics. When I look back to the Thirties and call on memories, it even seems that Moore invented a new moral virtue, a virtue of high civilization admittedly, which has its ancestor in Socrates' famous following of an argument wherever it may lead, but still with a quite distinctive modern and Moorean accent. Open-mindedness in discussion is to be associated with extreme literal clarity, with no rhetoric and the least possible use of metaphor, with an avoidance of technical terms wherever possible, and with extreme patience in step-by-step unfolding of the reasons that support any assertion made, together with all the qualifications that need to be added to preserve literal truth, however commonplace and disappointing the outcome. It is a style and a discipline that wring philosophical insights from the English language, pressed hard and repeatedly; as far as I know, the style has no counterpart in French or German. As Nietzsche suggested, cultivated caution and modesty in assertion are incompatible with the bold egotism of most German philosophy after Kant. This style of talking, particularly when applied to emotionally charged personal issues, was a gift to the world, not only to Bloomsbury, and it is still useful a long way from Cambridge.[5]

The writer is Stuart Hampshire, and in this passage he describes as an historical fact a more recent ideal of philosophical practice, which speaks to some of the motives and impulses that attract many into the field. The essence of the ideal remains Socratic: clarity and truth as a goal, with patience, persistence, precision, and a nonjudgmental openness to discussion and contention as the means.

Hampshire is right to describe this ideal as a "new moral virtue . . . of high civilization." It is a moral virtue because it imposes on one the obligation to subordinate the egocentric desires to prevail in argument, to shine in conversation, or to one-up one's opponent to the disinterested ethical requirements of impartiality, objectivity, and rationality in discussion. And it is a virtue of high civilization because it is not possible to achieve this virtue – or even to recognize it as a virtue – without already having cultivated and brought to fruition certain civilized dispositions of character, tastes, and values that override the desire to prevail. Thus this moral virtue stands at the very center of a "slave morality" that sublimates the desire to prevail to the imperatives of reason and the spirit. These imperatives, in turn, find expression in what Mill calls the higher pleasures of the intellect and moral and aesthetic sensibility. They presuppose the victory of "slave morality" in subjugating instinct and the exercise of power to the rule of reason and its attendant ethical values of fairness and impartiality in thought and action. This virtue of high civilization, then, presupposes both its participants' rationality and also their achievement of a equitable balance of power – however the material and social instruments of power may be distributed.

Thus this ideal can have meaning only for someone for whom basic psychological and spiritual needs for self-worth, and moral needs for the affirmation of self-rectitude are not so pressing that every dialectical encounter with others – whether written or conversational – is mined for its potential to satisfy them. So when we say of such a person that he is civilized, we may mean, among other things, that in conversation he is disposed to be generous in according credibility to his opponent's view, gracious in acknowledging its significance, patient in drawing forth its implications, and graceful in accepting its criticism of his own. Someone who has mastered this new moral virtue of high civilization is someone for whom philosophical practice expresses an ideal of personal *civility*, a civility made possible only by the control and sublimation of instinct, impulse, desire, and emotion.

The higher pleasure of doing philosophy in the style Hampshire describes is then the disinterested pleasure of thinking, considering, learning, and knowing as ends in themselves, and of giving these pleasures to and and receiving them from others involved in the same enterprise, in acts of communication. Plato was surely right to suggest that we are driven to seek erotic pleasure from others by the futile desire to merge, to become one with them. Erotic desire is ultimately futile for reasons of simple physics: we are each stuck in our own physical bodies, and you cannot achieve the desired unity by knocking two separate physical entities together, no matter how closely and repeatedly, and no matter how much fun it is to do the knocking.

Intellectual unity with another is a different matter altogether, however, and the kind Hampshire describes is particularly satisfying because it does not require either partner to submerge or abnegate herself in the will or convictions of the other. It does not require sharing the same opinions, or suppressing one's own worldview, or deferring or genuflecting to the other in order to achieve agreement. Rather, the enterprise is a collaborative one between equals who pool their philosophical resources. By contributing questions, amendments, refinements, criticisms, objections, examples, counterexamples, or elaborations in response to the other's philosophical assertions, we each extend and enrich both of our philosophical imaginations past their individual limits and into the other's domain. There are few intellectual pleasures more intense than the *Aha-Erlebnis* of finally understanding, after long and careful dialogue, what another person actually means – unless it is that of being understood oneself in that way.

The ground rules for succeeding in this enterprise are ethical ones. By making such assertions as clearly as I can, I extend to you an invitation to intellectual engagement; and I express trust, vulnerability and respect for your opinion in performing that act. I thereby challenge you to exercise your trained philosophical character dispositions – for impartiality, objectivity, and rationality – in examining my assertions; and to demonstrate your mastery of the enterprise in the act of engaging in it. This is the challenge to perform, in the practice of dialogue and conversation, at the ethical level made possible by our basic human capacities for language, logic and abstraction; and to bring those capacities themselves under the purview and guidance of our conception of right conduct. By engaging in the enterprise of philosophical dialogue, we challenge each other to observe the ethical and intellectual obligations of philosophical practice.

In this enterprise, I have failed if you feel crestfallen at having to concede a point, rather than inspired to elaborate upon it; or ashamed at having missed a point, rather than driven to persist in untangling it; or self-important for having made a point, rather than keen to test its soundness. After all, the goal of the enterprise is to inspire both of us with the force of the ideas we are examining, not to make either of us feel unequal to considering them, or smug for having introduced them. Too often we conceive of moral virtue as having to do only with such things as helping the needy, keeping promises, or loyalty in friendship – as though performing well in these areas relieved us of the obligation to refrain from making another person feel stupid, ashamed or crazy for voicing her thoughts; or ourselves feel superior for undermining them. When teachers fail to impart a love of philosophy to their undergraduate students, or drive graduate students, traumatized, out of their classes and out of the field, it is often because these elemental guidelines for conducting the enterprise – guidelines that express the simple truth that a love of philosophy is incompatible with feeling humiliated or trounced or arrogant or self-congratulatory for one's contributions to it – have been ignored. So this enterprise presupposes a basic and reciprocal respect for the minds, ideas and words of one's discussants, a respect that is expressed in attention to and interest in what they have to say.

Kant's concept of *Achtung* captures the intellectual attitude involved in this moral virtue of high civilization. The term is usually translated, in Kant's writings, as "respect"; and the object of *Achtung* is usually assumed to be exclusively the moral law. But Kant's account of reason in the first *Critique* makes quite clear that the moral law is not separate from the workings of theoretical reason more generally, but rather an application of it to the special case of first-personal action. We feel *Achtung* toward all the ways in which reason regulates our activity, both mental and physical. Moreover, in the *Groundwork* Kant makes it equally clear that he is not diverging from an important common, vernacular meaning of the term, which is closer to something like "respectful attention." When you and I are trying to get clear about the implications of a statement one of us has made – when we are fully engaged in the activity of "wring[ing] philosophical insights from the English language, pressed hard and repeatedly" – *Achtung* is what we feel for the intellectual process in which we are engaged and the insights we thereby bring forth.

And when Kant says that *Achtung* "impairs [*Abbruch tut*] self-love," he does not mean that *Achtung* crushes our egos or makes us feel ashamed of being the self-absorbed worms we know we are. He means, rather, that the value, significance, and power of the thing that compels our attention compels it so completely that we momentarily *forget* the constantly clamoring needs, demands and absorptions of the self; the object of our respectful attention overwhelms and silences them. For that moment we are mutually absorbed in the object of contemplation, or in actively responding to it – by acting, or by articulating it, or by evaluating its implications, or by reformulating or defending it – rather than trying to mine the discussion for transient satisfactions of our psychological cravings for self-aggrandizement. *Achtung* is an active, conative response to an abstract idea that overrides and outcompetes our subjective psychological needs as an object worthy of our attention.

These are the rare moments of intellectual self-transcendence in which together, through "extreme literal clarity, with no rhetoric and the least possible use of metaphor, with an avoidance of technical terms wherever possible, and with extreme patience in the step-by-step unfolding of the reasons that support any assertion made, together with all the qualifications that need to be added to preserve literal truth," we succeed in fashioning an idiolect subtle and flexible enough to satisfy and encompass all of the linguistic nuances we each bring to the project of verbally communicating our thoughts to each other. It is then that we achieve the only genuine unity with another of which we are capable. Alcibiades' drunken and complaining encomium to Socrates was also a eulogy to his own transient victory in achieving – even momentarily – the intellectual self-transcendence Socrates demanded.

Power and Philosophical Practice

Now I said that Hampshire described this Anglo-American update on the Socratic ideal as itself a historical fact. But is it? Here is a competing description of the same historical circumstance, from a rather different perspective:

> Victory was with those who could speak with the greatest appearance of clear, undoubting conviction and could best use the accents of infallibility. Moore . . . was a great master of this method – greeting one's remarks with a gasp of incredulity – Do you *really* think *that*, an expression of face as if to hear such a thing said reduced him to a state of wonder verging on imbecility, with his mouth wide open and wagging his head in the negative so violently that his hair shook. "*Oh!*" he would say, goggling at you as if either you or he must be mad; and no reply was possible. Strachey's methods were different; grim silence as if such a dreadful observation was beyond comment and the less said about it the better . . . [Woolf] was better at producing the effect that it was useless to argue with *him* than at crushing *you* . . . In practice it

was a kind of combat in which strength of character was really much
more valuable than subtlety of mind.[6]

Here the writer is John Maynard Keynes. Where Hampshire saw the
character dispositions of rationality in full flourishing, Keynes sees
psychological and emotional intimidation. Where Hampshire saw the
flowering of a moral virtue of high civilization – the flowering, in
Nietzsche's terms, of "slave morality," Keynes sees little more than a
less-than-subtle power struggle among *Übermenschen*, driven by the
instinct to win social status, even at the cost of philosophical integrity.
Who saw more clearly? The answer is important for calling into
question whether the character dispositions of rationality are as
central to philosophical practice as they are purported to be; and so,
more generally, whether the character dispositions of rationality *can
be* as central to the structure of the self as I, in this project, argue they
are.

There can be little doubt that Hampshire's version of the Socratic
ideal of philosophical dialogue requires of us a standard of intellectual
and moral conduct to which most of us are, most of the time,
intellectually and morally inadequate; and so that the ideal of rationality so valorized by a "slave morality" may be – for us – little more
than that. Here the moral inadequacy exacerbates the intellectual
inadequacy. It is difficult enough to keep in mind at one time more
than a few steps in an extended and complex philosophical argument,
or fully appreciate the two opposing views that must be reconciled, or
grasp the point of your opponent's criticism as he is voicing it while
you are mentally both formulating your refutation of it and refining
your view so as to accommodate it. But these purely intellectual
limitations are made so much worse by what Kant calls "certain
impulsions" of "the dear self" that obscure or interfere with the clarity
and sure-footedness of the reasoning process: the need to be right or
amusing at another's expense, the need to prove one's intelligence,
the need to triumph, or to secure one's authority, or to prove one's
superiority, or mark one's territory; or more viciously, the need to
intimidate one's opponent, to attack and crush her, shut her up,
express one's contempt for her, exact revenge, teach her a lesson, or
force her out of the dialogue. All of these needs exist on an ethical
continuum, from the merely regrettable or pathetic at one end to the
brutal or sadistic at the other. The essence of our moral inadequacy
to Hampshire's Socratic ideal of philosophical conduct is our temp-

tation to use even the limited skills of philosophical dialogue we have as a tool of self-aggrandizement or a weapon to bludgeon our opponent, rather than to arrive at recognizable truths we can both embrace.

This temptation finds vivid expression in certain familiar philosophical styles most of us have encountered at one time or another. For example, we have all at some point surely met – or been – the *Bulldozer*. The Bulldozer talks at you, at very great length, rather than to you; and seems to understand by "philosophical dialogue" what most people understand by "lecture." Indeed, Bulldozers may make excellent lecturers, and lecturing is an excellent training ground for bulldozing. The Bulldozer expounds at length his view, its historical antecedents, and its implications; anticipates your objections to it, enumerates each one, complete with examples, and refutes them; explains the views of his opponents and critiques them; and no doubt does much, much more than this, long after you have excused yourself and backed away with a muttered apology about needing to make a phone call. Sometimes the Bulldozer seems almost to induce in himself a trance state by the sound of his own words, and seems impervious to your ineffectual attempts to get a word in edgewise. And should you momentarily succeed in getting a word in edgewise, rest assured that there will not be many of those. For any one of them may set off a further volcanic eruption of speech in the Bulldozer, a shower of philosophical associations that must be pursued at that moment and to the fullest extent, relentlessly, wherever they may lead.

There is something alarmingly aimless and indiscriminate behind the compulsiveness of this performance, as though it were a Senate filibuster without a motion on the floor; as though the Bulldozer's greatest defeat would be to cede even the tiniest corner of verbal territory to someone else. Of course the experience of "conversing with" a Bulldozer is extremely irritating and oppressive, since one is being continually stymied in one's efforts to join the issues under scrutiny and make intellectual contact with one's discussant. But I think it is not difficult for any of us to imagine how it feels to *be* a Bulldozer, to feel driven to surround oneself stereophonically with the ongoing verbal demonstration of one's knowledge; to blanket every single square inch of the conceptual terrain, up to the horizon and beyond, with one's view of things; to fend off alien doubts, questions, and interjections of data into one's conceptual system by erecting around oneself a permanent screen of words and sounds so dense and wide that nothing and no one can penetrate it. Of course the Bulldozer himself may not think he is thwarting philosophical contact with others but instead enabling it; and may believe, even more tragically, that if he just says enough, he will surely command agreement in the end.

Then there is the *Bully*. Whereas the Bulldozer performs primarily for the sake of self-defense, the Bully performs more aggressively, in order to compel others' silent acquiescence. She may deploy familiar locutions designed to forestall objections or questions before they are raised: "Surely it is obvious that . . ." or "It is perfectly clear that . . ." or "Well, I take it that . . ." The message here is that anyone who would display such ignorance and lack of insight as to call these self-evident truths into question is too philosophically challenged to be taken seriously; and the intended effect is to intimidate the misguided into silence.

For example, I resorted to some of these bullying techniques earlier, in my discussion of Kant. "Kant's account of reason in the first *Critique* MAKES QUITE CLEAR that the moral law is not separate from the workings of theoretical reason more generally," I claimed; and "in the *Groundwork* Kant MAKES IT EQUALLY CLEAR that he is not diverging from an important common, vernacular meaning of the term *Achtung*." In both of these cases, I tried to double the barrage of intimidation, by brazenly combining claims of self-evidence with an appeal to authority. Why? Because even though I know these views to be controversial, I wanted you to swallow them on faith, for the moment, without questioning me, so I could go on and build on those assumptions the further points I wanted to make. Elsewhere[7] I do argue that a careful and unbiased look at the texts will support them. But I did not want to have to defend them here, or allow this General Introduction to the Project to turn into an exercise in Kant exegesis. So instead I finessed them through an attempt at intimidation; by insinuating, in effect, that ANYONE WHO'D TAKEN THE TIME TO STUDY THE TEXTS CAREFULLY could not fail to agree with my interpretation; and that any dissent from it would reveal only the dissenter's own scholarly turpitude. This is not philosophy. This is verbal harassment.

This kind of bullying may have many causes. It may result from a deficiency of "extreme patience in step-by-step unfolding of the reasons that support any assertion made." For Hampshire does not notice that this moral virtue of high civilization may be best suited to a mild, placid, even phlegmatic temperament, and may be largely unattainable for those of us who tend toward excitability, irritability, or an impatient desire to cut to the chase. But this does not excuse the indulgence of these tendencies at another's expense. After all, part of the point of philosophical training is to learn, not merely a prescribed set of texts and skills of reasoning, but also the *discipline* of philosophy. We are required to discipline our dispositions of attitude and motivation as well as of mind in its service. This is no more and no less than cultivation of the character dispositions of rationality requires.

Philosophical bullying may also result from a negligence encouraged by the structural demands of professionalism. Excelling in any of the various branches of philosophy demands specialization. This may lead us to underestimate the importance of securely grounding with "step-by-step unfolding of the reasons that support" those parts of our views that lead us into other philosophical subspecialties – as, for example, political philosophy may lead into philosophy of social science, logic may lead into philosophy of language, epistemology may lead into philosophy of science, metaethics may lead into philosophical psychology, or any of these may lead into metaphysics or the history of philosophy. And since the scarcity of jobs and limited professional resources often places us in a competitive rather than a collaborative relationship with our colleagues in other subspecialties, we may be tempted, on occasion, simply to ignore, dismiss, or bully our way out of the kind of careful attention to foundations that Hampshire recommends.

Furthermore, most of us entered this field because we needed to make a living doing something (true *Untertanen* that we are), and enjoyed doing philosophy enough to want to make a living doing it. As with any job on which our economic survival depends, we often have to balance the quality of our output against the time or space we have in which to do it. We are here to ply our trade, to speak authoritatively to the designated issues. And if what we have to say depends on unfounded or insufficiently argued assumptions, then (at least for the time being) so much the worse for those assumptions, and for those innocents who, not understanding the rules of the game – the allotted speaker time, the maximum acceptable article length, or the limited market demand for fat, ponderous books such as this one – would attempt to exercise quality control by calling those assumptions into question.

The Bully becomes a morally objectionable *Überbully* with the choice of more insulting or hurtful terms of evaluation, and with the shouting, stamping of feet, or even throwing of objects that sometimes accompanies his attempts to drive home a point. This performance shades into unadorned wrongdoing when these tactics of verbal intimidation include insinuated threats of professional retaliation or clear verbal abuse. Suggestions that holding a certain philosophical position is not conducive to tenure or reappointment, or that one will be dropped from a project for challenging received wisdom, or that raising objections to a senior colleague's view is offensive and inappropriate; as well as familiar locutions such as "Any idiot can see that . . .;" or, "That is the most ridiculous argument I've ever heard;" or, "What a deeply uninteresting claim;" or, "How can anyone be so dense as to believe that . . .?" are all among the Überbully's arsenal of verbal ammunition. Philosophers have been publicly and professionally humiliated for having argued a view that, in their critic's eyes, marked them as dim-witted, ill-read, poorly educated, lazy, devious, evasive, superficial, dull, ridiculous, dishonest, manipulative, or any combination of the above. Whereas the Bulldozer prevents you from contributing to the dialogue, the Überbully uses you and your philosophical contributions as a punching bag, trying to knock the stuffing out of them and scatter their remains to the wind.

It is tempting to explain this grade of lethal verbal aggression as an expression of arrogance or boorishness. But there is more to it than that. Like the Bully, the Überbully attempts to demolish you through verbal harassment, not rational philosophical analysis – in clear violation of the canonical rules of philosophical discourse. All we need to do is ask why either brand of bully feels the need to resort to these thuggish tactics when the canonical ones are available, in order to understand their brutal performances as an exhibition of felt philosophical inadequacy that expresses fear of professional humiliation. The frequency with which shame and fear emerge in these forms measures the suitability of the practice of philosophy to stand as a testimonial to our achievement of the Socratic/Hampshirean "moral virtue of high civilization," thereby as a testimonial to the victory of "slave morality," and thereby as a testimonial to the centrality of reason in the structure of the self.

There is also the philosophical style we may describe as the *Bull*. This one works best on students, or on colleagues who work in a different subspecialty than oneself. Like the Bulldozer and the Bullies, the Bull is designed to discourage questioning or dialogue, and silence dissent. The Bull may spew forth, with a great and rapid show of bombast, a torrent of technical or esoteric terminology, or inflated five-syllable abstractions. Or she may issue – again with no apology and much pomp – several incoherent, inconsistent, or mutually irrelevant assertions, and appear surprised at any suggestion of paradox. Or she may answer your pointed questions with a barrage of vague philosophical generalities that seem not to engage the issues at all. And the Bull may borrow some tactics from the Bully, in suggesting that any failure to grasp the overarching point of these turgid non sequiturs is merely a distressing symptom of your own philosophical incompetence. In this way the Bull uses the specialized tools of her trade to exclude you from participation in the private club to which she lets you know she belongs. The not-so-subtle message the Bull intends to communicate is: No Trespassers. Unlike the Bull's other philosophical utterances, this one is clear, easily grasped, and usually elicits compliance. It is not easy to remain involved in a discussion in which the suspicion quickly grows that one's discussant is talking nonsense.

And finally there is the *Bullfinch*, who simply flies away home. The Bullfinch avoids philosophical dialogue altogether, by declining to subject his views to philosophical scrutiny. Convinced of their veracity yet concerned to preserve their inviolability, the Bullfinch withdraws from philosophical engagement with unconverted others. Rather than argue his views, the Bullfinch at most will explain where he stands, ignoring retorts, criticisms, or opposing views by refusing to acknowledge their philosophical worth. The Bullfinch is more likely to view his own beliefs as so self-evidently true that it is beneath him to have to articulate or expose them to unconverted others in any form; and his opponent's beliefs as dangerous enough to justify getting rid of her at any cost. Thus the Bullfinch defends the sanctity of his convictions by refusing to defend them at all, instead retreating into silence, backhanded Machiavellian maneuvers, or flight. Or he may resort to cruder tools of psychological intimidation – of the sort Keynes describes – as more appropriate to his opponent. By refusing to engage in rational dialogue even as a weapon of intimidation, the Bullfinch thus approaches most nearly the explicit conduct of Nietzsche's *Übermensch*, for whom displays of power completely replace the Socratic ideal of rationality, and so express most clearly his unqualified contempt for his philosophical opponents.

Philosophy, Power, and Historical Circumstance

These brief character sketches do not exhaust the styles and strategies of intimidating philosophical practice, and there are more lethal ones than these: to treat philosophical contributions from others as though they had not been made; or as though they had been made by someone of higher professional status; or as autobiographical rather than philosophical in import; or as symptoms of mental illness; as well as the more subtle variants Keynes describes. The common motive that underlies all of these styles of dialogue is a desire to establish and maintain hierarchical *übermenschlichen* superiority, by silencing philosophical exchange rather than inviting it. This motive is not entirely foreign to any of us. But it is meant to stifle the exercise of rationality. As such, it is, in effect, an effort to obliterate the point and practice of philosophical dialogue altogether. It is worth asking what it is about the practice or profession of philosophy in general that kindles such an impulse to obliterate it; and how it is that this impulse can co-exist within the same field of inquiry as Hampshire's Socratic ideal. For this impulse does not signal merely our moral and intellectual inadequacy to the ideal. It expresses the lethal and ultimately suicidal desire to eradicate it.

We have certain external procedural devices for cloaking this suicidal impulse. There is the authoritarian device, of supplying spoken discussion with a strong-willed moderator; and the democratic device, of scrupulously invoking Robert's Rules of Order to govern every verbal contribution; and the juridical, testimony-cross-rebuttal-jury deliberation device, of the standard colloquium format. But if we were as civilized as Hampshire's description supposes, we would not need any of these external devices. We would not need a moderator to end filibusters or umpire foul balls because no one would be tempted to hog the allotted time or hit below the belt. We would not need Robert's Rules of Order because no one would be tempted to disrupt or exploit it. And we would not need the standard colloquium format because that format formalizes a dialectical procedure to which we would adhere naturally and spontaneously, as do Aristotle's temperate men to the mean and Kant's perfectly rational beings to the moral law. These devices are muzzles and restraining leashes designed to rein us in, not merely from expressing our philosophical enthusiasms too vehemently or at excessive length; but rather from too obviously lunging for the jugular under the guise of philosophical critique.[8] Sometimes it is as though in our serious philosophical activity we needed to be monitored and cued from the wings by an instructor in the basics of philosophical etiquette. It is as though there were no internalized voice of intellectual conscience to guide our philosophical behavior at all.

How is this lack of philosophical self-discipline to be understood? How are we to understand the frequent identification of personal and professional well-being with having at least temporarily obliterated one's philosophical enemies, and of personal and professional failure with having lost the war? And how are we to understand our own self-deception and lack of insight into the egoistic motives and meaning of such philosophical behavior – as though a punishing philosophical workover that verbally dices one's opponent into bite-size chunks were cognitively indistinguishable from the "cultivated caution and modesty in assertion" that Hampshire rightly applauds? Should we say that if we are incapable of practicing rational self-restraint and self-scrutiny in the circumscribed and rarified arena of philosophical dialogue, there is small hope for doing so in more complex fields of social interaction? Or should we say, rather, that it is because the philosophical arena is so small and morally insignificant that we have devoted so little attention to habituating ourselves to proceed in a temperate and civilized manner; and that our *übermenschlichen* barbarity here has no practical implications for our rational moral potential elsewhere?

The latter response is inadequate on several counts. First, the concept of rational philosophical dialogue as establishing metaethical conditions for comprehensive normative theory is too central to the moral and political views of too many major philosophers – Rawls, Hare, Dworkin, Rorty, and Habermas among them – to be dismissed as morally insignificant. If we cannot even succeed in discussing, in a rational and civilized manner, what we ought to do, it is not likely that we will succeed in figuring out what we ought to do, much less actually doing it. Second, talk is cheap; talk is the easy part of moral rectitude. If we can ever hold our tongue, choose our words, and exert ourselves to understand another and communicate successfully with her when our self-interest is at stake, then we may cultivate the rational disposition to do those things. The question then becomes whether we are less inclined to cultivate it when it is our purely philosophical interests that are at stake; and what that might reveal about the ability of philosophy – and so rationality – to give point and form to our lives. Certainly there are those for whom philosophy is merely an intellectual game.

Third, philosophy as the rational discipline *par excellence* has fashioned its own identity through the centrality of its involvement in the most elemental and universal ideals of human life: ideals of the good, the true, and the beautiful; of equality, rationality, and grace. These are the ideals that inspire the young to study philosophy, and that often sustain our allegiance to it as we grow older. That the intellectual skills with which we pursue research into these ideals can be so easily perverted by the Bulldozer, the Bullies, the Bull, and the Bullfinch in the service of the bad, the false, and the ugly is no minor matter. How a profession self-defined by its rationality and its idealism can generate suicidally self-repressive and self-abasing styles of practice demands explanation.

Earlier I suggested that part of the explanation is to be found in the economic conditions that have come to characterize the profession of academic philosophy since the late 1960s. These conditions have encouraged a possessive and authoritarian attitude toward philosophical ideas that is incompatible with the obligations of philosophical practice as Hampshire enumerates them. We have seen that these include a commitment to clarity, precision, and care in the development of an argument or view; and a methodological caution that eschews easy answers for the sake of a coherent thesis that is fully cognizant of significant objections and alternatives to the view being defended. But these obligations must compete with the mounting difficulty of finding long-term or permanent jobs in the field.

Up to the early 1960s philosophy was a small, homogeneous, economically secure academic enclave. As would befit a community of *Übermenschen*, Stevenson's emotivism vied with Ross's and Pritchard's intuitionism and Moore's non-naturalism as the metaethical views of choice. Kantian, rationality-based metaethical views were not in the competition. With Johnson's Great Society programs of the mid-1960s, philosophy began to open its doors to younger scholars showing the ethnic, gender, and class diversity that has always been representative of the population of the United States. But those programs in higher education funded this expanded academic population only briefly. Since then the resulting scarcity of jobs has become an increasingly serious problem for younger philosophers, newcomers and legatees alike. It has been a central professional fact of life since the late 1970s. Those of us who entered the professional side of the field as graduate students in the mid-1970s had studied, benefited from, and taken as models philosophical writings that uniformly predated this dearth of professional opportunities. But we had also received a letter from the American Philosophical Association, routinely sent to all aspiring graduate students, advising us that very few jobs were likely to be available upon receipt of the Ph.D. Under these circumstances, such aspiring graduate students have had three choices: (1) ignore the letter; (2) ignore those aspects of their previous philosophical training that conflict with it; or (3) try to adapt in ways that will allow them to compete successfully in the field. Clearly, the student who is both rationally self-interested and committed to philosophy will choose (3), and most who have survived professionally have done so.

For the most part the results have not been auspicious for the health of the field. The methodological caution that is essential to doing good philosophical work has been too often supplanted by an intellectual and philosophical timidity that is the antithesis of it. Understandably concerned to ensure their ability to continue and succeed professionally in the discipline to which they are committed, many younger philosophers in the past few decades have grown increasingly reluctant to fulfill the demands of the Oedipal drama that is essential to the flourishing of any intellectual discipline. In order to break new ground, younger thinkers must strive to study, absorb, elaborate, and then criticize and improve upon or replace the authoritative teachings on which their training is based. Otherwise they fail to achieve the critical independence and psychological and intellectual maturity that enable them to introduce new, stronger, and more comprehensively authoritative paradigms in their turn. Strawson's early critique of Russell's theory of descriptions, for example, or Rawls's rejection and displacement, as a young man in his early thirties, of Moore's philosophy of language-based metaethics, or Kripke's and Barcan Marcus's early repudiation of Quine's constraints on quantificational logic, or Kuhn's displacement of Popper's philosophy of science in the early 1960s, are only a few of the available contemporary models for playing out this drama in philosophy.

The obligations of philosophical practice as Epictetus and Hampshire enumerate them – and as Socrates exemplifies them – create an ideal context in which all of the characters in this drama can thrive. In attending only to the quality of philosophical contributions and not to the hierarchical position of those who make them, the "style of philosophical talking" Hampshire describes calls forth the best philosophical efforts of all parties, regardless of rank or stature. Careful, patient, and rational philosophical discussion is the great equalizer among discussants, the great leveler of professional hierarchy.[9] So younger philosophers can feel secure in the conviction that in subjecting the views of their elders to searching scrutiny and possible refutation, they are only doing what the obligations of philosophical practice demand.

This ideal of equality in rational dialogue comes into direct conflict with a reality in which professional survival is a scarce commodity doled out as reward in a zero-sum game. Where philosophical error translates as professional failure, the avoidance of professional failure requires the concealment of philosophical error at all costs. Under these circumstances there can be little place for the rational criticism and analysis of views, and so little place for unconstrained give-and-take among rational equals. These practices must be replaced by a system of patronage of the unempowered by the empowered, and mutual aggrandizement of the empowered by one another. It is because rational philosophical dialogue recognizes no professional hierarchy that other, extra-philosophical or even anti-philosophical measures must be invoked to maintain it under circumstances in which hierarchical status is the surest index of professional survival.

Philosophy as an academic discipline is correspondingly unusual in the obsessiveness and rigidity with which the character and composition of its traditional professional hierarchy has been guarded since the 1970s. In this traditional hierarchy, criticism from peers is received as an honor, whereas criticism from subordinates is resisted as insubordination; and novices, newcomers, provisional members, and interlopers tend to rank among the lowest subordinates of all. Accordingly, the more they diverge – in thought, appearance or pedigree – from the tradition, the closer to the bottom of the hierarchy they are likely to be found, and the more blatant the exercises of power that keep them there. Correspondingly more attention has been given to Kantian, rationality-based metaethical views since the 1970s, and many newcomers, provisional members, and interlopers – including particularly large numbers of women – are to be found among their proponents.

Younger thinkers who choose to diverge or defect rather than conform philosophically embark on a dangerous Oedipal drama in which they must confront and face down the wrath and resistance of their elders in order to prevail. By finally rejecting the views of those whom they have studied and by whom they may have been mentored and protected in the beginning stages of their career, younger scholars will often provoke disapproval, rejection or punitive professional retaliation from those who feel betrayed by their defection. They may risk their professional survival, advancement, and the powerful professional networks which the authoritative support of their mentors has supplied. This is of course an exceedingly painful and intimidating prospect for all concerned, elders and prodigal sons[10] alike. It is nevertheless necessary in order to advance the dialogue and ensure the intellectual health of the discipline.

The elders will survive this defection with their stature intact, as did Russell, Moore, Quine, and Popper; and eventually come to recognize their own example in that of their defectors. After all, they, too, were once defectors, and took the terrible risks they now discourage their own disciples from taking. Thus, those disciples need to demonstrate their respect for their elders, and the depth of their influence as role models, by similarly having the attachment and commitment to their own ideas, the energy and courage to probe their deepest implications, and a confidence in their value firm enough to impel them to this confrontation, despite the clear dangers to their professional self-interest. Otherwise these ideas become little more than disposable vehicles for promoting professional self-interest, of questionable value in themselves.

One might argue that this brand of naive intellectual bravado is in mercifully short supply under the best and most professionally secure of circumstances. But nerve fails all the more quickly as the threat of professional extinction becomes more real; and this failure of intellectual nerve has by now so completely pervaded the field of philosophy that it has generated its own set of professional conventions: a virtual culture of genuflection, relative to which merely to embark on the confrontation with one's elders is a serious and sometimes fatal breach of etiquette. So, for example, when I was a junior faculty member, a very senior and very eminent colleague reprimanded my efforts to defend the position developed in this project by informing me that it was "not [my] place to have views"; I once had a paper accepted for publication on the sole condition that I excise my critique of a major figure in the field; and had one rejected because a single negative referee's report, although acknowledged by the editor to be incoherent and self-contradictory, came from an important personage. Rather than take on the major thinkers, many have been encouraged or coerced to avoid the Oedipal confrontation altogether. The great, ongoing contentious debates that extended from Plato through Kant, Fichte, Hegel, Schopenhauer and on to the Vienna Circle, Russell, Wittgenstein, and Habermas seem to have been all but silenced by the repressive dictates of professionalism.

These genuflective norms of etiquette undergird the recommendations of professional self-interest, by encouraging and rewarding excessive deference to philosophical authority, by discouraging forthright argumentation and critique, and by undermining the intellectual and professional confidence of younger philosophers in their ability to develop their own views independently and survive confrontation with their elders. They thereby infantilize the unempowered, by stripping them of the very resources most essential, in the long term, to their own survival and flourishing: the character dispositions of rationality. It then would be unsurprising to discover that, when the unempowered were rewarded for their obedience with professional empowerment, the character dispositions of rationality were given both less exercise and less philosophical weight.

These norms of genuflection, necessitated by economic imperatives, create the authoritarian conditions under which the Bulldozer, the Bullies, the Bull, and the Bullfinch flourish. Like other artifacts of the culture of genuflection, they function to protect canonical or insecure philosophical territory using anti-philosophical weaponry, when pure philosophical dialogue itself is too subversive of established hierarchy or received interpretation to be tolerated. And through practice, repetition, and professional reward, these repressive philosophical styles are transmitted as role models from one generation of graduate students to the next, as legitimate modes of philosophical discourse. Ultimately they supplant the legitimate and civilized modes of philosophical discourse Hampshire describes with self-aggrandizing displays of power and domination, and corrupt the quality of philosophical ideas accordingly. In replacing the obligations of philosophical practice with the imperatives of professional survival, these styles bespeak more than our egoism. They bespeak our inability to transcend structural conflicts between the democratic prerequisites of a genuine philosophical meritocracy and the consequences of a market economy.

Philosophy as Exemplar of Rationality

Western philosophy has always found its source of value in its identification with rationality, originally the systematic rational inquiry practiced by Socrates. But as other disciplines – the natural sciences, psychology, sociology, political theory, anthropology – have gradually seceded from the formal discipline of philosophy and formulated their own rational methodologies, philosophy has repeatedly sought outside itself for its defining exemplar of rationality, and so for its source of intrinsic value. Up through the nineteenth century, Anglo-American analytic philosophy ignored the defection of the natural and social sciences and identified rationality with empirical rational inquiry, i.e., with scientific methodology. Traditional epistemology began to be upstaged by the newly emerging subspecialty of philosophy of science. At the beginning of this century, the melding of logic and mathematics of Russell and Whitehead's *Principia Mathematica* provided philosophy with another exemplar of rationality with which to identify: one of logical rigor, symbol, and system. Traditional speculative metaphysics received a corresponding boost in status at the same time that it took a drubbing from Logical Positivism. After the Second World War, philosophy turned to Frege, Wittgenstein, and Chomsky for yet another exemplar of rational philosophical method as linguistic analysis. Linguistic anthropology and sociology received correspondingly more attention from philosophers of language. And since the 1970s, philosophy has increasingly turned back to the sciences – this time to the emerging field of cognitive science – for its exemplar of rational methodology. The philosophy of mind and theory of action have flourished accordingly. Trade relations have thus run in both directions: the discipline of philosophy has exported and diversified its early conception of rationality as systematic Socratic inquiry into newly emerging research disciplines; and these, in turn, import back into the discipline of philosophy more highly specialized conceptions of their own.

The more the discipline of philosophy has succumbed to the political, economic, and professional pressures just described, the more stridently it has insisted upon these externally imported exemplars – sometimes singly, sometimes in tandem – as centrally definitive of the field and the practice of philosophy. And the more the discipline of philosophy as the practice of rationality *par excellence* has been threatened from any and all directions, and the more the specialized conceptions of rational methodology have proliferated, the more tenaciously philosophy has held onto its self-identification with rationality as such, adjusting its source of value according to how in particular rationality is conceived.

In the end, however, it is only philosophy's original identification with the systematic rational inquiry of Socrates – Epictetus' injunction to

> transgress in nothing the clear pronouncement of reason . . . to live as one who is mature and proficient, and let all that seems best to you be a law that you cannot transgress. . . . [to] attend to nothing but reason in all that [you] encounte[r]. . . . to live as one who would wish to be a Socrates.[11]

that remains impervious to defection, attack, or nonrational alternatives. It is impervious to defection because emerging fields that have defected have taken rational Socratic inquiry with them as their minimal foundations. It is impervious to attack because any such attack must presuppose its methods in order to be rationally intelligible. And it is impervious to nonrational alternatives because no such alternative competes with it on its own ground. Philosophy's greatest challenge, then, is to live up to its traditional, Socratic self-conception: conduct in all spheres that gives centrality to the character dispositions of rationality.

Under the historical circumstances earlier described, it is impossible to avoid calling into question the present-day adequacy of philosophy to meet this challenge, and so, its right to insist on its self-definition as an exemplar of rationality. Hence it is impossible to avoid questioning whether the character dispositions of rationality can be as central to the structure of the self as they seemed to be for Socrates and Epictetus. The problem would seem to be not that we so often violate Epictetus' injunction to "transgress in nothing the clear pronouncement of reason," but rather that we so often transgress that clear pronouncement in precisely those areas of conduct in which reason is purported to reign supreme. One explanation would be that philosophers have been guilty of self-serving pretensions to rationality all along; and that philosophical practice has never consisted of anything more than psychological intimidation and the flouting of power imbalances under the guise of rational dialogue. According to this view, Epictetus' entreaties would be addressed precisely to those in need of rationality as an inspiring ideal by which to modulate largely nonrational behavior.

But another possibility is that we must rather take special care now, in this particular historical and cultural epoch, to defend the centrality to philosophy of those character dispositions of rationality the exercise of which have been so traditionally definitive of its practice. It might be that these dispositions, and so the traditional practice of philosophy itself – and so its adequacy as an exemplar of rationality – are now under particularly severe attack, from both inside and outside the discipline, by concerted attempts to defend traditional power relations against the destabilizing effects of rational Socratic interrogation. The displacement of rationality from a central functional and valuational role in the way the structure of the self is conceived signals a move away from the "slave morality" that valorizes the character dispositions of rationality as essentially constitutive of human survival and flourishing. This displacement also signals a move toward alternative, *übermenschlichen* norms of behavior that implicitly condone freer and more blatant exercises of power in the service of desire, instinct, and emotion. It is no accident that this Gestalt shift occurs at an historical juncture when such exercises and displays of power are increasingly necessary to defend conventional social arrangements – both inside and outside the academy – against rational Socratic interrogation by individuals and communities traditionally disempowered by them. But it is then doubly ironical that the character dispositions of rationality themselves should be marshalled by some philosophers to justify them.

The philosophical use of reason to justify unreason then obliges those philosophers who explicitly value reason, rational interrogation, and the character dispositions of rationality more generally, as intrinsic goods, to defend them in turn. It requires us to reaffirm and protect these intrinsic goods as essential and definitive of philosophical practice, regardless of the express philosophical views on which they are honed. It requires us as well to realize these values in our philosophical practice, regardless of the professional repercussions. And it requires us to disregard those repercussions as secondary to the preservation of rational integrity. That is, the philosophical task is to demonstrate the deeply entrenched necessity of rationality to coherent thought and action, independently of the express metaethical views or valuation of rationality any particular philosopher might hold. That is my task in this project.

The Enterprise of Socratic Metaethics

In ethics, we distinguish between a *normative* and a *metaethical* theory. A normative moral theory tells us what we ought to do, and why. Thus it traditionally utilizes such prescriptive terms as "ought," "should," "good," "right," "valuable," or "desirable" (I offer an analysis of such terms in Volume II, *A Kantian Conception*). This is the *practical* part of a normative theory, also known as *casuistry*. Such a theory also contains a *value-theoretic* component that enlists certain states, conditions, or events that explain what is good, right, or desirable: friendship, for example; or love, or reason, or integrity. Value theories differ with respect to both content and structure (I say more about these distinctions in Volume I, chapter I).

By contrast, a metaethical theory seeks to unpack the metaphysical presuppositions of a normative theory: to what sorts of entities, if any, its prescriptive terms refer; whether it can be objectively true or not; what its scope of application might be; what conception of the agent, rationality, or human psychology it presupposes. Thus a metaethical theory is descriptive and analytical where a normative one is prescriptive and hortatory.

By comparison with the putative centrality of rationality to the practice of philosophy itself, the metaethical views philosophers expressly defend show wide variation in the role each assigns to rationality in the structure of the self. Here the value and function of reason ranges from the central to the peripheral, and the prominence of nonrational elements in the structure of the self varies accordingly. At one extreme, consider Subjectivism. Subjectivism essentially rejects truth and objectivity as possible goals for intellectual discourse on any subject. But any judgment in the categorical indicative mood implies – whether rightly or wrongly – the truth and objectivity of the judgment, including the judgment that truth and objectivity are impossible. So if that judgment, that truth and objectivity are impossible, is itself true and objectively valid, then it is false and objectively invalid. If it is false, then its negation, i.e., that truth and objectivity are not impossible, is true. So the truth of subjectivism implies its falsity. If, on the other hand, Subjectivism is neither true nor false, then it refers to nothing and expresses at best the speaker's emotional despair about the possibility of communication – a condition treated better in psychotherapy than in intellectual discourse. If this paradox of judgment strikes you as in any way troubling, or as detracting from the intelligibility of Subjectivism, then you have already accepted intellectual criteria of rational consistency that imply an aspiration to objective validity and truth. Only when these criteria are presupposed can meaningful or coherent discussion, on any topic whatsoever, proceed.

A fortiori, any judgment of specifically moral value aspires to be more than a mere emotive expression of the speaker's momentary feelings. It aspires to objective validity, and we signal this by stating our views publicly, defending them with evidence or reasoning, and subjecting them to critical analysis in light of standards of rationality and truth we implicitly accept. So, for example, suppose someone walks up to you and punches you in the nose. Your verbal reaction will surely include the statements that he had no right to do that, that his behavior was unwarranted and inappropriate, and that you did nothing to deserve it. It is not likely that you will then go on to add that of course these are just your opinions which have no objective validity and that there is no final truth of the matter. Rather, you express your beliefs in categorical indicative judgments, which you of course presume to be true, and which you can defend by appeal to facts you take to be obvious and values you take to be equally obvious. Of course, some of your presumptive judgments may be mistaken or false. But this does not entail that there is no fact of the matter as to whether they are or not.

The project of moral communication has not only to do with letting others know what we think, but also trying to command their acknowledgment that we are right. Those of us committed to the Socratic ideal prefer to command this acknowledgment through rational dialogue rather than emotional rhetoric, dissimulation, psychological manipulation, or threats of professional or social rewards withheld or punishments inflicted for dissenting. That is, we do our best to "live as one who would wish to be Socrates," rather than as a Bulldozer, Bully, Überbully, Bull, or Bullfinch. By relying on the force of rational dialogue to win agreement with our moral convictions, we try to command not only others' assent, but also their intellectual respect. In rational discussion, analysis, and argument, we reach beyond the circle of the converted to try and convert the unconvinced. We express respect for the rationality of the unconverted by appealing to it, rather than to their emotional, psychological, or social vulnerabilities, to convince them. And we receive the best confirmation of the truth of our moral convictions when others are rationally convinced, rather than manipulated or coerced or deceived, into adopting them. Call this the enterprise of *Socratic metaethics*. Socratic metaethics grounds moral convictions and judgments in the Socratic ideal of rational dialogue as a means for arriving at moral truth.

Within the enterprise of Socratic metaethics, there are many ways to proceed. One that has a long historical pedigree is what I will call Antirationalism.[12] In earlier historical periods this approach has emerged variously in normative theories such as Intuitionism or the Moral Sense Theory of the British Moralists. (Similarly, Virtue Theory claims allegiance to Aristotle, but on extremely shaky exegetical grounds.) As developed in the philosophy of Sir David Ross, Intuitionism stipulates the existence of an innate faculty of moral intuition, consultation of which tells us what moral principles we ought to follow in action.[13] More recent Antirationalists such as Annette Baier, Lawrence Blum, Michael Stocker, or Susan Wolf hark back to British Moral Sense Theorists such as Shaftesbury, Hutcheson, or the Hume of Book III of the *Treatise*, by repudiating the governing role of moral principle and instead appealing to moral emotion or sentiment to guide action.[14] (Similarly, the Noncognitivism of Gibbard, Raz, and Anderson reject the rationality of moral principle, but then resurrect rationality as a prescriptive criterion for moral emotions and attitudes.) In all cases, moral guidance is given by a nonrational component of the self: we ought to perform those actions we intuitively know to be right, or, respectively, feel most deeply. No consistent Antirationalist normative view can have a developed practical or casuistical component, because what any particular individual ought to do depends on her particular intuitions, feelings, or desires – not on impartially conceived principles. Nevertheless, the value-theoretic parts of these views are articulated and developed within the impartial normative constraints of Socratic metaethics.

The following discussion will contain much on the failings of Antirationalism. Here I call attention to just one reason why it is unpalatable *in practice* to anyone seriously interested in the enterprise of Socratic metaethics as a distinctive philosophical methodology. This is that it appeals to the authority of a first-personal, inaccessible experience in judging, not only what *one* should do, but what should be done *simpliciter* under particular circumstances. In consulting only one's moral emotions or intuitions about how to interpersonally resolve some hypothetical or actual moral problem that bears no obvious relation to one's own circumstances, one presumes to legislate how others should behave or feel on the basis of a moral foundation which is cognitively inaccessible to them, and therefore inaccessible to their evaluation.

Suppose, for example, that I discover that my best friend is dealing drugs to minors and decide, on the basis of my feelings about him, to protect our friendship rather than betray it by turning him in to the police. There is a great deal you and I may discuss about such a case. But without knowing, and without being able to experience directly the particular nature and quality of my feelings for this person, you may find my behavior simply indefensible. You may acknowledge and sympathize with the deep bonds of friendship and loyalty I am feeling, but find it nevertheless impossible to condone my claim that I just could not bring myself to destroy them by turning him in. You may think that no friendship, no matter how deep or meaningful, should count for so much that it outweighs the right of minors to be shielded from drug addiction before they are mature enough to make a rational choice. And since I cannot convey to you the direct quality of the experience of my friend on which my feelings are based, there is little I can say to defend my decision. Perhaps I may expect your pity or sympathy for my dilemma, but I cannot expect your respect or agreement. So unless you find me particularly compelling as a role model on nonrational grounds (say, my crucial presence in your upbringing; or my charisma, or broad sphere of social or professional influence; or your desire to stay in my good graces), I can provide you with no reason why the principles on which I acted (and even Antirationalists act on principles, even if they don't think about or formulate them) should govern your behavior under similar circumstances.

This is not a peculiarly Kantian objection. Unless a principle on which I act is formulated partially, i.e., with indexical operators, proper names and definite descriptions, we presume it to apply impartially; that is the way language works. Terms and principles have general application to the scope of referents they denote, unless their scopes are restricted explicitly by stipulation or fiat or context. So, for example, if I tell you that dogs are susceptible to gastric tortion, I am either mistaken or else using the term "dog" in an idiosyncratically restricted sense, to refer specifically to large dogs with cylindrical stomachs. Similarly, if I tell you I feel that friendship should come before social welfare, you will naturally take me to be doing more than merely emoting my personal feelings about this particular friend. You will naturally take me to be expressing a judgment that applies not only to my own behavior in this case, but to anyone's who must weigh the relative priority of friendship and social welfare. But since I am merely telling you what I feel, and since what I feel is not directly available to you, I offer you no available justificatory basis for evaluating the applicability of this principle to your behavior. Unless you have some special reason to be impressed with my feelings, you have no reason to be impressed with the principles on which I act. Antirationalism, then, subverts in practice the enterprise of Socratic metaethics on which it relies, by appealing to interpersonally inaccessible moral states to justify its moral judgments.

Ross's Intuitionism was couched in a metaethics that attempted to avoid this outcome, and contemporary Antirationalism may adopt a similar strategy. Ross argued that the principles we morally intuit as the outcome of careful and considered reflection on the circumstances in question were objectively valid, in the same way that mathematical intuitionists argue that the objects of mathematical intuition, such as the basic truths of arithmetic, are objectively valid. But this makes intuition, as well as its objects, even more cryptic and cognitively inaccessible than before. What if we have different moral intuitions about the same case? What if yours puts social welfare ahead of friendship? How do we determine which one of us is morally defective, and in what respect? The difficulty Intuitionists face in claiming an objectively valid status for the moral judgments they make is that intersubjective agreement can provide the only evidence for the mysterious mental capacities required to make them; and this, of course, makes the enterprise of Socratic metaethics itself unnecessary. Where rational dialogue becomes necessary to addressing the unconverted that lie outside one's circle of sympathizers, Intuitionism has nothing to say.

Contemporary Antirationalists might adopt a similar strategy, by claiming a certain veracity for moral emotions, based on their authenticity as a forthright expression of a person's most centrally defining values and projects. This would resolve Antirationalism into a species of Subjectivism: if a certain judgment authentically expresses my centrally defining values and projects, it is true, at least for me. I do not think this is an interesting use of the term "true," and will not pause to rehearse any more of the elementary objections to Subjectivism. Suffice it to raise the obvious problem, analogous to that faced by the Intuitionist, of how to dispose of the authentic feelings and judgments of the unconverted; or of a stormtrooper or lynch mob. Otherwise the basic objection stands: Antirationalism appeals for its persuasive power on interpersonally inaccessible moral states, and thereby sabotages the enterprise of Socratic metaethics on which it relies.

By contrast, *Rationalism* takes the enterprise of Socratic metaethics seriously as a methodological presupposition of *all* metaethics. The method of Rationalism is to try to justify a moral theory or principle by appeal to reason and argument as the currency of interpersonal communication. A Rationalist seeks to lead her reader or listener from weak and mutually acceptable premises to a substantive conclusion as to the most convincing substantive moral theory or principle, by way of argument, analysis, critique, and example interpersonally accessible to both. A Rationalist may appeal to imagination, personal experience, or certain feelings or perceptions or intuitions as reasons for or against a particular view; but she views reason – not the feelings or perceptions or intuitions or other responses invoked *as* reasons – as the final arbiter of rational dialogue.

In this undertaking, Rationalism is neither broadly democratic nor narrowly fascistic. A Rationalist does not try to gain adherents for her view by oversimplifying the theory or the arguments, or by obfuscating them with neologisms or inflated prose or grim silence in order to intimidate others into accepting it. In appealing to reason, Rationalism addresses itself only to those who are willing to exercise theirs. It does, however, assume that all competent adults can do so, *regardless of culture or environment*. In this, it is more democratic than Antirationalism, which demands intersubjective concurrence in substantive moral judgment as the only convincing evidence of the truth of those judgments, when in fact there is no necessary connection between intersubjective concurrence and truth at all. For these among other reasons, Rationalism defines the critical perspective adopted in this project. The argument proceeds by appeal to reasons and critical analysis, and most of the philosophers discussed here proceed similarly in defending their views – regardless of the substantive content of those views.

Rationality and the Structure of the Self

The main focus of discussion in both volumes of this project is with
two competing branches of Rationalism that differ with respect to the
role each assigns to rationality in the structure of the self. Both
branches agree upon the Socratic metaethical enterprise as a philosophical methodology. Both agree, as well, on the necessity of providing a metaethical conception of the subject as agent, as a foundation
for making normative claims about what subjects as agents should
do. And both agree upon the necessity of explaining what they think
moves subjects as agents to act, and in what they think acting
rationally consists. But each branch deploys different models of human
motivation and rationality as the shared, weak metaethical premises
on the basis of which to argue for these normative moral claims. The
first branch is what I will call the *Humean conception of the self*, the
second the *Kantian*. Thus both Humean and Kantian conceptions *in
fact* count as varieties of Rationalism according to this taxonomy,
regardless of the Antirationalist content some Humean views may
have.

By a "conception of the self," I mean an explanatory theoretical
model of the self that describes its dynamics and structure. A conception of the self is to be distinguished from a *self-conception*, which is
the same as a "personal self-image." The latter expresses the way or
ways in which an individual thinks of himself, for example, as nice,
well-intentioned, grumpy, loyal, fastidious, etc. It typically plays a
normative role in individual psychology: we try to live up to the ideal
individual we conceive ourselves to be, and regard negative attributes
as flaws or deviations from that ideal. Thus a self-conception is part of
one's normative moral theory. By contrast, a conception of the self
plays a descriptive, metaethical role in moral theory: it identifies and
describes the kind of individual to whom the theory purports to apply.
For example, a moral theory that urges general conformity to the
Golden Rule on the grounds that it best enables each individual to
promote her self-interest implicitly identifies those individuals to whom
the theory is addressed as desiring to promote their self-interest.
Similarly, a moral theory that recommends actions governed by the
dictates of reason presupposes reason as a significant motivational
factor in the relevant agents.

Traditionally, moral philosophers who write systematically and discursively always begin by describing their conception of human subjects as agents before they tell you what they think those agents ought to do. That is, they preface their normative claims with a metaethical conception of the self to which those claims are intended to apply. If they did not, we would have no way of gauging whether or not we ourselves were intended subjects of the theory. A conception of the self, then, provides a metaethical account of the psychological facts about human agents considered as subjects of normative moral principles.

My question in this project will not be that about which normative moral theory is uniquely correct. It will be the more foundational question of which metaethical conception of the self underlying normative moral theories provides the most accurate account of the psychological facts. If a moral theory's underlying conception of the self is falacious or largely inaccurate regarding the psychology of human nature, the question of the theory's validity for human beings can scarcely arise.

A conception of the self as I define it comprises two parts: first, it includes a *motivational model*. This explains what causes the self to act, and how. It identifies those events and states within the subject that constitute its capacity for agency; and it explains how, under certain specified conditions, those capacities are realized in agency. So, the motivational model in a conception of the self is an explanatory and causal model. Second, a conception of the self includes a *structural model*. This describes and charts the conditions of rational coherence and equilibrium within the self. It depicts that state of the self in which it functions as a unified psychological entity, and maintains psychological balance and integrity among its cognitive and conative components. Taken together, the structural and the motivational models explain what a unified subject is and how it is transformed into responsible agency.

The Humean and the Kantian conceptions of the self are each grounded to some extent, although not entirely, in the writings of Hume and Kant respectively. The first is the prevailing conception: Humean premises concerning motivation and rationality are widely accepted in such disparate fields as psychology, economics, decision theory, political theory, sociology, and, of course, philosophy. I believe that this conception is misguided in several respects, and in Volume I of this project I try to say why. The second branch of Rationalism in moral philosophy is less popular: Kantian premises regarding motivation and rationality are accepted in some areas of moral philosophy and social theory, but are not widely shared outside them. I believe that the full power of this conception of the self has not been sufficiently explored or exploited, and in Volume II I will try to begin to remedy this.

Relative to the enterprise of Socratic metaethics, my fundamental objection to the Humean conception of the self, and consequent allegiance to the Kantian, can be summarized quite simply: by insisting on desire as the sole cause of human action, the Humean conception of the self diminishes our conception of ourselves as rational agents, by failing to recognize or respect the ability of rational analysis and dialogue, as described above, to influence our behavior, even as it deploys and depends on them in philosophical discourse. This immediately raises the question, unanswerable within the traditional framework of metaethics itself, of what Humean moral philosophers take themselves to be accomplishing by discursively and rationally elaborating their views in print. If rationality is incapable of changing minds or motivating action, as Humeans frequently claim, what is the point of rationally defending their views in books and articles? Or is the point merely to get tenure and attract disciples motivated similarly by careerist considerations to adopt and promulgate one's views? Whereas Antirationalism subverts the enterprise of Socratic metaethics in practice while relying on it in theory, the Humean conception of the self subverts Socratic metaethics in theory while relying on it in practice.

We know from the historical examples mentioned earlier, as well as from personal experience, that the practice of normative moral philosophy often is not futile, its substantive views not motivationally impotent, and its practical consequences often far from inconsequential. The challenge is then to identify the metaethical conception of the self, rationality, and motivation that best explains its practical import. Are normative moral theories always adopted merely as a matter of convenience, in order to justify substantive policy decisions whose true *raison d'être* is the perpetuation of self-aggrandizing power relationships? Are they imported merely to legitimate pre-existing desires, sentiments, and political or social agendas, as the Humean conception implies? Or is it at least possible that they may themselves inspire and motivate the implementation of alternative agendas, disinterestedly and independently of the immediate self-interests and biases of their proponents? More concretely put: can reason itself inspire individuals other than Socrates to act and sacrifice in the service of rational social ideals?

Suppose it should transpire that the Humean conception of the self is, in fact, the most accurate explanatory model we can formulate. This would mean that, across nations as well as communities, subcultures, and individuals, human beings were *not* capable of marshalling the reserves of rationality to transcend the pursuit of self-interest, the gratification of desire, and the expression of instinct and emotion, in a shared vision of the good in the realization of which all can cooperate. Then all of our lives – not only those of the unempowered – would soon become even more nasty, brutish, and short than they have been in recent decades. It is here that Kant joins Hobbes in rejecting Nietzsche's *Übermensch*. A social order (however well serviced by *Untertanen* blinded by "slave morality") in which all fully empowered citizens were free to wield that power in the service of their instincts and desires would be no viable social order at all.

And *a fortiori*: should it transpire that philosophers were not capable of marshalling the character dispositions of rationality, so well exemplified by Socrates and described by Epictetus and Hampshire, to transcend the pursuit of professional self-aggrandizement in a shared vision of rational philosophical practice in which all could participate as equals, our professional practice would diverge more and more completely from the Socratic ideal of philosophical activity that led most of us to it, and poison our commitment to that activity accordingly. A philosophical practice in which all fully empowered participants were free to exploit that power in the service of personal desires would be no Socratic enterprise at all. This is the consequence to which the veracity of the Humean conception of the self would lead.

If, on the other hand, rational considerations can cause a change of mind or heart, then why should it not cause a change in behavior as well? A Kantian conception of the self acknowledges the motivational influence of rational argument on action from the outset. In speech and writing, Kantian moral philosophers exploit rationality unapologetically through appeals to conscience and reason, and reminders of who and what we are and where our responsibilities as rational agents lie.

The Humean conception is engendered by, but is not identical to, Hume's own conception of the self. Nor is it clear that it is embraced in its entirety by any one of its adherents. Rather, different facets of it are pressed into service to do different philosophical jobs: to explain behavior, for example; or predict preferences; or to analyze moral motivation, or freedom of the will. Thus the picture I shall sketch is a composite one, drawn from many different sources. This conception has been refined and elaborated to a high degree of detail in decision theory and the philosophy of mind, and its theoretical simplicity and apparent explanatory potency is attractive. But it has resulted in simplistic approaches to the understanding of human behavior in the social sciences, and it has generated enormous problems for moral philosophy.

This, shortly put, is the first, critical part of the view I shall try to defend, in three lines of argument: critical, historical/exegetical, and substantive. In Volume I, I offer *critical* arguments that enumerate some of the major internal and functional defects of the prevailing Humean conception of the self, with an eye to later highlighting the superior comprehensiveness, explanatory force, and suitability for moral theory of its suggested rival. Thus Volume I essentially is devoted to complaining about other people. I also offer *historical/ exegetical* arguments to demonstrate the limitations of Hume's own conception of rationality, and its imperviousness to face-saving charitable exegeses, in Chapters XI and XII.

The second, *substantive* part of this project that comprises Volume II argues that after having devoted two and a half centuries of attention to the Humean paradigm, it is now time to move on to a sustained consideration of the historically more recent, alternative conception of the self Kant proposed in response to these problems (which he, unlike us, saw right away). I suggest that we continue more deliberately the glacial process of collaborative refinement and elaboration of this alternative conception already begun, not only in Kantian moral philosophy, but in certain branches of cognitive psychology and social theory as well. My efforts in this project differ from those of most contemporary Kantian moral philosophers, in that I assume that Kant's moral writings by themselves are insufficient for developing a foundational conception of the self for moral philosophy. I believe that such a conception must be grounded in the conception of the self Kant actually develops in the *Critique of Pure Reason*. I adumbrate that conception, and make the case for the untapped richness of Kant's own conception of rationality and its potential as a resource for contemporary metaethics, in the first chapter of Volume II. Elsewhere[15] I offer a more extended treatment that explains in greater detail What Kant Really Meant.

The historical/exegetical arguments of Chapters XI and XII in Volume I and Chapter I in Volume II situate both the Humean conception and its rival in their proper historical contexts. The critical arguments and the historical/exegetical arguments are intended to motivate us to rethink our commitment to the prevailing paradigm, first by pointing out defects in its present formulation, and second, by scrutinizing the extent to which we may validly appeal to the authority of history and tradition in support of that formulation, and in support of the proposed alternative.

I then put Kant's conception to work in a contemporary form in the remaining chapters of Volume II, in a concerted campaign for the "slave morality" candidate. I build on the conclusions of Chapter I to offer substantive metaethical arguments that articulate and develop the motivational and structural models of the self that I claim undergird not only the range of moral theories most appropriate to the psychological facts about human beings, but also, therefore, our factual assumptions about the explanation of human behavior. Here the main theses are that the formal requirements of rational coherence structure the self, are a necessary condition of unified agency, and impose formal constraints on the range of ends human agents can rationally adopt.

Thus I claim that theoretical reason is motivationally effective in action, hence that the Humean model of motivation – the belief-desire model – is incomplete. I claim also that theoretical reason does imply substantive constraints on final ends that differentiate rational from irrational ones, hence that the Humean model of rationality – the expected utility-maximizing model – is incomplete. I argue that reason can therefore justify a certain *range* of normative moral theories as rational final ends, and can motivate us to adopt them. However, reason cannot show any one of these theories to be uniquely rational, nor that it is to be implied by the requirements of reason itself, as so many philosophers have thought. Rather, the appeal to reason, on which we as philosophers implicitly rely, presupposes a view of ourselves as socialized moral agents who are theoretically rational and therefore morally responsible.

This conception of the self opposes not only the Humean dictum that rationality is impotent to determine the ends we seek. It also opposes the Antirationalist stance that treats rationality in action as an impediment to personal authenticity. It implies that the Kantian conception of the self explains our actual moral behavior, including our reflective philosophical behavior, better than the prevailing Humean alternative, and that therefore it provides a more realistic and appropriate justificatory foundation for moral theory. These substantive arguments are intended to present an alternative way of conceptualizing our own behavior and conscious life as better suited not only to our aims in moral philosophy, but to explanation of the psychological facts as well.

I do not expect that any of these lines of argument will necessarily compel all, or perhaps even most, Humeans and Antirationalists to see the error of their ways or reform them accordingly. For in the end these arguments presuppose the *value* of rationality as the defining element in the structure of the self. They presuppose that one is prepared, not only to recognize rationality as definitive, but to valorize its character dispositions, as a "slave morality" does. As in any philosophical disagreement, philosophical opponents may ascribe to the same consideration cited as a reason a very different weight, and what is conclusive to one may be irrelevant to another, namely:

The Kantian	*The Antirationalist*	*The Humean*
But X is *irrational*!	But X is *irrational!*	But X is *irrational!*
But Y is *counterintuitive!*	**But Y is *counterintuitive!***	But Y is *counterintuitive!*
But Z is *unsatisfying!*	But Z is *unsatisfying!*	**But Z is *unsatisfying!***

So even if I succeed in making a plausible case that reason has that centrality, I have still relied on and presupposed the value of the very capacity I mean in my argument to valorize. A real Antirationalist who disparages the value of rationality will therefore accord little value to my rational arguments that rationality has value. If my reader is a real Humean for whom rationality has value but no motivational efficacy, my arguments will then provide no motivation to rethink his values, no matter how persuasive they are. Perhaps only Hobbes's astute – and rationally persuasive – observations on the necessary transience and instability of accumulated power might lead him to reconsider the value of the Socratic ideal.

Notes

This essay serves as the introduction in each volume of a two-volume work (nearing completion) entitled *Rationality and the Structure of the Self, Volume I: The Humean Conception* and *Volume II: A Kantian Conception.* A planned third volume, *Kant's Metaethics,* will appear separately. I am grateful to Professor Naomi Zack for her interest in the project's overview and motivation laid out in the following discussion.

1   Epictetus, *Enchiridion* LI. I have consulted two translations: P. E. Matheson (Oxford: Clarendon Press), reprinted in Jason L. Saunders (ed.) *Greek and Roman Philosophy after Aristotle* (New York: Free Press, 1966), p. 147, and George Long (Chicago: Henry Regnery, 1956), pp. 202–3.

2   Thomas Hobbes, *Leviathan,* ed. Michael Oakeshott (New York: Collier, 1977), pp. 75, 74.

3   Hobbes, *Leviathan,* ch. xlviii, note 1; see also ch. I.

4   The following discussion of Anglo-American philosophical practice has benefited from comments by Anita Allen, Houston Baker, Paul Boghossian, Ann Congleton, Ruth Anna Putnam and Kenneth Winkler, as well as by members of the audience at the 1994 Greater Philadelphia Philosophy Consortium symposium, "Philosophy as Performance" at which these remarks were originally presented.

5   Stuart Hampshire, "Liberator, Up to a Point," *New York Review of Books* XXXIV/5 (March 26, 1987), pp. 37–9.

6   John Maynard Keynes, "My Early Beliefs," in *Two Memoirs* (New York: Augustus M. Kelley, 1949), pp. 85, 88, quoted in Elizabeth Anderson, *Value in Ethics and Economics* (Cambridge, Mass.: Harvard University Press, 1993), p. 121.

7   *Kant's Metaethics,* in progress.

8   So much for Hampshire's injunctions against metaphor.

9   Indeed, there are few other fields in which the intellectual activity that centrally defines the discipline is so thoroughly inimical to professional hierarchy. Even in the natural sciences, such a hierarchy is justified to some extent by the training, experience, and accumulation of information and methodological resources required in order to ascend to its pinnacle. Only in philosophy (and perhaps mathematics) is it possible for some unschooled pipsqueak upstart to initiate a revolution in the field with an offhand, "Here's a thought!" issued from the safe haven of the armchair. Kripke's early work in modal logic would be an example; Parfit's on personal identity would be another.

10   I use this expression advisedly, since those who survive the confrontation are overwhelmingly male. The field numbers approximately 15,000 members. At last count, women occupied 8 percent, and African-

American women 0.001 percent, of all tenured positions. The punishments inflicted for their philosophical insubordination are correspondingly more virulent.

11   Epictetus, *Enchiridion* LI, footnote 1.

12   This is Thomas Nagel's term to characterize variants on the same group of views as I discuss here. See his *The Possibility of Altruism* (Oxford: Oxford University Press, 1975), p. 8. Chapter III of Volume I is devoted to a study of this work.

13   Sir David Ross, *The Right and the Good* (Oxford: Clarendon Press, 1938).

14   Annette Baier, *Moral Prejudices* (Cambridge: Harvard University Press, 1994); Lawrence Blum, *Friendship, Altruism and Morality* (Boston: Routledge and Kegan Paul, 1980); Susan Wolf, "Moral Saints," *Journal of Philosophy* 79/8 (1982); First Earl of Shaftesbury, "Selections" in *The British Moralists: 1650–1800* (Oxford: Clarendon Press, 1969) ; Francis Hutcheson, *Illustrations of the Moral Sense* (Cambridge, MA.: Harvard University Press); Hume, *A Treatise of Human Nature*, ed. L. A. Selby-Bigge (Oxford: Clarendon Press, 1978), Book III.

15   In Volume II, footnote 7.

See the figure in the Appendix to this chapter for the author's schematic location of her project of Socratic metaethics. [Ed.]

Appendix

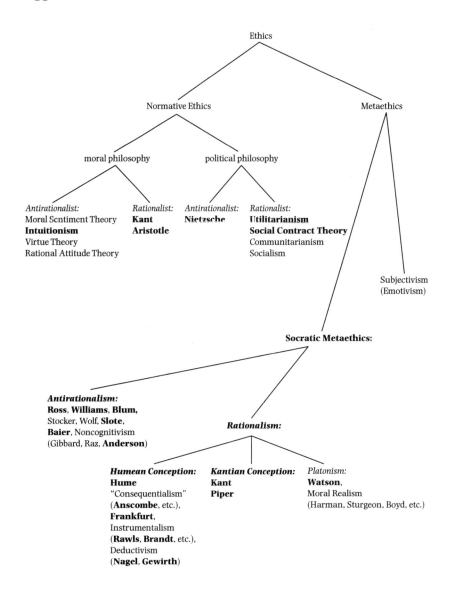

A Taxonomy of Ethics

Views discussed in this project are in boldface.

PART 2

Activism and Application

CHAPTER 5

Interview with Angela Y. Davis

GEORGE YANCY

George Yancy: When and where were you born?

Angela Y. Davis: I was born January 26, 1944 in Birmingham, Alabama.

Yancy: How did the pervasiveness of segregation in Birmingham, Alabama impact your early childhood consciousness?

Davis: Fortunately, I learned how to challenge the ubiquitous segregation in Birmingham at a very young age. I am very thankful to my parents for having reared me for as long as I can remember to think in a critical way about the conditions of our lives. My mother and father always pointed out that while we might have been living in circumstances within which Black people (or Negroes, as we were called then), were deemed inferior, that was not, in fact, the way it was supposed to be. So, in a sense, I grew up with an awareness of the need to contest, rather than simply accept, the given. I have often been asked to describe my path to political activism. I usually point out that there was no one pivotal event in my life. My activism is how I learned to live in the world.

Yancy: While at Carrie A. Tuggle Elementary School, I understand that you were introduced to the works of Frederick Douglass, Sojourner Truth, and Harriet Tubman. How did these figures impact your consciousness early on?

Davis: Living in a segregated environment, attending segregated schools, I imagine our teachers sought ways to transform conditions that were destined to have a negative impact on the students into experiences and lessons that were affirmative. I am thankful that I had the opportunity to participate at a very early age in what we eventually came to call Black History Month. From the time I was in the first grade we celebrated what we then called Negro History Week. We were always required to do projects, which meant doing some kind of minimal research on prominent Black figures, contemporary and historical. Whenever we sang the "Star Spangled Banner," we also sang the "Negro National Anthem." So I learned "Lift Every Voice and Sing" when I was 3 or 4 years old. I think this attempt to build community within the context of segregation was what motivated many people to fight back. It certainly played a role in *my* early motivation to protest racism. As children, we knew that people like Frederick Douglass and Sojourner Truth and Harriet Tubman fought for Black people as a whole, which helped to give us a sense of community. Within this stringently segregated environment, we acquired a sense of "our people," and of freedom as our people's destiny.

Yancy: Talk about the shaping of your early critical consciousness.

Davis: When I was very young I had the opportunity to visit New York during the summers, to move in and out of the South. My mother was doing graduate work at New York University for her MA degree, and she would take all of us – her four children – to New York every summer. In New York we had the opportunity to get to know and make friends with people of all different ethnic and racial backgrounds. Traveling back and forth also gave me a consciousness of possibilities that went beyond what was deemed possible in Birmingham, Alabama. So I decided to seek ways of moving beyond those restrictive conditions – and by the time I was in high school I investigated concrete possibilities of continuing my schooling outside the South. Also – and this was important in shaping my consciousness – my mother was very close friends with a number of people who were involved in radical politics, Black people who were members of the Communist Party. She had worked with these individuals in organizations in the South prior to the McCarthy era. During these trips to New York, we spent time with Black people who by that time had really put their lives on the line. This was during the late forties and early fifties, during the McCarthy era. My parents' friends were in great danger on a daily basis, and I remember being aware of this, and knowing that it was a result of their work for racial and economic justice. These experiences helped to arm me with a vision of what it meant to be in active opposition to an unjust society.

Yancy: So, it was the early political praxis of your mother and father that really helped to shape your consciousness early on?

Davis: Yes, absolutely.

Yancy: Given that your mother and father were both teachers, I assume that you were exposed to books at a young age.

Davis: My father was a teacher for quite some time until the challenges of supporting a family led him to look for more lucrative employment. We all grew up, my sister, brothers, and I, in a learning environment. In a sense, books were the most important toys we received. There was one book that I remember I found particularly fascinating. It was a dictionary – a huge book for a child – that my parents bought for me. I remember reading every single page of that dictionary when I was about 4 years old. My mother encouraged all of us to read. She began teaching me to read when I was 3 or so. By the time I was 4 I had a regular reading schedule. When I went to school at 5, I was much more advanced than any of the other children in my class. My mother was actually quite astounding in that respect. Under her tutelage, my sister's daughter began to read when she was 2. I think that this is probably a testament to my mother's perseverance and ability [more] than anything else.

Yancy: Would you say that you evidenced a philosophical disposition early on?

Davis: In the sense that we all have potential to engage philosophically with the world, I would say yes. I explain this philosophical disposition as a consequence of my parents' encouragement to think critically about our social environment, in other words, not to assume that the appearances in our lives constituted ultimate realities. Our parents encouraged us to look beyond appearances and to think about possibilities, to think about ways in which we could, with our own agency, intervene and transform the world. In this sense my own philosophical disposition initially expressed itself not so much as a specific mode of thought, but rather as a quotidian way of living in the world.

Yancy: Why did you want to be a physician and what led you to give up this ambition?

Davis: I wanted to do something that was unique at that time, something that was extraordinary, something that was not generally offered to Black people – especially Black women – as a possibility during the forties and fifties. I became very fascinated at an early age with the children's hospital adjacent to the nursery school I attended. I wanted to help others, I felt moved by a deep desire to heal. I don't think that I've abandoned that vocation. Rather, I've found other ways of carrying it out.

Yancy: Hence, this theme of healing is still in place.

Davis: Yes. Anti-racist activism, for example, is very much about social healing. Education and the production of knowledge can also be motivated by a desire to heal. I should also mention, in this context, that I have been working with the National Black Women's Health Project for over ten years. This is the way I have come to think about and work toward healing today.

Yancy: And how we come to think about things differently is often mediated by distance.

Davis: Absolutely.

Yancy: While attending Elisabeth Irwin High School, though at this time you did not understand scientific socialism, you became acquainted with the idea that there could be an ideal socioeconomic society. What factors shaped your consciousness such that you were even receptive to this notion?

Davis: My receptivity to Marxism is very much related to the way I was reared. If I learned as a very young child that racism was fundamentally wrong and that it was possible to recreate a world in which racial justice prevailed, I also was encouraged to think critically about what we now call whiteness. As difficult as it may have been to separate racism from an essentialist notion of whiteness, I do remember struggling hard as a child to understand how white people might extricate themselves from the racism that infected their attitudes. As a child, what I learned from my peers was that white people were evil, that the reason we were treated the way we were was because white people were inherently bad. But my mother constantly urged me to think about white people and racism in very different terms. I think she drew upon a universalistic vision. I actually remember that I would say, "Mother, there's a white man at the door," or "There's a white woman on the telephone who wants to speak with you." And my mother would always say, "There's a *man* at the door" or "There's a *woman* who wants to speak with you."

I would problematize that now, but it was very helpful, at that age, in making me think more deeply about what it meant to engage in oppositional practice against racism. When I eventually lived in New York with a white family of prominent progressives – William Howard and Mary Jane Melish – and was attending a school that was overwhelmingly white, I struggled with this more universal vision of humanity and with ways of thinking about the project of making things better in the South. I discovered the notion of a working class – a multiracial working class – serving as an historical agent of changing the world. At the same time, as I have already mentioned, many of my mother's friends were members of the Communist Party. Consequently many of my own friends in New York – the children of my mother's friends – were politically active at 14 or 15: Bettina Aptheker, for example, who is the daughter of Herbert and Fay Aptheker; Mary Lou Patterson, the daughter of William L. and Louise T. Patterson; Margaret Burnham, who is the daughter of Louis M. and Dorothy Burnham. Herbert Aptheker is the prominent historian who wrote pioneering texts in Black Studies; William Patterson defended the Scottsboro Nine and, with Paul Robeson, presented the Petition Against Genocide to the United Nations; Louis Burnham was the editor of the *Guardian*, the newspaper which was at that time connected to the Party. So my social life, as it took shape in relation to the friends I already had, was very much a political life. I eventually became involved in what was the youth organization of the Communist Party. At the same time, I was attending a progressive high school where we were able to study Marx and read the *Communist Manifesto* in the eleventh grade. I make these points because I don't think my own political vision came from within as much as it was shaped by external forces, by the particular historical conjunctures where I fortunately found myself.

Yancy: What was it about the *Communist Manifesto* that "hit you like a bolt of lightning," as you state in your autobiography?

Davis: Well, you know, "Workers of the world, unite! You have nothing to lose but your chains." It gave me a way to think about the world, about my experiences growing up in the South, that made a great deal of sense. It provided me with a way to conceptualize and yet to transcend much of the pain I had experienced. It is very hard to think about one's past except through the lens of one's present insights, so I guess today I would say that it gave me some basic conceptual tools with which to think about what we now call intersectionality, or the relationship between race and class. Gender was something that we had not yet learned to think about back then. But from a very early age I was struggling with a way of thinking about white people that did not universally demonize whiteness. My exposure to the *Communist Manifesto* gave me some fundamental conceptual tools with which to think about social change in a way that moved beyond an exclusive focus on race.

Yancy: Had you remained in the South, what would have been the trajectory of your sociopolitical consciousness?

Davis: I think that I probably would have become involved in the Civil Rights Movement as it unfolded in the South from 1960 onward. I went to New York in September of 1959, and I remember very vividly the moment of the first sit-ins in February of 1960. I had been in New York just a few months, and I desperately wanted to go back home. I had the feeling that somehow I had made a wrong decision to leave Birmingham – wrong in a world historical sense. I felt that I had given up my chance to be a part of these earth-shaking, historical events. I can remember telephoning my parents, talking to my mother and crying because I wanted so much to return. From the moment of the first sit-ins, I would often think about the way my life might have unfolded had I not gone to New York. I don't know whether things would have been substantively different. Indeed, I might have been shaped by a different set of circumstances, but I like to think that I would have pursued a similar political vocation even though some things in my life probably would have been very different.

Yancy: While in high school had you encountered any books by African-American authors?

Davis: Yes. I think that the most influential work I encountered was James Baldwin's *Fire Next Time*. It helped me to think more deeply about the way that the Civil Rights Movement exploded. I went on to read as many of his works as I could find. Later, when I went to college, I had the opportunity to hear Baldwin speak. He has always been a model for me in the way he related his work as an artist and as a writer to the social movements emerging around him.

Yancy: You heard him speak while you were at Brandeis University, right?

Davis: Yes. I heard him speak in the middle of the Vietnam War. As a matter of fact, I heard him and Herbert Marcuse speak during the same critical period of the US troop buildup in Vietnam. These were two individuals who clearly used their knowledge to illuminate and contest political injustices – and to encourage people to engage in collective struggles for change. I think of both Baldwin and Marcuse as mentors who helped me to conceptualize a relationship between theory and practice, a challenge that I continue to struggle with today.

Yancy: Before coming to Herbert Marcuse to ask him to help you to draw up a bibliography on basic works in philosophy, what got you initially interested in philosophy?

Davis: I became interested in French literature in college. As a matter of fact, my initial interest developed in high school when I was compelled to do a very intensive program in French in order to catch up with my classmates who had already taken two years of French by their junior year in high school. In my junior year, I took an intensive tutorial which required me to basically learn three years of French in one year, so that I could take the regular courses with my classmates during my senior year. That was a very serious challenge, particularly since I had never given a great deal of thought to learning a foreign language – this was not encouraged in the high school I attended in Birmingham, Alabama. But by the time I finished that tutorial I had become deeply interested in French literature and, as a matter of fact, I decided to major in French literature when I entered Brandeis University.

During my third year, I participated in a junior-year-abroad program that allowed me to study at the Sorbonne. The focus of my studies was contemporary French literature, which meant that I took a course on the novel, one on the theater, a course on contemporary French poetry, and a course on contemporary French ideas. It was in that course on contemporary French ideas that I was introduced to the philosophical works of Sartre and the works of phenomenologists like Merleau-Ponty. By the time I completed that year in France I realized that I was most interested in the realm of ideas. This is what led me to philosophy. When I returned to Brandeis the following year to complete my studies there, I also began an intensive study of western philosophy with Herbert Marcuse.

Yancy: I imagine that your philosophical predisposition was reinforced as a result of reading philosophically oriented French literature.

Davis: Absolutely.

Yancy: While studying philosophy at Johann Wolfgang von Goethe University in Frankfurt, Germany, under Theodor Adorno and Jürgen Habermas, in what philosophical manner did each of these thinkers shape your own philosophical reflections?

Davis: Because I had, during the previous year, done work with Marcuse, I had an established interest in the German idealist tradition, in particular. That's why I decided to go to Germany to study. What I hoped to learn from Adorno was the way in which one can draw productively on the tradition of German idealism in order to develop the basis for a critical theory of society. I was most interested in ways in which philosophy could serve as a basis for developing a critique of society and how that critique of society could figure into the development of practical strategies for the radical transformation of society. Of course, Adorno at that point had assumed a somewhat more conservative posture, particularly with respect to the relationship between theory and practice.

I have to point out that this was a period of intense student activism in Germany as well as in other parts of Europe – in France, for example. And it was a period during which the student movement was taking shape in the United States, the anti-war movement was developing, and of course the Black Liberation Movement was moving into a different phase. And all of these dynamics were very much connected with my own philosophical interests. I never saw philosophy as separate from a social critique or from social activism. Oscar Negt, as a young professor at the time, was involved in the work of the German Socialist Student Organization, SDS (*Sozialistischer Deutscher Studentenbund*), the organization with which I was working. From Negt's example, I was able to understand how one could do academic work and at the same time connect one's scholarly research to the struggle for radical social transformation.

I also attended lectures by Habermas, who by that time had become quite critical of the student movement. Although previously he had written on the emergence of the German student movement, during this period – which one might characterize as the most militant phase of that movement – he began to express extremely conservative criticisms of the SDS. So what I found most interesting about my stay in Germany was the way in which it was possible to develop very interesting ways of mediating organizing work and scholarly work.

Herbert Marcuse visited Europe on several occasions, and the most important reason I eventually decided to return to the United States and work closely with him was because he maintained a sense of the connectedness between emerging social movements and his larger philosophical project. At that time, Adorno wasn't very interested in such a project. Adorno took the position that if in fact the revolution had not occurred, it was an indication of a flaw that was deeply rooted in the theoretical process and that the critical question was not so much how to continue the organizing or activist work, but how to examine the theoretical weaknesses. He therefore called for a retreat into theory. Since this was an era of international uprisings and new social movements, I found myself fundamentally at odds with Adorno and all the more drawn to Marcuse.

Yancy: How does Critical Theory offer a philosophical framework helpful to Black struggle here in America?

Davis: Critical Theory envisions philosophy not so much as an abstract or general engagement with questions of human existence; rather, it envisions a productive relationship between philosophy and other disciplines – for example, sociology, cultural studies, feminist theory, African-American studies – and the use of this knowledge in projects to radically transform society. Critical Theory, as formulated and founded by the Frankfurt School – which included Horkheimer and Marcuse – has as its goal the transformation of society, not simply the transformation of ideas, but social transformation and thus the reduction and elimination of human misery. It was on the basis of this insistence on the social implementation of critical ideas that I was able to envision a relationship between philosophy and Black liberation.

Yancy: Within the context of the academy, what is the role of the African-American female philosopher?

Davis: That is a very broad question, particularly since philosophy has a vast range of definitions in the United States. I can talk about the philosophical project of attempting to bring together feminist theory and Black Studies, and employing philosophical

ideas in ways that place African-American women as much at
the center of liberatory discourse and praxis as African–American
men, etc. I am not suggesting that every Black woman philosopher would see this as her project. But I do think that it is
important to insist on gender analyses within Black philosophical
projects, as well as in organizing efforts in Black communities.

Yancy: How can African-American philosophers come to see their
departments as sites for struggle?

Davis: I think that is an important question in the US, particularly
in philosophy departments where race is not always considered
an appropriate subject for philosophical inquiry, especially given
the popular philosophical emphasis on color blindness in contemporary US society. I think that African-American philosophers as
well as other philosophers of color – and white philosophers who
consider themselves socially progressive – need to insist upon
integrating into the curriculum courses that foreground race and
courses that focus on African-American historical interests.
When I first began to teach philosophy at UCLA, there was not a
single course that had anything to do with African-American
ideas. So I designed a course entitled "Recurring Philosophical
Themes in Black Literature," in which, for example, I asked
students to read Frederick Douglass's depiction of the master–
slave relationship and to compare it with the relevant passages
in Hegel's *Phenomenology*. I also encouraged students to identify
philosophical themes in the work of Ann Petry and other Black
women writers. This was prior to the emergence of critical studies
of African-American literature. I found that it was extremely
important to legitimate the production of philosophical knowledge in sites that are not normally considered *the* philosophical
sites. And, of course, this was in 1969, nearly thirty years ago.
Today, there has been some progress, but it's clear – especially in
philosophy departments where faculty and students struggle to
legitimize philosophical knowledge that is produced in places that
aren't considered essentially philosophical – that there is an
ongoing struggle to legitimize alternative sites of knowledge
production.

Yancy: Do you privilege your Marxist identity over your racial
identity?

Davis: No. I've never been able to figure out how one goes about
making those decisions about which part of one's identity should

take precedence. Marxism has assisted me in developing clarity regarding the relationship between race, class, and gender. So I see these identities as very much interconnected and wouldn't want to develop a hierarchical approach to them.

Yancy: And I assume that you also non-hierarchically integrate your feminist identity as well?

Davis: Absolutely.

Yancy: In what direction should Black feminist theory move?

Davis: I would respond to that question by arguing that Black feminist theory is not a unitary theory, that there is no such thing as Black feminist theory. Patricia Hill Collins in her path-breaking work, *Black Feminist Thought*, does create this sort of encyclopedic approach to Black feminist thought, but I don't know if we can simply argue that every Black woman who has produced important knowledge can be considered a Black feminist. I really do appreciate her effort to identify non-scholarly or non-academic sites for the production of important Black feminist ideas. I would say that one of the challenges for Black feminist theories is to engage the category of class in a way that allows us to understand the production of Black feminist insight in the workplace and in organizing efforts – particularly in the latter nineties with the demise of so many social movements. I think that it's extremely important to rehabilitate the role of the organizer. And, therefore, I like works like Joy James's *Transcending the Talented Tenth*, in which she offers an innovative analysis of the Black intelligentsia. I really like the way she looks at women like Ella Baker and Charlene Mitchell as having produced important knowledge for Black communities. I think this is one of the directions in which Black feminist theories need to move.

Yancy: What are some of the difficulties preventing the formation of a united women's movement?

Davis: I don't think that we need a united women's movement because I think that there are political questions and issues that can't be reconciled by deploying a universal category of "womanhood" or "sisterhood." Historically, there has been a rather naive approach to women's unity, just as there has been a rather naive approach to Black unity. I don't think that it's possible to ground unity solely in race or gender. Unity needs to be produced politically, around issues and political projects. So I would suggest that we need to do a lot of work not only around coalition building – which is the approach that is most often taken – but around, for example, women of color formations that have emerged on the grass-roots level and on college campuses, that demonstrate how unity can be produced around political projects. I don't think that unity should be sought simply for the sake of unity.

Yancy: Did you find the American Communist Party just as sexist as you found the Black Panther Party?

Davis: When I joined the Communist Party, which coincided with my activism in the Black Panther Party, the women's movement was just beginning to take shape, and I guess I would say that both of these organizations were probably equally influenced by sexist and patriarchal ideas. I wouldn't say that one was more sexist than the other, although patriarchal influences may have been differently expressed. I was initially impressed by the fact that women did achieve leadership positions in the Black Panther Party, although that in itself was very complicated. After the publication of Elaine Brown's book, *A Taste of Power*, stories that I had not heard about the organization at the time came to light. Within the Communist Party USA, on the other hand, there was a continuous struggle to legitimize the leadership of women and to find ways to integrate a gender approach into the class analysis of the Party. At the same time, many women's leadership positions were gendered as female. For example, women tended to be organizational secretaries rather than district organizers. Within both the CPUSA and the BPP, extremely important contestations over gender took place. This is how I see that history through the conceptual prism of the present. In other words, we did not then possess the conceptual tools for gender analysis that we possess today, and we couldn't benefit from the history of social movements around gender as we can today. So, I would characterize both organizations as sites of extremely intense, passionate, and often productive contestations over gender.

Yancy: You have critiqued the Million Man March in terms of its masculinist and hierarchical structure. How do Black women challenge such a structure without themselves creating their own feminist and hierarchical structure? In short, how do we best merge both Black male and female discourse and action?

Davis: I should point out that the critique that I represented of the

Million Man March was one that was formulated by an *ad hoc* group of Black women and men. It was not meant to be a critique proposed solely by women. It was meant to be a feminist critique. The men who participated in our *ad hoc* committee – and who have gone on to become involved in a loosely knit network that we call African-American Agenda 2000 – argued as much for the inclusion of women as the women did. As a matter of fact, drawing from my own involvement with feminist struggles, I would say that the most interesting and productive battles have never been gender wars – not struggles between women and men – but rather struggles over the *role* of women and struggles over the acknowledgment of gender. Men and women have positioned themselves on both sides of those struggles.

In terms of the Million Man March, we were not simply concerned with the explicit exclusion of women. We were most concerned, I think, with the representation of the March as providing a strategy of salvation for the Black community, which positioned men in the privileged role. This led to the marginalization of issues like the impact of the criminal justice system on women, the impact of drugs on women, etc. The masculinist approach prevented us from engaging in a national conversation around the gendered character of our struggles in Black communities. And, at the same time, many of us were concerned that the politics of the March did not place the struggle for the emancipation of the Black community within a global context. In particular, the organizers of the March did not acknowledge the extent to which transnational capitalism plays a structural role in the impoverishment of Black communities. The March did not attempt to encourage, for example, an awareness of the relationship between capitalist globalization and the rising numbers of Black men and women consigned to live out their lives within the prison industrial complex.

Yancy: I have a question related to your essay "Black Women and Music: A Historical Legacy of Struggle." Do you see Sister Souljah and Queen Latifah as operating within the same discursive space as such singers as Ma Rainey, Bessie Smith, and Billie Holiday?

Davis: That's a complicated question because historical conditions have changed. During the 1920s – the classic blues era – the recording industry was at an embryonic stage. Therefore, the process through which decisions were made regarding which songs got to be recorded, how they were distributed, etc., was very different from the contemporary process of the production and distribution of popular music. What I find most interesting about the work of the early blues women is that at a time when there were few public discourses on gender, women's blues served as a site for explicit and provocative conversations about Black gender politics. I argue in my forthcoming book on this issue [*Blues Legacies and Black Feminism*] that Black women blues singers allow us to see the emergence of a politics of gender produced by Black working-class women at a time when research on Black feminist traditions generally relies on written texts produced by figures such as Mary Church Terrell and Ida B. Wells. I argue that through music an aesthetic community was forged, which allowed for the development of a Black working-class discourse on gender and sexuality.

Today, however, things are quite different, particularly because hip-hop artists are forced to contend with a very different process of production. Moreover, the commodification of their work happens through a process that is far more complicated than during the early stages of the recording industry when people basically could record what they wanted to record. The audience for that music was almost exclusively a Black audience. The records were sold in community places like barbershops and hair salons. Precisely because of the segregation of the music, far fewer market-driven restrictions intervened. But I do think that in hip-hop culture today, the political consciousness of young people, particularly young Black people, is shaped much more through the cultural politics of hip-hop than through social movements.

So, I think that it is important to look at the contributions of artists like Latifah and Souljah. But it is also important to recognize the way that some of these aesthetic struggles are staged. When one recognizes that Yo Yo, for example, who served as a feminist counterpart to Ice Cube – and who responded to the misogynist pronouncements in his work – was "discovered" by Ice Cube, and that their conversation was largely motivated by market considerations, one must question the implications of that exchange, even though on the surface it may have had some value. Cultural politics are far more complicated today. Nevertheless, rap music is an important site of political struggle, and it is essential to take it seriously rather than simply to advocate discarding it because of its misogyny or its oftentimes naive nationalism. Look at artists like Michael Franti, for example, who used to be with the Disposable Heroes of Hiphoprisy and now leads Spearhead. He is a wonderful artist who does a remarkable job contesting misogyny and homophobia, along with racism. So I do think that cultural politics, as Stuart Hall argues, must be taken seriously.

Yancy: Since the collapse of the USSR, have you thought about the work of Karl Marx or Marxism any differently?

Davis: Well, since the collapse of the Soviet Union and of the European socialist countries, I have become even more convinced of the importance of studying the work of Karl Marx and developing the kinds of anti-capitalist analyses that will hopefully push us beyond this historical period during which capitalism is assumed to be hegemonic. Because the socialist experiment in countries like the Soviet Union and the German Democratic Republic did not work, this does not mean that socialism is no longer a part of the historical agenda, and it certainly does not imply the historical triumph of capitalism. As a matter of fact, I would argue that in the aftermath of the collapse of the socialist countries, the expansive globalization of capital has led to a predicament in which the everyday lives of people are even more directly and intimately affected by capital than, say, twenty years ago. The project of developing explicitly anti-capitalist theories and practices is of greater importance now than ever before.

Yancy: Briefly, what are some of the psychological dimensions of being hunted by the state?

Davis: Well, first of all, it was a very difficult situation to find oneself in. And I can't say that I wasn't extremely afraid. Fear was something that I had to deal with daily during that period. I imagine that I was able to overcome that intense fear for my life by focusing on *why* the state was conducting this massive search for me. It didn't make sense that they were hunting me for the threat that I posed as an individual. I realized that there was a symbolic value to their focus on me, which turned the FBI hunt into a generic assault on potentially radical Black women. This insight came later, when I discovered how many thousands and thousands of Black women had been stopped or arrested by police.

The circulation of my photograph on the FBI "Wanted" poster

helped to create a generic image of the radical Black woman with the large "Afro," which made vast numbers of African-American women vulnerable to the state. I always tend to deal with my deeply individual and personal fears by attempting to understand the larger implications. The fact that so many people did organize around my case assisted me to move beyond that fear, which otherwise might have become all-consuming.

Yancy: As an African-American woman philosopher, who is Angela Y. Davis?

Davis: That is a question that I am constantly working on. I think I can say, however, that for many decades the theme of my work, of my life, has been the attempt to use whatever knowledge, skills, and wisdom I may have acquired to advance emancipatory theory and practice. As I've already said, my philosophical inclination was a gift that resulted from the conditions of my childhood. It emerged from the way in which I was compelled to learn how to be critical of the environment in which I grew up and, at the same time, to seek ways of transforming that critique into political practice. I don't think that part of me has changed over the last fifty years. But I also need to acknowledge that whatever I am and whatever I become is always related to developments outside of myself. I see myself and my work as connected with a collective effort to bring about radical social change.

As a teacher, for example, I work with as many students of color as possible, both undergraduates and graduates. We don't have a Black Studies Program at UC Santa Cruz, so I often end up serving as adviser for undergraduates who want to create an independent Black Studies major. Of course I also work with a number of organizations. In the National Black Women's Health Project, I have helped develop a political framework for the conceptualization of Black women's health as physical, psychological, emotional, and spiritual. I also work with organizations like the Prison Activist Resource Center, and I currently am involved in organizing a national conference on the prison industrial complex that will be held in the fall of 1998. For at least thirty years, I have worked collectively in defense of prisoners' rights and to challenge racism and political repression in the criminal justice system as well as in the larger society.

At the end of the day, I am not so much concerned about my own personal influence as I am concerned with carrying out a legacy and doing my best to guarantee that that legacy lives on with future generations. I see myself, along with many other people, as a part of a tradition of struggle, and this is what I try to convey to students, workers, and prisoners. Therefore I am most concerned with how my ideas and experiences can be productively used within collective contexts. I'm far less interested in claiming ownership of my ideas and experiences than I am in ensuring that this tradition remains a vital one, and that it is transformed in productive and progressive ways by each new generation.

CHAPTER 6

That Alchemical Bering Strait Theory!
or
Introducing America's Indigenous Sovereign Nations Worldviews to Informal Logic Courses

ANNE SCHULHERR WATERS

Introduction

American Indian Sovereign Nations students are bi-cultural; to be bi-cultural is to hold both native-centric and Eurocentric worldviews. American Indians in academic institutions must translate information from their sovereign nation's standpoint to a Euro-American stand-point, and vice versa. Critical Thinking courses can help facilitate this skill. Incorporating American Indian philosophy into critical thinking and logic courses empowers Native American learning, and non-native understanding. Using examples students can identify with in logic courses makes materials more accessible to them, and assists in the learning process. Incorporating culturally relevant material also serves to reinforce a sense of self-identity and self-esteem. In this paper I present examples from my personal teaching experience in logic classes, and my work with indigenous students. As an educator I am privileged to have opportunities to teach western philosophy, American Indian studies, and American Indian philosophy to American Indian Sovereign Nations students. When I incorporate American Indian philosophy into courses, this means I am incorporating it into logic, epistemology, metaphysics, ethics, social and political theory, jurisprudence, and the history of western philosophy.

It is my position that when I teach, my identity as a philosopher, lawyer, feminist, lesbian, woman of color, Jew, and American Indian, when appropriate, not be left out of the dialogue. Just as my being a Jew is relevant to a discussion of the European Jewish Holocaust, so also my being an American Indian Indigenist[1] is relevant to a discussion of the American Indian Holocaust. Placing identity information about myself into the classroom setting, and using a variety of culturally relevant content for my examples, opens a space for cultural safety. This safe space allows all students more comfort to name and share their own culturcentric perspectives. It gives rise to diverse voices.

Being able to share a cultural perspective empowers people. Thus the praxis of my teaching reinforces my belief that cultural inclusion is practically useful, and hence culturally appropriate for all students. This praxis is especially useful for some American Indian students, who, because of bicultural mores, otherwise might not as readily apprehend an Eurocentric explanation, or join in the discussion. That is, where all or most examples are from a Eurocentric perspective, Indigenous students feel left out, and falsely represented. This chilly climate forms the basis for exclusion, and a flight from academic education.

Before providing examples of incorporating American Indian philosophy into informal logic courses, I should briefly explain what I mean by "American Indian philosophy." In the Americas, a carefully thought-out meaning of "American Indian philosophy"[2] might include all ideas that spring from, are about, or affect pre-colonial and postcolonial thought and experience of nations indigenous to the Americas. It is a fluid and malleable concept, and ought to be defined and clarified by Americas' Indigenist philosophers. Philosophical thought by or about Americas' Indigenous Nations reaches across all disciplines, and views the world from American Indian-centered perspectives. It may include, but need not be exclusive to, oral or written "testimony" about indigenous experience and worldviews, from the past, of the present, or in the future.

We can thus distinguish Indigenous Nations philosophy of the Americas from, for example, African-American, European-American, and Asian American philosophies, as well as philosophies indigenous to continents other than the Americas. Indigenous philosophies, and we, as philosophers of continents around the globe, "stand on our own feet, in our own right," as do philosophies and philosophers of non-indigenous cultures.

We can talk about philosophies of Indigenous Nations in the Americas with or without making it a subset of "American philosophy." Thus "American philosophy," although having many roots in Americas' Indigenist thought, can be separated out from an American Indian Indigenous philosophy by the former's tradition of hosting Eurocentric, rather than indigenous values and experience.

With respect to who is American Indian, Native American, Indigenous, Indian, or member of a Sovereign Nation, this is a matter of philosophical interest, because racist political agendas have focused on external identification processes, rather than more easily sustained notions of kinship and geography. Indian identities also spring from tribal sovereignty, community resources, and self-identification.[3] And, although non-indigenous individuals may speak "with" sisters and brothers about identity, they may not speak "for" us.[4]

In 1996, Highlands University in Las Vegas, New Mexico, hosted a conference on Native American philosophy.[5] Viola Cordova[6] was not able to attend, but she did send in a paper that was printed in the program. In this paper she explicates a Native American philosophical framework that seeks to define Native American philosophy.

Whatever Native American philosophy may be defined as, Viola claims, it must be *for* Native Americans. Her other two definitional parameters are that it must be *by* and *about* Native Americans. For Viola then, a Native American philosophy must benefit Native Americans if it is to be *meaningful* to Native Americans. I believe that my work incorporating Native American ideas, and ideas about Native Americans (and other groups as well) into my courses, benefits Native Americans (and others as well). In this context, "meaningful" means that the experience speaks to us, does not marginalize us, and has healing potential for us.

Teaching American Indian-centered Informal Logic

Students normally begin a logic course by first identifying the parts of an argument, that is, the premise(s) and conclusion. Then they study the difference between deductive and inductive reasoning patterns in arguments. In most courses (as in my own), before tackling formal logic, we examine and learn about an array of some twenty to thirty informal fallacies (out of the possible one hundred plus informal fallacies). I present fallacies in the following order: begging the question; false cause; false analogy; hasty generalization; authority; suppressed evidence; composition and division; false dichotomy; signs; ignorance; and slippery slope.

Prior to discussing specific informal fallacies, I discuss the Bering Strait land bridge migration theory. I do this because throughout the course we can use this theory as a reference point for locating fallacious reasoning. This also gives me another opportunity to discuss the nature of scientific theory and the foundational reasoning of the hypothetico-deductive pattern. I use this example to talk about the function of theories generally, in the context of the coherence, correspondence, and pragmatic theories of truth. This method lays an epistemic foundation so that students will have a background understanding of why some premises of some arguments will be accepted by some individuals, and not by others.

Begging the question

To assume the truth of the Bering Strait land bridge theory may "beg the question," or assume that which is in need of proof. As a theory, it is plagued by incompleteness of evidence. Its reasoning assumes that since Sovereign Indigenous Nations have not, in a western sense of scientific proof, proved that they are indigenous, they cannot be. That is, because American Indians have not "proved" that they always lived in the Americas, westerners conclude that they are not indigenous. Arguing that what can't be proven to exist, must not exist, Eurocentrics politically argue that American Indians did not originate in, but were only the earliest inhabitants of, the Americas.

There remains however, no evidence to support this argument; mere intuition convinces students that lack of proof for "one thing" does not thereby prove its opposite true! (Lack of proof that I love you does not prove I don't love you!) Further valuing our intuitions, it is easy for students to see how background values of scientists can operate: for what purports to rest as proof in this theory, may be no more than an intention that western science will eradicate Indigenist land claims. Yet because the indigeneity of American Indians cannot be proven, the Bering Strait land bridge theory may equally support a reverse migration theory, multiple coinciding migrations, or even the arrival of some Sovereign Nations, and not others.

Assuming that which is in need of proof to support the land bridge theory itself (that there are no nations that originated in the Americas, hence American Indians are of imported cultures; they migrated into the land rather than always being there), plays to the political advantage of Euro-american land claims. In this way, Eurocentric science denies credibility to other "just so" stories of American Indian origin that are older, and have more coherence than, the Bering Strait theory. Americas' Indigenous Nations may view such a ploy as being arrogantly insulting, morally reprehensible, and scientifically repugnant.

We may now zoom in on the exact logic. The Bering Strait theory runs something like this: (1) Evidence suggests migration took place between the Asian and North American continents. The second premise is taken either as (a) a religious dogma, or (b) a scientific fact, and then an inference is drawn denying indigenous roots to American Indians: (2) (a), Humans were created by a Hebrew god in the Middle East, from where they dispersed throughout the world; or (2) (b), Since remains only of Cro-Magnon man, not of earlier hominids, have been discovered in the western hemisphere, human beings could not have evolved in the North American continent, but must have eventually reached it from Africa, via Asia and the land bridge.[7]

In class I discuss some contravening arguments. I show how both of the second premises to the argument (i.e., both (a) and (b)) beg the question. Each is assuming the truth of something not proved to be true, namely religious dogma or scientific fact. In this context we can talk about the coherence of American Indian creation stories, the nature of religion and science as tools of knowing, and refer back to our different concepts of coherence, correspondence, and pragmatic truth.

Generally, I explain to students how assumptions of one culture, or religious group, may differ from those of others, and thus give rise to disparate theories (or beliefs). In this way, we "open up" the practical effects of recognizing that some premises will hold for some persons, but will not be acceptable for others, and that no cultural group has a monopoly on human knowledge.

The question of the origin of Americas' indigenous groups then, remains unproven except by means of a western, or Eurocentric, religious dogma, or science. From a standpoint outside this Eurocentric position however, religious dogma and science proof "go begging" for verification. Explaining this "begging the question" fallacy puts knowledge systems themselves up for grabs, and effectively sensitizes students as to why it is important to respect traditions other than our own. It also gives an academic credibility and sensitivity to the cultural origins and intuitions of American Indian students.

Teaching such controversial topics empowers students to think seriously about arguments. And what happens when students then go to their anthropology courses, leaves smoke in the halls. Thus I warn students that my arguments will not be the same as others they will encounter, but that studying logic provides them with tools of analysis. They then understand that it is their choice to decide which religious theories, if any, they will accept; and how they may work with and talk about scientific theories, without having to believe them.

There are many variations on the land bridge argument, and I encourage students to look at the different possibilities that could be suggested by the very same evidence that scientists cite to prove their theory. I especially like to let them explore the "reverse migration theory," i.e., that nations in Siberia originated in the Americas.[8] Also, I ask them to think about the possibility of numerous migrations of various groups to and from the continents. This praxis encourages students to think of alternative inferences drawn from same premises, thus expanding their critical thinking skills.

False cause

The Bering Strait theory presents us with another fallacy, the "false cause" (*post hoc ergo propter hoc*). I offer the following example: S represents "we see evidence of the early presence of humans in Asia and Africa" and A represents 'we later see presence of humans in the Americas; (l) 'S' and (2) 'A', therefore S caused A. This argument builds into itself a temporal causal connection. To arrive at the conclusion, unannounced premises must be supplied: (3) There is a particular type of causal connection between S and A such that S is sufficient for A; (4) Humans are indigenous only to Africa; and (5) There have never been humans indigenous to any of the Americas. Of course, each one of these missing premises also stands in need of being proved.

This argument can also operate as an example of a *non causa* variety of the false cause fallacy. Again, a presumed premise supports the argument. In this case all that is needed is (5) above. Just because

Europeans did not know of the Americas, nor produce any data about indigenous groups, does not prove anything about it not being inhabited by indigenous groups.

Another good example of a false cause argument in this context is the claim: (1) Indigenous nations people caught many diseases from the Europeans, therefore 'Disease caused the dramatic drop in Indigenous population. While it is true that many Indigenous Nations people did die of disease, as a result of European contact, it is not true that disease was the only cause of the population drop. Nor is it true that contracting a disease like smallpox was only a matter of personal contact with Europeans.

Smallpox-infected blankets and infected handkerchiefs from smallpox hospitals were saved, only to be intentionally and maliciously given to Indigenous Nations by the calvary. Given that the calvary expected the disease to spread with deadly effectiveness, the motive for introducing it must have been genocide. So also, after periodic surrender by American Indians, massacres of them still took place; American Indians were massacred whether they surrendered after fighting, whether they resisted, or whether they submitted without fighting. From the fifteenth century onward, Euro-American colonial entrepreneurs captured Indigenous people to be used as slaves both internally and via exportation to other European colonies.[9] A broad view of this population decline suggests that intentional genocide, the systematic extermination of Indigenous culture, in the context of the encroachment of European immigrants and soldiers, was the main cause of population reduction. Thus, the argument posing disease only, or primarily, as the cause of indigenous population decline, is a *non causa* variety of the false cause fallacy because it fails to cite other causes. In failing to claim all of the causes the analysis has brought forth necessary, but perhaps not sufficient, causal reasoning.

False analogy

Before introducing the fallacy of "false analogy," I have found it helpful to give an example of a good analogy, showing why and how it functions inferentially. I present an argument that genocide was policy against Australian indigenous groups. I ask whether we can analogize from the claim of an holocaust in Australia to the same claim about the Americas. Not only can students see the similarity, as we discuss the particular techniques, but they are also then able to construct an analogy about American Indians as members of a group subject to a policy of extermination, or genocide, perpetrated by Eurocolonists.[10]

An upbeat example of a false analogy pertains to the great diversity of the Americas' Indigenous cuisine. The similarity of some food in two Indigenous cultures does not allow us to analogize to other characteristics. For example, it is not possible to analogize from the claim that "Indigenous Nations of the Southwest of North America eat chilis," to the conclusion "hence Indigenous Nations of the Northeast of North American also eat chilis!" That some characteristics may be similar in these cultures, for example, origin in the Americas, rhythmic music, a colonization of historic importance, an oral history tradition, etc., does not mean other characteristics will be similar.

One of the benefits of examining how the false analogy works, is that it helps students to see how some stereotypes are created, and enables some students to break away from the notion that "all Indians are alike" or even "all x's are y's" where x is a group and y is an accidental group characteristic. The indigenous students also have an opportunity to reveal aspects of their culture that are unique, helping to break down stereotypical images and ideas. Using this content, I can educate both American Indian and non-indigenous students about logic, achieve a cultural sensitivity and respect for different cultures, and positively affirm indigenous students' experience in academia.

Hasty generalization

Hasty generalizations frequently create stereotypes about American Indians, and other cultural groups. The processes of creating stereotypes, by false analogy or hasty generalization, are the same, whether about race, ethnicity, sex, gender, class, age, or disability. Most non-dominant power groups, from the point of view of the powerful, which is most frequently the media, are seen as either ignorant or immoral; this standpoint validates the ruling power of the dominant elite.

Cross-cultural communications improve when students understand that misinformation about the world may be rooted in stereotypes passed from generation to generation, culture to culture, and in a silent partnership of the media and the public that maintain, continually reinforce, and recreate stereotypes.[11] Discrimination is sometimes the result of an unconscious cultural process feeding prejudices about persons of non-dominant culture groups. Understanding how these processes work, and how to intervene when they operate, is a process of critical thinking.

Both Indigenous and non-indigenous stereotypes influence literary, social, biological, anthropological, archeological, historical, medical, legal, philosophical, and other ideas, both about individual persons and groups of persons. The problem with stereotypes from a critical thinking perspective is that they mask information necessary for reasoned inferences. Individuals, by attributing characteristics of one person to a group of persons, can distort and suppress information that is needed to draw correct conclusions, if that information does not support the stereotype.

Perpetuating false information, or masking pertinent information by making hasty generalizations, is how some social scientists ignore the anomalous facts they come across, because they are inconvenient. Not using the method of generalization might discredit assumptions, or create anomalies, that could eventually result in a paradigm shift within a particular theory. Sometimes a theory, in shifting its paradigm, may get rid of racist, sexist, elitist, or other internal assumptions that supported group oppression.[12] Theories about race, sex, and genetics are especially susceptible to manipulation via generalized assumptions when dominant groups want to keep non-dominant groups in a subordinated legal or social status.

Appeal to authority

In presenting the fallacy of arguing from authority, an analogy is drawn to how stereotypes can affect even "properly credentialed" authorities, and cause otherwise reasonable persons to make a false authority fallacy. For example, suppose person *A* is a member of a legally or socially subordinated group, and has a law degree. Suppose person *B* is a member of a legally or socially dominant group, and also has a law degree. Though *A* may be a much better lawyer than *B*, *A*'s membership in the subordinated group may act, in *C*'s consciousness, as a social and or personal stigma, falsely and unfairly suggesting that *A* would be a less competent or moral lawyer than *B*. Thus *C* may cite *B*'s argument in a court of tribal law, thinking it to be a more worthy argument. In fact, the better argument may be *A*'s argument. If *B* practices civil law, and *A* practices tribal law, *A* would be more likely to have a preferred argument for tribal court. Thus *C* would have cited a wrong, or false authority. Moreover, what gave rise to citing the false authority was an outcome of stereotypic thinking patterns.

Another example I like to use is about an anthropologist who claims to be an authority about a culture to which the anthropologist does not belong. This context provides an opportunity to teach what I refer to as "the field of denotation and connotation." This problem can be introduced with an example of a person from one culture pointing to, for example, a rabbit, and announcing "gavagai," meaning rabbit ears. Yet a person from another culture, the outsider (anthropologist) interprets the word as "the entire rabbit". Problems of outside authorities can also occur when there is no similar concept in the outsider's language, but the outsider alleges to have a word that correlates to the meaning. A person becomes a cultural authority by living in a culture. Admittedly, a person can read about a culture, study a culture, guess about a culture, or even dance a cultural dance. But cultural authorities must be the persons living and breathing in the culture. This is because such persons have daily contact with people having practices and beliefs associated with their own. Thus, they are more attuned to changes taking place within a culture, for example, shifts of meaning, practices, intent, and affect.

Authority issues prevail when origin theories and stories are ascribed by archaeologists, without consulting or giving credence to the knowledge base of individual cultural members. For example, although the Bering Strait land bridge theory, as explanation for the origin of American Indians contradicts all American Indian origin stories, it is still taught as fact by many disciplines. Thus, who "counts" as an authority figure for whom with respect to this theory becomes a political, rather than an academic issue. It is helpful to all students to discuss the politics of citing to authorities. Just as Euro-American culture proclaims authorities on certain issues, so also America's Indigenous Nations assert their own authorities. And American Indian students have a right to hold and protect their sacred beliefs, without having them belittled by academics. Given the process of colonization in the Americas, who counts as an authority for American Indian students may present a moral problem to Euro-Americans. This of course raises issues about gate-keeping, and the role of authority in gate-keeping cultural information.

Suppressed evidence

A "suppressed evidence" fallacy may operate at a macro-level of education, in the context of teaching Euro-American-centred disciplines to American Indian students. Specific examples, like teaching the Bering Strait theory, has the potential to project false information about Indigenous Nations. When information about Indigenous Nations is not adequately assessed, or portrayed, relevant information is suppressed.

The fallacy of suppressed evidence occurs whenever providing information previously not provided would change the conclusion of the arguer. Thus, identifying American Indians as aboriginal, or first inhabitants, may tell part of the truth, but would suppress the idea that they originated in America. Whether intentional or not, suppressing relevant information about opposing theories supports textbook status quo theory, and at the same time implicitly castes doubt upon Indigenous sources of information, and Indigenous people's ideas about their own origins.

Correct sign interpretation

The problem of inferring information from "signs" can be taught in the context of discussing received messages on billboards, in movies, and television, which depict a false reality about American Indians. Parodies of stereotypes operate to create misinformation that denigrates the character of all indigenous persons. The real, day-to-day harm that these signs perpetrate (intentionally or not) can be discussed by both indigenous and non-indigenous students in a supportive learning environment. Such an environment provides an opportunity to expose blatant cultural racism, sexism, and classism, and whether the media forces the participation of passive observers.

Definitional power

A good example that shows how the power of definition and signs can work together to suppress information, and thus portray a false reality, is historical markers across the Americas. At many sites where Indigenous Nations surrendered, and then were summarily massacred, the Federal United States government has incorrectly put up signs saying that these are sites of battlefields. In many instances no battles were ever fought. For example, no battle was fought at Wounded Knee Creek, South Dakota, on December 29, 1890; rather, a genocidal massacre of North American Indians by the USA military government took place. This example presents the injustice of false naming via signs that present misinformation by way of false definition. In this context we can also again talk about "begging the question," this time by assuming a definition of the word "battle" that would include "massacre." Obviously, using definitions like this, which fail to depict accurate assessments of reality, begs the question.

False compositions and divisions

Fallacies of composition and division are appropriate tools students can use to show, once again, how stereotypes arise. The first is the false reasoning from attributes of the parts of the whole to attributes of the whole itself. A good example of "composition" can be provided by drawing from an Indigenous student's experience of education. Attaining a knowledge base required for an academic degree may enhance American Indians' understanding of a Euro-American perspective, or a Eurocentric culture. From this fact, however, it should not be inferred that attaining many degrees will enhance the student insights even more; there may be a saturation point with respect to attaining a framework of interpretive analysis. Just like the anthropologist, one cannot "get into" or "put on" another's culture. One can dress differently, act differently, dance differently, and perhaps even grasp the language, but cannot live another's cultural experience.

Another example of a composition fallacy might be the claim that because some characteristic is true of some particular American Indian, it is true of a nation. And finally, if one were to suggest that if ingesting one toke of peyote makes a person feel good, having many of them will made the person feel absolutely wonderful, the logic of composition has been misapplied! In fact, it may make them ill, or paranoid, or even pass out!

With respect to the fallacy of division, the inverse of the previous example of peyote may be used. To argue that because many tokes of peyote may make one sick, thus one toke may make someone ill, is to commit the fallacy of stating that a characteristic that is true of the whole, must also be true of the part, which does not follow. So also, things that may be true of certain Indigenous Nations, may not be true about any individual member of that nation. To suggest otherwise may lead to another stereotype, another fallacy.

The false dichotomy

Another fallacy portrayed in the context of American Indian stereo-types is the false dichotomy. Some persons, it can be argued, think that America's Indigenous persons are either American Indian or European. This dichotomy is false because it fails to take account of the complexity of race and ethnic identity politics. Some native nations citizens may identify as both, or as mixed. Some American Indians may also identify differently under different contexts. This example can open a discussion of philosophy of the self, identity politics, nationalism, and critical race and ethnic theory.

Slippery slopes

Finally, the "slippery slope" fallacy, the assumption that a tendency gets progressively worse, like something accelerating downhill, can be portrayed by examining the fear of many Euro-Americans with respect to Americas' Indigenous Nations' treaty rights. In asking that our treaties be recognized, respected, honored, and acted upon, many Americans fear that reparation of lands for one tribe will set a precedent for all tribes, arguing that the next thing you know they will take over and force all non-indigenous persons to leave the Americas. Quite plainly, granting reparations to Indigenous Nations, by recognizing treaty rights, does not lead to an extermination of non-indigenous persons in the Americas. Indigenous Nations have a 500 year history of accommodating the land space needs of Euro-Americans. It is only "fair," some argue, that the USA government now accommodate Indigenous Nations with respect to land issues and space. The evidence of our centuries of co-existence ought to preclude such slippery slope backlash thinking. Yet many persons, for whatever personal reasons, perpetuate this type of slippery slope argument with respect to native rights, as well as rights of other non-dominant groups of persons, who may have justified reason for reparations from the United States government.

Presenting the slippery slope in this context can lead to discussions of historical injustices in the Americas, causal relationships among these injustices, the social and political contexts of these injustices, and the contemporary power of European nation-states, and the United States, to correct these injustices. It can also lead into another direction, the use of slippery slope arguments against granting equal rights to non-dominant groups of lower race and economic class, the elderly, physically or mentally challenged, different gendered, and historically or politically disadvantaged and disenfranchised ethnic groups.

Conclusion

I have presented some of the informal fallacies and content that I use in critical thinking classes that incorporate an indigenous perspective. Many more can be developed. My intent has been to show a methodology of curriculum development that encourages indigenous students to more actively participate, and thereby sharpen, their creative thinking skills. Eventually, in the process of the course, students come to grasp and articulate relationships between fallacious reasoning and oppression. They begin to understand the importance of intuitive reasoning, and the problems associated with reasoning from false or incomplete premises. They also get a glimmer of what it means to disagree with others as a result of having different underlying assumptions or belief systems. And if I have done nothing else during a semester, this last thing, in itself, justifies my method and content. In this way, I believe I am "doing" native philosophy of the Americas: it is being done by, for, and about Native Americans! And yes, it also benefits non-native students who learn something about not only logic, but their hosts, the Indigenous Sovereign Nations still inhabiting our home, turtle island.

Perhaps I am not doing all that I could. For example, a textbook could be written utilizing examples that incorporate experiences of our multiracial and multiethnic populations in the Americas. Perhaps in the future I or someone else will find the time to write such a book. But this is a beginning. It is one nick in the walls of boundaries that unnecessarily divide students one from another in classrooms. And, in the spirit of doing "insurgent scholarship" it has revolutionary potential to provide students with tools for both living and doing philosophy.

Notes

1   An American Indian Indigenist is a person who advocates for the claims of American Indians, i.e. on behalf of the claims and beliefs of descendants of the original Peoples of the Americas, for example as a member of a political movement. He or she need not be indigenous to the Americas. A person who is descended from the Original Peoples of the Americas is Indigenous. "Indigenous," in the sense I use of "always having been there," is to be distinguished from "aboriginal": the first to inhabit a region.

2   When I use the term "philosophy" I also mean to include the notion of "doing philosophy" as an activity. I use the term in a broad sense.

3   On American Indian identity, see Ward Churchill, "The Crucible of American Indian Identity," in Duane Champagne (ed.) *Contemporary Native American Cultural Issues* (Walnut Creek: AltaMira, 1999), p. 39.

4   Lorraine Brundige has recently written a paper asking non-natives to dialogue "with us, not for us."

5   Although it was advertised as the first ever Native American philosophy conference, only one person identified as a Native American Ph.D. philosopher presented. That individual was invited only after the organizers of the conference were contacted with a query about Native American participation. The American Philosophical Association (APA) at the time of writing, identified only two American Indian Ph.D. philosophers (conversation with Anita Silvers, and also with Eric Hoffman, at the APA Pacific Division Meeting, Berkeley, California, Spring 1999). This does not include persons I would include as philosophers, for example, Vine Deloria Jr., who has engaged in indigenist philosophical thought from an American Indian perspective for many years, and many other historical "message carriers" from one generation to another. However it does raise a question about why there have been no Native American Ph.D. philosophers prior to this date.

6   In 1992, Viola Cordova became one of two American Indian scholars to receive a Ph.D. in philosophy; the other was myself. From 1992 to 1997 Viola had been teaching at the University of Alaska, and I at the Albuquerque Community College in New Mexico. At the time of writing this, we are both writing and speaking, though neither is employed full-time as a philosopher.

7   These epistemic arguments are taken up, and convincingly argued against, by Vine Deloria Jr., in *Red Earth, White Lies: Native Americans and the Myth of Scientific Fact* (Golden, CO: Fulcrum Publishing, 1997).

8   Jeffrey Goodman, *American Genesis: The American Indian and the Origins of Modern Man* (New York: Summit Books, 1981).

9 Regarding disease, massacre, and enslaving of Indigenous Nations, see Ward Churchill, *A Little Matter of Genocide: Holocaust and Denial in the Americas, 1492 to Present* (San Francisco: City Lights, 1997); and Russell Thornton, *American Indian Holocaust and Survival: A Population History Since 1492* (Norman: University of Oklahoma, 1987). Both texts quote from official correspondence from Sir Jeffrey Amherst, commander-in-chief of the British forces, to his subordinate, Bouquet. Thornton writes, "In 1763 ... Amherst ... wrote in the postscript of a letter to Bouquet the suggestion that smallpox be sent among the disaffected tribes. Bouquet replied, also in a postscript, 'I will try to innoculate the[m] ... with some blankets that may fall into their hands, and take care not to get the disease myself' ... Amherst replied, 'You will do well to try to innoculate the Indians by means of blankets as well as to try every other method that can serve to extirpate this execrable race.' On June 24, Captain Ecuyer, of the Royal Americans, noted in his journal: 'Out of our regard for them ... we gave them two blankets and a handkerchief out of the smallpox hospital. I hope it will have the desired effect' (Stearn and Stearn, 1945: pp. 44–5)" (Thornton, pp. 78–9).

10 The "one exception to the rule" fallacy can also be examined in this context. The claim is that Indigenous persons were not all killed, their descendants live, hence there was no genocide. In this context I can talk about the power of definition, and that the definition of genocide, according to the International Trials at Nuremberg after World War II, rejected this model. It was rejected on the grounds that a few exceptions do not disprove the overall context and motivation, nor the intentional suppression of evidence. Also, the significant reduction of population by disease, massacre, and discontinuity enforced on the remaining nations, was itself enough to claim a holocaust. See Churchill and Thornton above.

11 Regarding the transfer of false consciousness and cultural groups, see Naomi Zack, *Thinking About Race* (Belmont: Wadsworth 1998), especially ch. 10 (p. 88): "as the media ... reaches out to give the public what it wants, and the public reaches out to its media to find out what it wants, they form a partnership of creating and re-creating stereotypes and myths."

12 I refer here to a Popperian sense of discrediting (falsifying) a theory, and a Kuhnian sense of a theory paradigm shift.

CHAPTER 7

The Libertarian Role Model and the Burden of Uplifting the Race

BARBARA HALL

As an African American, do I have certain obligations to all other African Americans *per se*? Am I, for instance, obliged to lead my life in a manner which they as a group believe reflects positively on the race?

As a liberal, it would be very easy for me to maintain that I owe nothing to the blanket group, African Americans. How could all of these others (whom I do not know, but with whom I share a common ethnicity) possibly come to have tenable expectations of me? What viable claims are there that might place limits on my liberties only because I also am African American?

Such a notion offends my liberal sensibilities. Yet, I *do* believe that I have special obligations to the group "African Americans." I believe that I owe them some sort of fidelity and that I must make a positive contribution to and for others in the group. I also believe it morally appropriate to criticize any African Americans who do not do so.

Can my position be justified? Is it appropriate in a liberal society for members of a subgroup to exact special requirements of its members which may well infringe upon some of the freedoms guaranteed by the larger society? More specifically, do I have a special duty to try to support and uplift my race or group?[1] Can I be condemned for not striving to do so? Can I be censured for attitudes or behavior deemed degrading by and to the group? What does it even mean, to "uplift" or "degrade" the race? These are some of the questions that precipitate this paper.

Liberalism and Communities

In a liberal society such as ours there is much discourse about the rights and freedoms of individuals. Indeed, it was the twin ideals of liberty and rugged individualism that served as the cornerstones upon which this country was founded. According to the liberal tradition, restrictions placed upon the rights or actions of individuals are only justifiable to the extent that those actions represent a palpable "harm to others."[2] Thus, anyone ought to be free to do as she pleases as long as she does not act to harm another.

Recent critics of traditional liberal political philosophy have argued that the basic tenets of liberalism (at least as conventionally conceived) are mistaken, for they do not take into account the important role of community in defining the person's relationship to and function within her society.[3] Human beings, they suggest, are social creatures who develop and operate within group settings. We are not atomistic beings, but are communal in nature. This fact, they argue, suggests that a primary focus on individual rights is inadequate (if not incorrect) for portraying the various collective influences that characterize people within a societal context.

What has resulted from this discussion of the rights of groups (specifically those of minority groups) is a much richer dialogue, which recognizes and gives validity to the rights claimed by some ethnic groups. Even some liberals acknowledge that the significance of group membership for individuals should be properly recognized.[4] Thus they endeavor to find ways to interpret liberalism that give cogent recognition to the social and political value of groups.

I do not question the moral or legal appropriateness of group rights. There can be little doubt that individuals may suffer harms strictly because of their group membership(s). Thus, their rights as a collective are violated and subject to remedy.

My concern, here, is not about justifying the rights claims of groups as opposed to the rights claims of individuals. Rather, it is about an individual member's obligations or moral responsibilities to her particular subgroup (racial, ethnic, gender, etc.). The philosophical topic of group rights addresses the legitimacy of subgroup legal claims upon the larger society. My concern, however, is with the legitimacy of a subgroup's moral claims upon its own members.

My inquiry concerns the possibilities and limitations of a liberal ideology within a communitarian structure. While liberalism's emphasis is on the individual "I," and communitarian ideals emphasize the communal "we," there appears to be no *necessary* disjuncture between the two ideologies. (That is, not if both sides are willing to compromise on their positions.) The primacy of the "I" versus the sway of the "we" is a dilemma with which, perhaps, every member of a distinct group wrestles at some time.

Liberals are apprehensive of the restrictions that may sometimes be placed upon individuals by the larger group. Indeed, it is just this issue, which Kymlicka calls "internal restrictions" that fuels the philosophically popular debate between liberals and communitarians.[5] But the matter of what *legal* constraints a group may or may not impose upon the liberties of its members is not what I wish to consider here.

The question I ask is, "Should my status, *per se*, as a member of a particular group carry with it certain *moral* obligations to the others in my group? If so, what justifies the imposition of these obligations?"

Perhaps the philosophical literature on voluntariness and responsibility might shed light on the issue. After all, imposition of legal or moral responsibilities seem to require some type of voluntary consent (implied or explicit) from the obligatee.

A resolution is not to be found so quickly, however. This is because, ultimately, my question concerns persons who have not volunteered, or could not have volunteered, to belong to a designated group. These are inescapable "mandatory" memberships. The question of whether membership alone in these groups carries with it certain obligations and responsibilities to the other members is, therefore, a perplexing one because group memberships, while not coerced, are also not freely chosen.

Moral Obligations, Responsibility and Voluntariness

Most writers agree that under a just system of rules, S's legal and moral responsibilities for some thing or event X or to some person P should be conditioned upon some voluntary (knowing and willing) choice of S vis-à-vis X or P.[6] If Steve decides to speed through the red traffic signal and police officer Tom sees him, then Steve (having broken the law) will be held responsible to the extent that the law requires. Or, say that Johnny willingly throws a rock that shatters the windshield of Dave's pick-up truck, we may say that he deserves to be held responsible for his action because, in choosing to throw the rock, Johnny has "earned" the responsibility of compensating Dave for the destruction of his windshield.

By contrast, it would not be fair for Betsy randomly to select some stranger off the street and proclaim that he, henceforth, will have total responsibility for providing food and shelter for her two children. Betsy is tired. She just wants to get away. She's decided to move to Paris and pursue her dream of becoming an existentialist poet. Suppose this stranger learns that Betsy is lawfully able to carry out her plan. He, therefore, has no legal recourse to stop her. The stranger would justifiably feel victimized. Betsy has forced upon him responsibilities that he does not deserve on the basis of his actions or choices.

Responsibility as liability, then, is something that has to be merited or deserved. It is earned in a negative way, i.e., imposed as a burden, rather than awarded as a prize. What is imposed, foremost, is blame – blame for bringing about an undesirable state of affairs, one which warrants correction by the person responsible.[7] Given this, my question becomes, "When can a person be said to merit the blame or condemnation of her group for failing to meet some special moral obligation entailed by her as a group membership?"

H. L. A. Hart, I believe, provides a useful starting point from which to discuss the types of moral responsibilities group memberships can impose. Hart, speaking of "role responsibility" says:

> [W]henever a person occupies a distinctive place or office in a social organization, to which specific duties are attached to provide for the welfare of others or to advance in some specific way the aims or purposes of the organization, he is properly said to be responsibile for the performance of these duties, or for doing what is necessary to fulfill them. Such duties are a person's responsibilities.[8]

It is the person's "role" or status as a group member that is the catalyst for the imposition of responsibilities.

Hart uses the example of a sea captain as someone who, because of his role, has acquired certain responsibilities. These responsibilities are for and to his passengers. His role gives him the responsibility for things like their safety and well-being.

There is a distinction between the group to which the captain belongs (the group which imposes the obligations on him as one of their own: the sea captains) and the group for which he is directly responsible (passengers). So, the people for whom the captain is responsible are not the members of his own group; but, instead, are members of another group, "passengers." In this situation a failure satisfy one's obligations only indirectly affects one's own group. It is the *other* group for which one has responsibility that is directly harmed by any malfeasance.

When some member(s) of group *A* has responsibilities for the members of a group *B*, I will say that this person's responsibilities are "other directed." These sort of "other-directed" obligations are acquired when a person chooses to be a part of a group whose membership entails these responsibilities. The choice of certain careers or vocations imposes special obligations (e.g. in the case of a doctor, lawyer, airplane pilot, etc.). These positions obligate their practitioners as *individuals qua group members*.

Perhaps, most of the time the responsibilities we incur are not a result of our group memberships; rather they are the responsibilities of *individuals qua individuals*. For instance, when I promise my neighbor that I will feed her cat while she is on vacation, I am, as an individual promise-maker agreeing to take on the responsibilities of caring for her cat.

However, as I said earlier, my concern in this paper is with the responsibilities of individuals *qua* group members, and not with the "other-directed" type of role responsibilities just discussed. I am, again, more puzzled by the responsibilities that are associated with individuals and the obligations they have to the members of their own group. These are "self-directed" obligations because the individual, herself, is a part of the group.

If I am Tiger Woods and all I want to do is play golf, ought I, nevertheless, feel obligated or be compelled to visibly support African-American causes? What if I have no political consciousness or simply wish to lead a private and quiet life of my own choosing? Do I owe something special to African Americans merely because I am one of them? Suppose I wish to adopt an attitude of true "color-blindness" and, thus, feel no special affiliation with or obligation to the others of my race?

I believe that some types of special obligations to one's group can be justified given certain facts about the group and its situation within the larger society. Before I discuss this, however, I would like to identify some of the kinds of moral obligations a group might presumably impose on its members.

Role Model Responsibility

A person might be expected to serve as a role model for other members of the group. A particular individual because of her accomplishments might be expected to serve as a source of inspiration for others in the group who aspire to succeed. Perhaps, more importantly, she might be expected to provide inspiration for those in the group who have no "positive" aspirations. When oppressive social conditions have fostered a sense of hopelessness and futility, the presence of successful group members could certainly inspire others. How might a person fulfill or fail to fulfill her role model responsibilities? What kinds of things are expected of a role model?

A role model must (presumably) be someone whom a majority of group members believe would be an appropriate person for others, especially the young, to emulate. Thus, a role model is likely to be someone of whom high moral standards are expected. A role model must also be someone of whom group members speak with pride: they are proud that he or she is "one of them."

So, it is not only the secular achievements of the potential role model that are important, but also the "uprightness" with which she leads her life. All successful group members may become candidates for role model status; however, only those who lead the proper types of lives are actually deemed to be role models. Success as determined by (but not limited to) the fame, popularity, economic, or political accomplishments of the individual.

A successful member is expected to lead the kind of life that will be agreeable to group members, and to society in general. For instance: she must not engage in criminal activities; behave rudely or violently towards others; she will not be seen falling down drunk in public, etc. What is expected is (at least) a certain moral uprightness and conformity.[9]

Someone whose lifestyle keeps her from being an acceptable role model will be a suitable candidate for moral repudiation by the group. After all, what is expected is that others will want to emulate her and this should be a positive thing – something to "up-lift" the group. Someone whose behavior is not uplifting may well be seen as detrimental to the group if emulating her behavior would be seen as damaging the group's interests or well-being.

These are merely general guidelines. It will not be uncontroversial who or what constitutes appropriate role model material. An excellent example of a "proper" role model was baseball great, Jackie Robinson. Because of him, young African-American boys began to dream of playing major-league baseball and of being like Jackie. His moral character and disposition were viewed as impeccable by African Americans and non-African Americans alike. He was the sort of person that any mother could want her son to grow up to be.

Reputation Responsibility

A second type of responsibility that a group could place upon its members is more common. It is placed upon *any and every* member of the group, not just the recognized successful ones. These obligations are self-directed, but they necessarily involve those who are not group members: it is the responsibility of every member of the group to enhance, redeem, or otherwise, not to damage, the image and reputation of the group.

This is a responsibility that would belong to every member because every member is taken to be an ambassador of the group. This "ambassadorship" is imposed by persons outside of the group. The common name for this phenomenon is "stereotyping." Except in rare instances, the role of ambassador is not chosen and cannot be relinquished.[10] Given that an individual group member is stereotyped as a representative of the whole, what the group would demand is that in the company of these outsiders the member must exhibit socially exemplary behavior.[11] This is because he is an ambassador and, so, a reflection of the group *in toto*. A bad assessment of "one" reflects poorly on the whole.

Ultimately, the person's responsibility is to or for her group. However, she can only satisfy this responsibility by having a positive influence on those who are outside of the group. For it is these others who judge the group *in toto* on the basis of any contact with individual members. Every group member is charged with recognizing this fact and, thereafter, comporting him- or herself in a manner that will lead to a positive assessment by non-group-members. (Here, I must emphasize that I shall not be commenting on the moral propriety of this type of judgment. It is the mere *fact* of the judgment upon which I base my discussion.)

An African American who is said to be "a credit to his or her race" is someone who has succeeded to some extent in redeeming or enhancing the image of the group. Someone who is foolish, slovenly, ignorant, or dishonest, anyone who displays traits not deemed acceptable by the larger dominant society embarrasses the group, "makes everybody look bad." For example, violent, criminal behavior by a few persons is likely be seen as a hallmark of the group.[12] Given this fact, those individuals whose actions are deleterious "tarnish" the whole and may well be subject to their moral denunciation: for the iniquity of the acts themselves, but more precisely, for the damage done to the group's reputation.

The role model and good reputation responsibilities may be the most common kinds of group-dictated obligations. There are surely others. These, however, are sufficient for my purposes.

Presumptions of Responsibility

The fact that each member "owes" something to her group has typically been accepted without question. Early African-American thinkers took for granted that African Americans should strive to "uplift the race." They often differed about how to accomplish this end; but that there was an obligation to try was always assumed.[13]

Jews who do not support Jewish causes are censured by the more ardent group-oriented members. Latinos who do not maintain some aspect of their heritage are frowned upon by other Latinos. Indeed, terms such as "oreo cookie", "apple", "coconut" are sometimes used by the members of various groups as pejorative descriptions of those members who do not seem to demonstrate the requisite dedication or loyalty to their groups. (These people are believed to be "colored on the outside, but white on the inside.")

Is it fair for groups to attempt to pressure their members into some kind of conformity – into becoming "loyal" members of the group? Earlier, I discussed the topic of voluntariness. It does *not* seem unfair for some groups to have conditions of membership so that someone who is unwilling or unable to meet the conditions can and may be censured by or excluded from the group. What divides those groups that seem justified in making demands of their members from groups whose membership obligations pose a problem for anyone with liberal inclinations is that membership in the former type of group is optional or voluntary, while membership in the latter type of group can be virtually inescapable. That is, a person cannot voluntarily become a member of the group, nor can she (in many cases) voluntarily or involuntarily leave the group. Let us look more closely at the notion of a compulsory membership.

Compulsory Memberships

Liberalism places a high value on personal freedom and individual rights. But I, an African American, did not choose to become African American. Nor is it true that should I decide that the conditions for remaining an African American are too difficult I can just get out and become something else. (I am, I suppose, fortunate that I do not dislike being an African American!)[14]

Like it or not, some individuals are "stuck" with their group identity. Sometimes racial group memberships do have a voluntary flavor in that particular individuals may be able to conceal their identities as members of the group. They can escape the group and, hence, whatever discrimination or disapproval that comes with being identified as a member. But are they right when they "pass" as someone not in the group?

Up until recent times it was not uncommon for some African-American individuals who bore no physically discernable traces of their African ancestry to "pass" as white or not-Negro. That is, they either implicitly or explicitly declared themselves to be white by living, working, and marrying into the segregated white society that was hostile to blacks.

To the extent that there are physical characteristics deemed to be peculiar to or identifiable with a certain group, anyone possessing these characteristics will be "tied to" the group. One might further claim that anyone who does not possess these attributes, or anyone who may be able to significantly disguise or alter them, is not really "stuck with" her group identity. So, if red hair is a hallmark of a group and red hair is easy to dye, then anyone who does not disguise her red hair is, in essence, voluntarily choosing to be (remain) a member of that red-haired group. Indeed, former New York Congressman Adam Clayton Powell who had little if any visible African American features often said that he was nobler than most African Americans because he could and did choose to be identified as African American. Thus, he surmised, he voluntarily chose to endure the cruelties perpetrated upon members of the race when he could have lived a privileged life as a white man.[15]

Too much emphasis on physical characteristics, however, might lead to a confusion in distinguishing ethnic groups from mere collectives. The people who are left-handed comprise the collective of left-handed individuals. A collective is some group whose members share a (physical, etc.) characteristic. An ethnic group, however, is a group linked by more than just particular characteristics. It has been argued this additional factor is the group's shared history the legacy of which can be linked to some definable characteristic of the group.[16] So the history of Jewish people is a history from which religious persecution is inextricable; the history of Latinos in America is a history of discrimination involving language and culture; and the history of African Americans is one in which persecution is intimately linked with skin color.

Justifying Special Obligations

Can the view that a person has special moral obligations to his ethnic/ racial/gender group be justified within a liberal framework? A careful study of the literature will reveal that liberals find it problematic to justify even the basic notion of political obligation.[17] Thus, an attempt to find justification for *special* obligations may prove extra difficult for a person with liberal sentiments.

For our purposes, let us assume that the liberal justifications for political obligation are unproblematic. They still cannot provide justification for the imposition of special obligations on members of subgroups by other subgroup members. This is because these justifications attempt to reconcile political obligations with some sort of voluntariness.[18] But, as I noted earlier, the types of obligations with which I am concerned are mandatory or non-consensual in nature.

So how might one go about looking for a justification of special obligations? There are, I believe, certain conditions that have to obtain before one can be said to have acquired special obligations. The first and most important one is that one must belong to a subgroup that has experienced, and continues to experience, some sort of oppression from the larger group.[19] This requirement seems necessary if the demands of the subgroup are to have any sort of moral pull. Certainly a subgroup making demands "just for the heck of it" would seem to have a less weighty claim than a group whose claims are based on a need to oppose oppressive conditions.

Secondly, the oppression must be the intentional result of the dominant group's expression of its dislike of some feature or intrinsic characteristic of the subgroup. That is, the subgroup suffers because of who or what its members are. Accidental or arbitrary infliction of suffering certainly seems less evil than does intentional and purposeful oppression.

Thirdly, *fairly or not*, individual members of the subgroup are viewed by those outside of the group as being representative of the group *in toto* (i.e., they are stereotyped as ambassadors).

Fourthly, *fairly or not*, individuals inside the group must share a sense of identity with each other. That is, they embrace and triumph in the laudable achievements of other group members; similarly, they feel shame and disappointment at iniquitous acts of other members.

Rightly or wrongly, these four conditions together place individual subgroup members in a position of necessarily affecting (negatively or positively) the interests of the other members. Given this, I contend that subgroup members (because of the way the world is) simply cannot divorce themselves or their actions from the group. If this point is correct then they must acknowledge and accept the added responsibility entailed by their having to carry the interests and welfare of other group members with them. The moral justification for this position is clearly utilitarian. If, for reasons beyond my control or not, my actions will cause further harm to my group (a group that has already been harmed), then I ought to acknowledge this and to act in a way that is not harmful to the group.

For example, if I find myself in the position of being the sole African American on the board of directors of multinational Corporation QW then I *ought* not to lie and steal. I ought not to do so for the same reasons that *any* person in such a position ought not to do so, but, (and here is the critical difference between me and Peter Davis, a fellow board member and white male) *I ought not to do so for the added reason that I am viewed as a representative of my race (a group that has endured injustices), and my conduct may well harmfully affect the prospects of future and other African Americans at multinational Corporation QW.*

I am not suggesting that it is *right* that I should be viewed as a racial ambassador. I am suggesting that given I am thrust into this situation it would be wrong for me to deny or ignore the associated responsibilities. I am arguing that I ought not to "mess things up" for other group members whose fortunes (rightly or wrongly) may well be in my hands (even if this is true only because we are all African Americans). I believe that I must acknowledge the possible widespread consequences of my behavior and that if I fail to do so, I may be subject to condemnation for not doing so.

Where does this leave my argument? I have not given reasons for holding that as a subgroup member I have special obligations to do affirmative acts to "uplift" my group. At most, I have provided reasons for suggesting that I have special obligations *not* to act in ways that can be detrimental to the group. I also believe that I have obligations to affirmatively act to better the group; however, I shall explore those at another time.

Notes

My discussion concerns traditionally liberal values and issues. I use the term "libertarian" here to connote a form of "ultra" liberalism in which individual liberty is decreed the supreme good.

1   I am assuming that "support and uplift" can be defined; and will attempt to do so shortly.
2   See Joel Feinberg, *Harm to Others* (New York: Oxford University Press, 1984).
3   For example, Iris Young, *Justice and the Politics of Difference* (Princeton: Princeton University Press, 1990).
4   See Will Kymlica, *Multicultural Citizenship* (New York: Oxford University Press, 1995).
5   Ibid., pp. 34–44.
6   Cf. H. L. A. Hart, *Punishment and Responsibility* (New York: Oxford University Press, 1968).
7   There may, of course, also be obligations imposed by non-members. But the issue which interests me concerns the legitimacy of the claims of the group to whom the obligations are believed owed, namely the individual's own group.
8   Hart, *Punishment and Responsibility*, p. 213.
9   I take there to be a crucial distinction between moral conformity and political conformity. Thus, while a person's political views may be radical compared to mainstream African-American thought, I suggest that it is only her departure from accepted moral standards that should affect her

suitability as a role model. If this distinction is not made, one could argue that a role model is just a "good Negro" who does not "rock the boat."

10   This is an important thesis of my paper, which will be discussed in more detail shortly.

11   Jackie Robinson was selected to play in the white major leagues not because he was the most talented player in the Negro leagues. Rather, it was because he was a good Negro ambassador. He had the temperament to endure the racism directed his way. He was able to show white America that (the group) blacks could play with whites without "messing things up." Cf. Jules Tygiel, *Baseball's Great Experiment: Jackie Robinson and his Legacy* (New York: Vintage Press, 1983) and Robert Peterson, *Only the Ball was White: A History of Legendary Black Players and All Black Professional Teams* (New York: Oxford University Press, 1970). (Note: Robinson's demeanor was seen as a moral virtue, although the context in which he found himself was a political one.)

12   Cornel West and others have written about the difficulty that an African-American male has in hailing a taxi in Manhattan. Even in business attire he is suspect. Cf. Cornel West, *Race Matters*, (Boston: Beacon Press, 1993). The black criminals who rob taxi drivers have made it virtually impossible for any African-American male to flag down a taxi. Whites robbers, on the other hand, do not seem to have affected the ability of white males to get a cab.

13   Neither Booker Washington nor W. E. B. DuBois doubted that individuals should work to better the condition of the race. They only differed as to the means. Cf. W. E. B. DuBois, *The Souls of Black Folk* (New York: Signet Classic/Penguin Books, 1995).

14   Perhaps the term "black" would be more appropriate than "African American" which is technically considered a designation of nationality rather than a racial classification. People do, of course, change nationalities all of the time. The term "African American", however, should (for my purposes) be considered a racial designation, because it is commonly used as such and because, historically and primarily, it has been the physical features of African peoples that have marked them for unjust treatment.

15   Wil Haygood, "Keeping the Faith," in *American Legacy*, 3/4, Winter (1998). Is there a difference in the moral status or obligations of those who are "tied to" the group and those who may "pass"? If I am correct in holding that anyone who is an African American has special obligations to other African Americans, then anyone who rejects these obligations is morally culpable. If this person is someone who is "tied to" the group, he will still not be able to escape the abuse and injustice directed at him because of his obvious features. However, if this person is

someone who may "pass", then he could hide his identity and avoid the derisiveness. Such a person, however, seems to be more morally culpable because he can and does abandon his own kind.

16   Cf. Tommy L. Lott, "DuBois on the Invention of Race," in John P. Pittman (ed.) *African-American Perspectives and Philosophical Traditions* (New York: Routledge, 1997). While physical characteristics alone are not necessary or sufficient to place one in a particular group, they do provide those in and out of the group with a means of recognition.

17   See for example C. Wellman, "Associative Allegiances and Political Obligations," in *Social Theory and Practice* 23/2, Summer (1997).

18   The consent theory, for example, holds that citizens are obligated because they can implicitly or tacitly consent to be obligated by their actions. See Wellman, "Associative Allegiances."

19   The idea that oppression was the key element was suggested to me in a brief conversation with Keith Lehrer.

I would like to thank Jim Humber for his insightful comments on this paper. Special thanks, also, to Naomi.

CHAPTER 8

Interracial Marriage: Folk Ethics in Contemporary Philosophy

ANITA L. ALLEN

Introduction

In 1967, *Loving* v. *Virginia* settled the question of the constitutionality of laws prohibiting marriages between persons of different races.[1] In *Loving*, the United States Supreme Court determined that state laws banning "miscegenation" violate the Equal Protection Clause of the Fourteenth Amendment. Since *Loving*, a higher percentage of Americans have married across racial lines.[2] The rate of black/white inter-marriage, the type of intermarriage centrally at issue in the *Loving* case, has quadrupled.[3] As the number of mixed race families and offspring has grown, the number of theorists who question the very idea of race and racial classification has also grown.[4]

On the evidence of the foregoing observations, it is tempting to conclude that law, theory, and social practice are united in support of interracial marriage. Marriage between blacks and whites, however, remains comparatively rare and significantly controversial.[5] The 1990 census showed that 97.6 percent of married black women are married to black men, down only slightly from 99.1 percent in 1960.[6] Homogamy is typical for blacks of both sexes. The tendency of blacks to marry other blacks may be due to the unavailability of willing partners of other races. But the story is more complex than other races' antipathy towards blacks. Some African Americans view mar-riage between blacks and whites as a *moral* problem best avoided. They describe hetergamy as potentially disloyal, inconsiderate, and self-hating. Interracial intimacy is an *emotional* problem for some blacks, too. In a study conducted by University of Michigan psychologist Ruby Beale, black women ranked "seeing an interracial couple" as the second leading cause of stress in their lives, ahead of "racism, housework, economic worries and more than 100 other potential causes of stress" that she measured.[7]

Loving v. *Virginia* was a legally and morally just decision, an important milestone in American's quest for racial equality and marital privacy. Without impugning the justice of *Loving*, I would like to assess the perspective of some, but not all, African Americans that marriage between blacks and whites is a moral problem. A minority some 24 million strong, mainstream blacks deserve to have their perspectives on marriage taken seriously by moral philosophers, I believe. I try to take them seriously here. In addition to examining blacks' perspectives on interracial marriage, I would also like to comment on the role I believe the study of population-group specific ethics – we might call them "folk ethics" – could play in academic philosophy. As a philosophy-trained law professor, I am less than ideally situated to comment on future directions for philosophical research and pedagogy. My comments must be construed as those of an interdisciplinarian.

I will be unable to address all of the interesting and important issues relating to interracial friendship, sex, and marriage suggested by my discussion. I reserve for others the tasks of examining, for example: (1) how members of other population groups view interracial marriage; (2) how members of all population groups who choose not to marry, but value intimacy, view interracial friendship, sex, or partnership; and (3) how gay men and lesbians view interracial homosexual relationships. My focus is thus perspectives, commonly, but not universally, held among African Americans, on the kind of relationship that was centrally at issue in *Loving*: governmentally sanctioned heterosexual marriage between blacks and whites.

Marry Black!

Many African Americans are morally troubled by marriage between blacks and whites.[8] The African Americans I have in mind are ordinary men and women, but especially women,[9] of all social and economic classes. They include students and professionals, some of whom date and marry interracially. They are not the kinds of people who would be classified as racists or racial separatists. They are the ordinary black people whom whites know as congenial co-workers and neighbors, as well the ordinary people living in urban or rural communities that whites seldom penetrate.

The ethics of interracial marriage is a frequent topic of discussion and debate among African Americans.[10] Film-maker Spike Lee tried to capture the controversial nature of interracial intimacy among professional and middle-class blacks in the commercially successful movie *Jungle Fever*.[11] Highly educated black women are more likely to out-marry than other black women.[12] It is important to emphasize, however, that while many educated blacks are comfortable with interracial intimacy, highly educated blacks number among those most deeply troubled by it. A black professor once told me that she would feel insulted if a white man asked to date her, because she would regard the invitation as insensitive to the many good reasons black women have for not trusting white men. Lack of trust in other ethnic groups is not unique to blacks, highly educated or otherwise. A white Jewish philosopher told me that she could not marry a non-Jew because she feared he might reveal repressed anti-Semitism in a moment of anger or disappointment.

The moral qualms I am attributing to African Americans surface in books and films about black life, and on the pages of magazines and newspapers marketed to blacks.[13] Discussions of interracial intimacy in the popular press are sometimes prompted by the rise to fame of a mixed-race beauty, performer, or athlete; and sometimes by the coupling of a prominent black with a prominent white.[14] The interracial marriage of entertainer Sammy Davis Jr. raised eyebrows in the early 1960s, but it was entertainers Whoopi Goldberg, Diana Ross, O. J. Simpson, Alfre Woodard, Angela Bassett, James Earl Jones, and Cuba Gooding Jr. who troubled star-watchers in the 1990s.[15] In the nationally circulated black press, the stance that people should be free to date and marry whomever they like coexists with the stance that blacks have a special obligation to seek black mates. Experts urge black women who are tempted to cross the color line to give older, younger, and lower-income black men a chance before giving up on the possibility of finding a suitable black mate.[16] The overall message of the black press seems to be that, intermarriage can work, but it is best for blacks who marry to "marry black," even if finding a black mate requires extra effort and sacrifice.

The story I am telling may be unfamiliar to my readers who are unfamiliar with one or another segment of African American society, including African-American readers whose exposure to black society has been limited by integration or an international upbringing. But it is a familiar enough *type* of story. Generalized into a story of intergroup intimacy conflicting with intra-group loyalty, the story I am telling is familiar as the basis of romantic tragedy, in Shakespeare's *Romeo and Juliet*, for example. Generalized into a story about a practice that is legal, but morally controversial, the story I am telling should be familiar to philosophers who write about issues such as abortion, capital punishment, and affirmative action. But whereas the ethical controversies about abortion, capital punishment and affirmative action have been repeatedly debated by mainstream professional philosophers in numerous books and articles, mixed marriage controversies have not. The case, it seems, is closed.

Case Closed

In the United States today we describe marriage as a private matter, and yet we see the justice of public regulation of marriage. It is only right that public laws should ban certain kinds of marriage – for example, incestuous marriage between children and adults.[17] The constitution has been interpreted to permit government to regulate marriage in the public interest. More than a hundred years ago, in *Reynolds* v. *United States*, the Supreme Court held that Mormon polygamy could be outlawed consistently with religious liberty and equality.[18] Some recent immigrants believe the law should be reformed to recognize polygamous unions formed abroad;[19] but the most ripe area for legal reform today is same-sex marriage. The constitutionality of laws prohibiting same-sex marriage has yet to be decided by the Supreme Court. Some gay and lesbian advocates of same-sex marriage fear the ghost of *Reynolds*, even as they fight for their *Loving* v. *Virginia*. In the meantime, a national conversation about same-sex marriage is ongoing in statehouses and courtrooms.[20]

There was once something of a national conversation about interracial marriage. Like today's conversation about gay and lesbian marriage, it was a conversation full of hate, prejudice, and biological misinformation.[21] At their best, discussions of interracial marriage focused on the demands of equality and privacy or the practical consequences of defying taboos and upsetting traditions. At their worst they focused on the supposed intellectual and moral inferiority of blacks. For blacks, the ban on interracial marriage had been seen as a powerful symbol of exclusion and inequality, particularly in the South where interracial sex was commonplace despite the ban on interracial marriage. As explained by legal historian A. Leon Higginbotham, the laws and customs of the South penalized blacks more severely than they penalized whites suspected of interracial sex.[22] The legal incapacity of white men to marry black women brought shame on black women who wanted to have sex with white men, and permitted white men to sexually exploit black women.

The national conversation about interracial marriage abruptly stopped when the Supreme Court handed down the *Loving* decision during the height of the civil rights movement. Although few blacks wanted to marry whites in 1967 and few had the opportunity, *Loving* seemed a fitting complement to the Civil Rights Act of 1964. Blacks had no reason to oppose the new marital freedom law, and whites who opposed the law were silenced by the finality of a Supreme Court decree that echoed the overall direction of national integration policy.

By the time respected journals such as *Philosophy and Public Affairs*, *Philosophical Forum* and *Ethics* emerged as consistent platforms for practical and applied ethics, the morality of interracial marriage had ceased to be a politically viable topic for analysis. Philosophers apparently thought there was good reason to oppose abortion after *Roe* v. *Wade*,[23] because abortion destroys human potential; affirmative action for diversity after *Bakke* v. *Regents*,[24] because diversity policies are amenable to characterization as unjust reverse discrimination; and anti-sodomy laws after *Bowers* v. *Hardwick*,[25] because such laws allow police to single out gay men for harassment. We can only assume, though, that philosophers did not think there were comparably good, publicly debatable reasons to oppose interracial marriage after *Loving*.

It does not follow from the premise that *Loving* was correctly decided as a matter of legal or moral justice, that there are no good reasons for questioning the morality of all or some interracial marriages. Many people believe the law justly permits individuals to choose abortion, even though they believe abortion is nearly always an immoral choice. Many blacks believe the law justly permits interracial marriage, even though (they believe) interracial marriage is nearly always a morally irresponsible choice. In fact, interracial marriage raises a number of important moral questions about the requirements of self-respect and group membership. African Americans (and other minority group members, I might add) actively and routinely struggle with questions

about the morality of out-marriage premised on group-specific obligations of solidarity and care.[26]

Although I understand the prudential basis of philosophers' reserve,
philosophers who support *Loving* as just law should not have been,
and should not be, reluctant to acknowledge the moral issues it left
behind. In a democratic society founded on deliberative ideals,[27] there
are good and plentiful reasons meaningfully to acknowledge the moral
issues left behind after a major legal pronouncement. In some
instances, to grapple with the moral issues left behind is simply an
important way of acknowledging the ethical lives of the millions of
fellow citizens with whom one shares responsibility for democratic
government. Understanding how blacks view interracial marriage is
of practical value to understanding blacks' evaluation of criminal
defendants, political candidates, judicial nominees, workplace dating
bans, adoption policies, the rate of black male incarceration, and
artistic depictions of black life.[28]

Segregation as Community Builder

Segregation by race perpetuates cultural differences that impair the
formation of personal and intimate relationships among blacks and
whites who might otherwise live, work or attend school together.[29]
Segregation slows the dissolution of old animosities between the races.
Segregation sustains prejudice and stereotyping. Past and present
racial segregation helps to explain both the low rate of black out-
marriage, and the moral qualms blacks feel about out-marriage to
whites.

Because public accommodations and workplaces are often racially
integrated, it is easy to overlook the fact that blacks and whites live
substantially segregated lives. In some areas of the country, residential
and school segregation is as extensive as it was prior to the Civil
Rights Act of 1964.[30] A 1997 survey of whites with school-age
children showed that 41 percent of whites would object to sending
their children to a school in which more than half the children were
black.[31] Overall, blacks of all social classes (poor, middle-class and
affluent) tend to live in segregated, virtually all black communities.[32]
Housing segregation by race is not a wholly voluntary pattern.[33]
Economic factors limit choice and mobility – you live where you can
afford to live. Fear that prejudice and racism will lead to violence

limits choice and mobility – you live where it is safe to live. Well-off blacks seek middle-class and affluent majority black communities, hoping thereby to achieve comfort, acceptance, and community – you live where you expect to flourish. Most American public school children attend schools that are virtually all white or all minority.[34] Schools are segregated because housing is segregated. Compounding the segregation in housing and schools, religious institutions and certain businesses (hair salons, funeral parlors) are often segregated by race.

Segregation is a cloud with a silver lining. Racial segregation based on appearance (skin color, facial features, hair texture, language etc.) or known ancestry (African, etc.) has contributed to the ability of blacks all over the United States to become a culturally vibrant population group. Black society has produced great music, visual art, entertainers, athletes, language styles, and cuisines. Many blacks have common interests, experiences, and viewpoints. Rich and poor blacks, rural and urban blacks, recent immigrant and slave-ancestry blacks feel a subjective affinity for one another despite radically different lifestyles and languages. Blacks use the terms "black community," "black culture," and "black society" to emphasize the matrix of cultural and historical ties binding a population group that is strikingly decentralized and diverse. Being part of the black community, culture, or society does not require any affirmative act of admission. If you have black African ancestry and North American roots or aspirations, you belong. You belong even if one of your parents is not black, and even if you grew up in a white neighborhood or in a white adoptive or foster home. Many African Americans treat black society, which would include their extended families, as where they come from: their community of origin.

A sense of belonging to the African-American community is the basis of attributions of obligation. Philosophers will recall the conception of having special obligations to one's community of origin found in Plato's *Crito*.[35] Socrates was about to be put to death for allegedly corrupting the youth of Athens. When good friends offered him an opportunity to escape from prison and live safely abroad, Socrates refused. He argued that he owed a debt of gratitude to his community of origin for all it had done for him, and that that debt meant he could not turn his back on the community when it wrongly adjudicated him to be a criminal. Moreover, Socrates argued, a disobedient escape from prison would set a bad example to the young, rendering him guilty in fact of the crime of which he was accused. Unlike Athens, the black community is not a geographically situated polity with its own systems of laws. Nonetheless, many blacks feel an obligation to the black community analogous to the obligation Socrates felt toward Athens: an obligation to further the group's collective welfare and to yield to its collective judgments, even when that means foregoing personal liberties and sharing resources. I know blacks who deny having any special obligations to black community, but whose behavior towards other blacks suggests that they are constrained by implicit acceptance of a kind of "second order" obligation to respect the fact that other blacks extend community membership to them.

Why Interracial Marriage Is a Moral Issue

To take African Americans' ethical critique of out-marriage seriously, one must try to understand its implicit premises. As I shall interpret it, the critique is premised on the belief that membership in the black community imposes moral obligations, including obligations about the choice of intimate partners. These obligations are unassumed, non-voluntary obligations.[36] Three very general moral imperatives appear to lie behind disapproval of out-marriage: (1) respect and care for your community of origin; (2) respect and care for your family and friends; (3) respect and care for yourself. I will try to elaborate each imperative, invoking the considerations that African-American critics of interracial marriage put forward. Following my elaboration of each imperative, I will go on, in the next section, to explain why I believe African Americans should view marriages between blacks and whites as moral challenges rather than moral mistakes.

Respect and care for your community of origin

As previously observed, many African Americans view themselves as constituting a community. The community in question is not a geographical one, narrowly conceived, because blacks who live hundreds and thousands of miles apart belong to the same community. The community is constituted by cultural and historical affinities that exist whether or not individual blacks attach meaning to them. Loyalty and solidarity, evidenced through involvement with, or participation in, the community is one of the obligations imposed by the black community on blacks.

In general, it is wrong to turn one's back on one's community. We have seen this principle at work among members of the ethnic minority groups "cleansed" from their homelands in Eastern Europe. This ethical notion is strongly held in the United States, sometimes adduced to justify capital punishment for traitors and compulsory military service. Other applications of the notion would justify demands for community service of lesser proportions, such as contributing time and money to charity or holding public office. Opponents of out-marriage construe it as turning one's back on one's community. To in-marry is to validate the community by acknowledging that it can provide one with people of character, beauty, and resources suitable for the intimate relationships most vital to flourishing. To in-marry is to validate the community by signaling an intent to perpetuate the community through childbearing and child-rearing. To in-marry is to be an involved participant in the community through central life activities.

What then does it mean to out-marry? Focusing on the obligations of black men to date black women and utilizing metaphors of war, psychology professor Dr Halford Fairchild summed up the respect-and-care-for-one's-community-based objection to interracial marriage with unusual passion:

> I feel it is irresponsible for Black men to cross date in today's day and time . . . It's nice to date whom you want, to say that all is equal, but life is not equal. Black people are defined as inferior and put in second class status. We must recognize our debt to each other. For Black men to date and marry White women in the face of our lingering debt to each other is irresponsible. The brother has sold out. We have a responsibility to each other. We are under siege. We are at war. To sleep with the enemy is treason, racial treason.[37]

To out-marry is to express disappointment with the human products of one's community, to deny the worthiness of perpetuating one's culture and to reject the significance of community loyalty and solidarity.

Respect and care for your family and friends

Intimate friends and family ties are of special importance to most people. Moreover, in a society in which government presupposes the existence of family networks to provide childcare, sick-care, and elder care, family members may need us, as well as want us. One ought therefore to build a life that includes one's parents, siblings, and other kin. One should avoid designing a life that distances rather than brings together; that hurts rather than pleases; that introduces stresses and tensions into settings that have the potential, otherwise, for uninhibited devotion. It is one thing to go to college and to work with people of all races, but to introduce the political divisions and social division present elsewhere in the society into the home and family is a mistake, particularly if one will thereby loose one's capacity to be an effective member of the family. To in-marry is to signal a willingness to remain involved; to not shift cultural alliances; to not distance oneself.

To out-marry is to invite distance and division. Out-marriage can cause complications that separate a person from his or her family and friends:

> Research and personal accounts indicate that interracial couples experience considerable hostility in the workplace, in their social lives and even in their extended families. And Black/White marriages are more likely to face prejudice than other interracial pairings.[38]

We marry to meld worlds, hoping the whole will be greater than or equal to the sum of its parts. Melded lives can bring a bounty of new kinship, friendships, and holiday celebrations. But if friends and families resist a spouse who is a cultural outsider, or if prejudice and xenophobia abound, interracial couples may find that they are socially diminished, rather than enlarged by their marriages. The result can be a melded life together that feels like a net loss.

The loss of society that can come from interracial marriages is not a result of the behavior and attitudes of persons exogenous to the relationship. A white person married to a black person may feel uncomfortable around blacks other than his or her beloved spouse, including his or her beloved's black family and friends; *mutatis mutandis*, a black person married to a white person. Suppose a white professional man joins through marriage an African American family that includes, as they often do, siblings of vastly dissimilar education and employment: a welfare mom, a doctor, and a marine. He marries the sibling who is a doctor. If the white spouse is from a solidly upper middle-class segregated white background, he may be quite unable to relate to the welfare mom and the marine, let alone the father who never went to college, the cousin just released from prison, and the aunt who "shouts" in church. White men also may have trouble understanding the sense of responsibility their successful black partners may feel with respect to family members in addition to her own children, siblings and parents. Whites may not understand extended family loyalties that extend far down the kinship chain to nieces and nephews, to great aunts, and even to "play" cousins or "play" aunts. Even blacks and whites of the same income group and professional class may find that they bring to the marriage inconsistent culturally specific social expectations. The ideal of melded lives may be impossible for some interracial couples to approximate. Thanks to rampant segregation, to out-marry is to invite conflict, stress, and disappointment.

Respect and care for yourself

One ought to love oneself. It is wrong to be ashamed of what you are and to devalue your own immutable characteristics. These are important ethical ideas. For some blacks, to in-marry is to announce pride in their racial heritage. It is to announce that "I have no problems with my color, my nose, my lips, my shape, my hair, nor with similar traits in others." In-marriages announce that, "Should I choose to bear children, I will be glad to pass on my African traits." To in-marry is to demand and get the best for oneself – namely, a partner who can easily comprehend one's value, humor, and needs. To out-marry is to imply a need for white approval and validation; regret about what one is; and aversion to the traits one would pass on to offspring were one to in-marry and bear children. It does not appear that African Americans believe whites and blacks are incapable of loving one another. But I have heard blacks suggest that blacks who marry whites are selling themselves short. (This suggestion often is made about the attractive, affluent blacks who become intimately involved with what are considered less attractive or affluent whites.) To out-marry is to sell oneself short by giving up the opportunity to share one's life with a true peer, someone capable of deep, culturally-based understanding of who one is and what one values.

Defending Interracial Marriage

How does one reply to the powerful moral concerns African Americans raise against interracial marriage? "That's private!" would be a poor response, ignoring rather than engaging the claims of community debt African Americans make with respect to one another. Liberals respond inadequately, therefore, if they reply simply that everyone has a right to marry whomever he or she wants to, racial difference notwithstanding. You love who you love and isn't it great when love defies segregation! Some African Americans who choose white spouses undoubtedly do so feeling morally justified by just the kind of liberal considerations cited. They feel their autonomous, legal choice of spouse is no one's business. They may even feel that they are doing America a favor.

Liberals do better who acknowledge the practical adversities interracial couples face and cause, but stress the ideals of romantic love and toleration that interracial marriages often instantiate. Because so many African Americans embrace the seemingly unliberal notions that race is a basis of community and community a source of unassumed obligations of solidarity and care, I want to try and frame a response to the case against out-marriage that reconciles interracial marriages between blacks and whites with black community-centered concerns about respect and care. I believe interracial intimacy and out-marriage can be defended within a framework that takes seriously (without necessarily sharing) African-American concerns and values relating to communities of origin.

First, interracial marriage is consistent with the principle of respecting and caring for the black community. Interracial marriage would not be consistent with this important principle if the practice were intended to injure blacks or in fact injured blacks. Black/white out-marriage is a product of integrated association rather than of efforts to harm, demean, or offend blacks. Interracial intimacy is normally the product of living, working, or playing in desegregated environments. If people from different racial communities are thrown together, despite overall segregated housing and social patterns, a few will form attachments to people of other races. Many middle-

and upper middle-class blacks live in majority white neighborhoods, and work in majority white environments. Many blacks in the military raise families in multicultural and international settings. As young adults, many blacks who have led heretofore segregated lives attend majority white colleges and universities, and undertake fields of study that are populated mainly by whites and other non-blacks. Extensive contact with whites in these contexts can result in close friendships, sexual attraction, and a desire to marry.[39]

Second, interracial marriages have not rendered black cultural life less vital. This is partly because out-marriage has not shown signs of ending the pervasive segregation that regenerates black cultural life, and partly because blacks who out-marry make contributions to the black community comparable to those they would have made in any case. Out-marriage is always evidence that segregation has been ineffective. Those who come into contact with happy out-marriages may be moved towards greater racial tolerance. And yet out-marriage – still rare when viewed as an overall percentage of black marriage – has done little to change the fact of pervasive segregation. Indeed, a black woman married to a white man may end up living as the only black in a white community, or a white woman married to a black man, may wind up as the only white in a circle of blacks. Blacks who out-marry are not thereby lost to the black community, even if they do come to reside in majority white neighborhoods. Some of the most prominent contributors to African-American art, culture, politics and social life have been married to whites or are products of interracial marriages.[40] Indeed Marion Wright Edelman, the best known children's advocate in the United States is an African-American woman married to a white lawyer she met while working as a civil rights lawyer in the South.[41] The offspring of mixed marriages typically identify themselves as blacks and are more likely to be black identified or bi-cultural than to be black outsiders. Mindful of the moral concerns I am discussing, blacks who out-marry may possess active fears about being lost to the community that lead them to eagerly embrace opportunities for contributing to the black community through their employment, volunteer work or philanthropy.

Some of the moral opposition to black out-marriage is based on the presumption that out-marriage signals a deficit of black identity that will naturally lead to a diminished willingness to be involved as participants in black life. Blacks who marry whites may live in majority white neighborhoods and come to take on some of the external affects or lifestyles associated with European America. But this says nothing about their core identities. They may have strong black identities. Identity issues are real among African Americans who live in isolation from other blacks. I believe it is possible for a black person to wish she were white, "act white," and even to forget that she is black;[42] but these possibilities result from integrated life-styles that can be a product of black wealth, military service, and residential or schooling choices, unrelated to out-marriage.

The fear of genocide through interracial marriage is an important dimension of blacks' moral preferences for in-marriage. The consequences of interracial sex and marriages pressured the federal government to change its still clumsy racial categorization practices on the decennial census forms;[43] but interracial marriages have done nothing at all to water down African-American culture or to erode the existence of a distinct population group. Could it some day? Suppose over time there came to be fewer people in the United States with distinctively visible African features and ancestries because of interracial procreation. This development alone would not signal the end of an African-American community or culture.

Segregation and in-marriage have, without a doubt, made African-American culture the rich and distinct culture that it is. The continued existence of an African-American culture (or a series of African-American subcultures) is not dependent upon the perpetuation of a group of people who will forever look substantially different from whites and non-white minorities. There could be pride enough for a joyous Black History Month celebration even though what it meant to be African American no longer had substantially to do with skin color, facial features, and curl patterns. The existence of an Irish-American culture is not mainly dependent upon the ability to tell, on the basis of appearance alone, who is Irish. African-American culture and community will die out, not if blacks become tan or beige, but instead, if blacks cease to identify with one another on the basis of common interests and heritage. Whether interracial marriage makes loss of common identity significantly more likely is hard to say. Clearly, all African Americans, not only the small number who out-marry, must take some responsibility for preserving worthwhile cultural products and institutions. For those who out-marry, meeting this responsibility may be more difficult, and in that respect, represent a special moral challenge. Overcoming obstacles to black community participation erected by blacks hostile towards out-marrying fellow blacks and their families is part of the special challenge.

The obligation of respect and care for family and friends, and the obligation of respect and care for self are not addressed by claims that interracial unions do not destroy black identity and erode the basis of vital community life. The ultimately stronger arguments against interracial marriage may be those that focus on the harm to the interracial couple and their families. Interracial marriage is clearly a moral challenge for the individuals who choose it and for their families. African Americans value romantic love and obligations to respect the romantic choices and aspirations of family members and friends. When the love object is of another race, those obligations do not go away. Reciprocal obligations of respect and care suggests that the marrying couple will need to take measures to accommodate the reasonable concerns and emotional needs of family members, and family members will have to take steps to accommodate the reason-able concerns and emotional needs of the marrying couple.

Romantic love is typified by a placement of the object of love at the center of the universe: nothing and no one matter more than the beloved. Inflicting emotional pain and depriving needy people of emotional and financial support in violation of settled expectations are moral injuries, whether resulting from interracial marriage or other intentional acts. The *Guess Who's Coming to Dinner* model of interracial marriage is insensitive and irresponsible. Under this model, one springs (or inflicts) a new spouse or fiancée on unsuspecting families and lets the chips fall where they may.[44] This approach may serve only to exacerbate the moral challenges ahead. Every person, family, and relationship is a little different. Interracial marriage will be a morally acceptable choice in some situations, and the morally optimal choice in others. Interracial marriage is a morally bad choice for people who have good reason to believe the marriage will not work because they or their spouse would be permanently or substantially isolated from their families and friends as a result of their marriage.

Folk Ethics and Philosophical Inclusion

The example of black/white interracial marriage illustrates three key points I would like to make about the limitations of academic moral philosophy. First, moral issues that are quite central to one group may be peripheral to another group in the same city, state, and nation. Indeed, one of the ways in which a culture is defined is by reference to its core concerns and controversies. We can speak of African-American culture, Korean-American culture, Jewish culture, and so on, in part because there are people – blacks, Koreans, Jews – worrying about different things over tables heaped with different kinds of foods. The late philosopher Richard Brandt once wrote a book about Hopi ethics. In general, American moral philosophers have shied away from particularistic ethical studies.

Second, to the extent that moral philosophers rigidly devote themselves to what they consider "classical" problems, "universal" principles, and "major" national issues, they preserve a divide between the discipline of ethics and real, lived ethics – folk ethics, if you will. There are problems we have that we share with Socrates and Mill; but we have unique problems and variations on unique problems that merit elaboration. One adverse consequence of the neglect of folk ethics is a loss of opportunities for cultural self-understanding, and cultural cross-engagement in scholarship and teaching. Another may be the loss of opportunities to forge distinctly American ethical philosophies.

Third, there may be a relationship between the openness of philosophy to explorations of ethical perspectives that not all groups share and the racial diversification of the field. The number of African Americans seeking advanced degrees in philosophy is small compared to the numbers seeking degrees in law, medicine, education, communication, engineering, psychology, English, and history. I have heard it speculated that blacks reject philosophy because they are not interested in (or competent at) subjects at its core like logic or metaphysics. I believe African Americans would be more interested in (and competent at) mastering the foundations of philosophy, including logic and metaphysics, if they expected the hard climb beyond the foundations to be worth the energy expended.

My (admittedly) limited experience suggests that some African Americans' keen interest in moral matters (aspects of moral justice, for example) is dulled by philosophy teachers who will not or cannot engage *their* issues. To overcome this problem, we might encourage young blacks to approach their foundational studies in philosophy and the standard ethics curriculum with a sense of play, as intellectual gamesmanship, waiting for the day when they will be able to make a unique and heartfelt mark on the field. I have not had much luck with such encouragement. Gamesmanship (and anything that looks like gamesmanship) may lack appeal to those who come to philosophy urgently in search of greater understanding of self and society, understanding they believe they need to navigate the university and the world with their sanity, dignity, and intelligence intact. Introducing African-American and other folk ethics into standard philosophy curricula could be helpful in attempts to diversity and extend the reach of the discipline.

The significance of interracial marriage to African Americans was my starting place and focus, but it has become clear that the reasons African Americans have reservations about interracial marriage, will pertain to other groups as well. In the "folk ethics" of particular groups, something of the universal obtains. When a Jewish friend told me she would not consider marrying a non-Jew, I knew exactly what she meant: she does not trust Gentile men, just as some of my black women friends do not trust white men. Out-marriage is an issue for many minority group members and many whites, too.[45] When moral qualms about out-marriage are based on controversial notions such as the existence of non-assumed obligations following from group membership, even the most traditional philosophers should stand up and take notice. Academic philosophy – both teaching and research – will be enriched by expanding the portals to incorporate distinctly minority perspectives on major social and political institutions. If people of color are to "do" philosophy, philosophers must be willing to "do" people of color. When we give minorities' issues their due we dignify them as moral agents with morally and intellectually significant lives. We increase our capacity to understand perspectives that may bear on public life. At the same time, we give everyone a chance to see how general philosophical problems play out in actual, living human societies.

Notes

1 *Loving* v. *Virginia*, 388 US 1 (1967). The case concerned a white man and a black woman who returned to their home state of Virginia after getting married in the District of Columbia. Once back in Virginia, the Lovings were convicted of violating a Virginia statute that criminalized marriages between blacks and whites. The Lovings' pleaded guilty and

were sentenced to a year in jail. The criminal trial court suspended the sentence on the condition that the couple agreed to leave Virginia. A 1996 film, *Mr and Mrs Loving*, tells their story.

2   Interracial marriages "skyrocketed by more than 800 percent" between 1960 and 1990 (Michael Lind, "The Beige and the Black," *New York Times Magazine*, August 16, 1998, pp. 38–9). US Bureau of Census, *Current Population Reports*, show 1,260,000 interracial married couples (all races) in 1996 and 651,000 (all races) in 1980. See note 4, below.

3   In discussing interracial marriage here, I will use "African American" and "black" as synonyms. Of course, some blacks residing in the United States are not American by birth, but recent arrivals from countries in Africa, such as South Africa, Ghana, or Nigeria, or from other countries with black populations, such as France, Great Britain, Jamaica, or Haiti.

> Black-white marriages have risen from a reported 51,000 in 1960 (when they were still illegal in many states), to 311,000 in 1997. Marriages between white men and black women, though still uncommon, rose from 27,000 [*sic*] in 1980 to 122,000 in 1995. Although black out-marriage rates have risen, they remain much lower than out-marriage rates for Hispanics, Asians and American Indians. For the 25–34 age group, only 8 percent of black men marry outside their race. Less than 4 percent of black women do. (Michael Lind, "The Beige and the Black")

Lind got one of his numbers wrong. The actual number of marriages between white men and black women reported in US Bureau of the Census data for 1980 was 45,000, not 27,000. The number of black/ white interracial married couples nearly doubled between 1980 and 1996. See US Bureau of the Census, *Current Population Reports*, p. 20–4888, and earlier reports; and unpublished data, "No. 62. Married Couples of Same or Mixed Races and Origins: 1980 to 1996." According to Douglas Besharov and Timothy Sullivan, 10 percent of black men who marry now marry a white woman; and about 5 percent of black women who marry now marry a white man. See "Interracial Marriages Rise," *Michigan Chronicle*, 60/16 (1997), p. 8-D, citing research by Besharov and Sullivan unveiled in the July/August issue of *The New Democrat*. Their numbers are higher than most other authorities.

In the social science literature, marriage between persons belonging to different groups, including interracial marriage, is sometimes called "out-marriage," and between persons of the same group, "in-marriage." I will use the phrase "out-marriage" to mean marrying outside of one's ethnic, racial, or similar population group. In-marriage is a kind of "homogamy"; out-marriage, "hetergamy." Hypogamy is marriage to

200   *Anita L. Allen*

someone of a lower social status; hypergamy, marriage to someone of a higher social status. Hypogamy in black/white relationships is the focus of George A. Yancey and Sherelyn W. Yancey, "Black–White Differences in the Use of Personal Advertisements for Seeking Interracial Relationships," *Journal of Black Studies* 27/5 (1997), p. 650.

4   Philosophers who have questioned race and racial classification include Naomi Zack, *Race and Mixed Race* (Philadelphia: Temple University Press, 1993), and Anthony Appiah, who with political theorist Amy Gutman, wrote *Color Conscious: The Political Morality of Race* (Princeton, NJ: Princeton University Press, 1996). Social scientist Glen Loury is a well-known advocate of a "transracial humanism." See "Interracial Marriages Rise," *Michigan Chronicle* 60/16 (1997), p. 8-D, describing Loury's views.

The periodical *Interrace* is a forum for celebrating multiracial people and racially integrated families. See Laura Daniels, "Aren't They All Mixed Marriages," *Interrace* 8/2 (1997), p. 9. See also Traci Nelson, "Of Many Colors," *Interrrace* 43/16 (1998). The pages of *Interrace* exude optimism about the color-blind society. Not all commentators are optimistic that intermarriage will end pernicious color distinctions. See Lind, "The Beige and the Black," arguing that prejudice against blacks may lead to a "beige" majority and a black minority, rather than the uniformly intermixed "beige" society.

5   The black out-marriage rates have risen, but they remain significantly lower than the out-marriage rates for Hispanics, Asians, and American Indians. Among younger adults only 8 percent of black men and less than 4 percent of black women out-marry. See Lind, "The Beige and the Black," p. 38. According to Dr Larry E. Davis, *Black and Single* (New York: One World/Ballantine/Random House, 1998) the rate is 2 percent for African-American women, and 5 percent for African-American men, compared to 40 percent for Hispanic Americans and 60 percent for Asian Americans.

To summarize the various data cited in this paper, the percentage of black women of all ages who out-marry is between 2 and 5 percent; black men, between 5 and 10 percent.

6   "I, Thee, We, Them," *The Economist* 347/8073 (1998), p. 31 (Population of America report indicates that interracial marriage is still rare).

7   For white women the second leading stressor was housework (Richard Morin, "Unconventional Wisdom, New Facts and Hot Stats from the Social Sciences," *Washington Post*, June 29, 1997, p. C-05).

8   See Yanick St Jean, "Let People Speak for Themselves: Interracial Unions and the General Social Survey," *Journal of Black Studies* 28/398 (1998), p. 17; Yanick St Jean and Robert E. Parker, "Disapproval of Interracial Unions: The Case of Black Females," in Cardell K. Jacobson (ed.) *America Families: Issues in Race and Ethnicity* (New York: Garland Publishing,

1995), p. 344. Seeking to explain why black women disapprove marriages between whites and blacks, St Jean and Parker suggest that "in order to safeguard their reputation, women of color might overconform to expected rules of behavior and avoid engaging even in casual friendships with white males." They also suggest that "disapproval may be a . . . form of social protest, rather than pure conformity to societal rules." St Jean and Parker assessed data from a study in which 10.3 percent of black females over 35 and 10.26 percent of black women who were strongly religious said they favored laws banning intermarriage (p. 347). The same study showed more than 16 percent of black women without high school degrees favoring the ban! (p. 347) These striking numbers nonetheless corroborate my claim that most African Americans support the *Loving* decision, whatever their moral stand on interracial marriage.

Interracial marriage troubles some, but a study of factors in mate selection suggests that "nonracial factors are more important than racial factors for spouse selection." See Richard Lewis Jr., George Yancey, Siri S. Bletzer, "Racial and Nonracial factors that Influence Spouse Choice in Black/White Marriages," *Journal of Black Studies* 29/1 (1997), p. 60.

9 See Pamela S. Paset and Ronald D. Taylor, "Black and White Women's Attitudes Toward Interracial Marriage," *Psychological Reports* 69 (1991), pp. 753–4. See also Ben Gose, "Public Debate over a Private Choice," *Chronicle of Higher Education,* May 10, 1996, describing how black women at a major university created a "wall of shame" onto which they inscribed the names of blacks involved in intimate relationships with whites.

10 Cf. Davis, *Black and Single.* Davis asserts that "interracial dating is a topic that manages to stay in the forefront of Black romance." Davis thinks blacks spend too much time debating interracial intimacy, given the low rate of interracial marriage: "Given these realities, it would be a better use of the time we spend thinking about interracial dating to instead create greater life opportunities for Black people, and to expand our notions of the "acceptable" Black partner" (p. 175).

11 Spike Lee, *Jungle Fever* (Universal, 1991). The term "jungle fever" refers to the irrational interracial sexual attraction that stems from the sense of novelty and the exotic. Lee's film seems to express skepticism about whether typical black/white relationships can survive the "jungle fever" stage.

12 See Richard Morin, "Unconventional Wisdom, New Facts and Hot Stats from the Social Sciences," *Washington Post,* June 29, 1997, p. C-05. According to Morin, the Michigan study indicated that "better educated, higher income black women were more likely to say they were bothered by seeing an interracial couple." See also Lawrence Otis Graham, *Our Kind of People, Inside America's Black Upper Class* (New York: Harper-

Collins,1999), p. 15. Graham maintains that out-marriage is shunned by educated black elites. The traditional rule of thumb among black elites is, he says, "emulate them [whites], but don't marry them" (p. 15). But see Zhenchao Qian, "Breaking the Racial Barriers: Variations in Interracial Marriage Between 1980 and 1990," *Demography* 34/2 (1997), pp. 263–76, arguing that the odds of interracial marriage increase with couple's educational attainment. See also "News and Views: The Effect of Higher Education on Interracial Marriage," *Journal of Blacks in Higher Education*, June 30, 1997, p. 55, reporting that: "For black women, 3 percent of those who had only a high school education married nonblack men. But 5 percent of black women college graduates and 6 percent of black women with graduate degrees married outside their race."

13 *Jet* and *Ebony* are popular black-oriented "coffee table" magazines profiling African Americans in politics, entertainment, sports, and business. Several articles on the topic of interracial marriage have appeared in recent years in these magazines. See, e.g., "Why More Black Women Are Dating White Men," *Jet* 92/22 (1997), p. 12; "Why Interracial Marriages Are Increasing," *Jet* 90/3 (1996), p. 12; "New Survey Shows Attitudes More Open Toward Interracial Relationships," *Jet* 88/21 (1995), p. 22; "Black Men and White Women: What's Behind the Furor?," *Ebony* 50/1 (1994), p. 44.

14 An article on interracial unions in the *National Review* appears to have been influenced by the phenomenon of golfer Tiger Woods, the offspring of a marriage between an Asian and a black. Steve Sailer, "Is Love Color-Blind?," *National Review* 49/13 (1997), p. 30.

15 Black man/white woman relationships provoke greatest hostility. See "Black Men and White Women, What's Behind the Furor?" The interracial marriage of celebrity O. J. Simpson was much discussed during the pendency of his prosecution for his ex-wife's murder in the "trial of the century." When a jury dominated by black women acquitted Simpson, it was speculated that black women were unable to empathize with a white women married to an allegedly abusive black.

16 See the advice of Dr. Larry E. Davis, cited in note 10, above. But see Audrey Cobb, "Black Women Losing the Dating Game," *Jacksonville Free Press* 12/39 (1998), p. 3 ("Why are we told to marry down, when white women are not told the same thing? . . . I want to be in a relationship with someone who is an equal in every way – or someone I can learn something from.").

17 Leigh B. Bienen, "Defining Incest," *Northwest University Law Review* (1999), forthcoming.

18 *Reynolds* v. *United States*, 98 US 145 (1878).

19 Barbara Crosettes, "Testing the Limits of Tolerance as Cultures Mix: Does

Freedom Mean Accepting Rituals that Repel the West?" *New York Times*, March 6, 1999.

20 The most discussed case has been *Baehr* v. *Lewin* 852 P.2d 44 (DC Hawaii 1993), holding that a gay marriage ban may violate equal protection. But see *Dean* v. *District of Columbia*, 653 A.2d 307 (DC 1985) (same-sex couple may be denied marriage license).

21 William Eskridge, *The Case for Same-Sex Marriage* (New York: Free Press, 1996).

22 A. Leon Higginbotham, *In the Matter of Color: Race and the American Legal Process* (New York: Oxford University Press, 1978).

23 *Roe* v. *Wade*, 410 US 113 (1973).

24 *Bakke* v. *Regents of the University of California*, 438 US 265, 313 (1978).

25 *Bowers* v. *Hardwick*, 478 US 186 (1986).

26 Michael Sandel defends a "republican" vision of democratic life that embraces non-voluntary moral obligations to groups that are constitutive of a person's identity. See Michael J. Sandel, *Democracy's Discontent* (Cambridge, MA.: Harvard University Press, 1996).

27 Jon Elster, *Deliberative Democracy* (Cambridge: Cambridge University Press, 1998); Amy Gutman and Dennis Thompson, *Democracy and Disagreement* (Cambridge, MA.: Harvard University Press, 1996).

28 A black person opposed to interracial intimacy might have a harder time warming to a black candidate for office or the leadership of a black public official who is married to a non-black. – be he a Thurgood Marshall (his second wife was a Asian) or a Clarence Thomas (his wife is white).

29 The University of Michigan has compiled a series of helpful studies of American segregation and the impact of diversity in education in *The Compelling Need for Diversity in Higher Education*, a compilation of expert testimony by Thomas Sugrue, Eric Foner, Albert Camarillo, Patricia Gurin, William Bowen, Claude Steele, Derek Bok, Kent Syverud, and Robert Webster in *Gratz et al.* v. *Bollinger*, No. 97–75231 (E. D. Mich) and *Grutter et al.* v. *Bollinger et al.*, No. 97–75928 (E. D. Mich).

30 See the report by Thomas Sugrue et al., in *Compelling Need for Diversity*; *Gratz et al.* v. *Bollinger*, No. 97–75231 (E. D. Mich); *Grutter et al.* v. *Bollinger et al.*, No 97–75928 (E. D. Mich).

31 "Vital Signs: Statistics that Measure the State of Racial Equality," *Journal of Blacks in Higher Education*, September 30, 1997, p. 99. A Gallup Organization survey cited in this article reports that 61 percent of whites approve of interracial marriage, a dramatic change since 1958 when only 4 percent approved. Although whites say they approve interracial marriage many prefer not to live in the same neighborhoods as blacks and to send their children to schools with a small percentage of blacks or with no blacks.

32   Ibid.

33   See the report by Thomas Sugrue et al., in *Compelling Need for Diversity*; *Gratz et al. v. Bollinger*, No. 97–75231 (E. D. Mich); *Grutter, et al. v. Bollinger*, et al. No 97–75928 (E. D. Mich).

34   Ibid.

35   Plato, *Crito*, in *Plato: Collected Dialogues*, ed. Edith Hamilton (Princeton: Princeton University Press, 1963). Socrates makes a number of arguments to Crito, including one that bases obligation on implicit consent. Socrates tells Crito that were he to escape, fellow Athenians could say that he was "breaking covenants and undertakings" (p. 38). However Socrates also relies on the argument the community presents him with: that he is bound by the expectations of his community simply because it is his community; "you were our child and servant, both you and your ancestors" (p. 36). It is this reciprocity/identity strand, rather than the more dominant consent/contract strand in the argument for loyalty to the community that I emphasize here.

36   See Michael Sandel, *Democracy's Discontent*.

37   See "Black Men and White Women, What's Behind the Furor?"

38   Ibid.

39   Surveys suggest that military service greatly enhances the prospects for interracial marriage. About 14 percent of black men and 10 percent of black women who serve in the military marry non-blacks. See "News and Views: The Effect of Higher Education on Interracial Marriage," p. 55.

40   F. James Davis, *Who is Black?* (University Park, PA.; Pennsylvania State University, 1991).

41   Marion Wright Edelman heads the Children's Defense Fund, in Washington, DC. She and her husband Peter Edelman have three high-achieving sons. See Mary McCory, "Voting with Conscience, and Feet," *Washington Post*, September 17, 1996, p. A2; Barbara Kessler, "Jonah Edelman," *Dallas Morning News*, March 23, 1997, p. 1.J.

42   Anita L. Allen, "Forgetting Yourself," in *Feminists Rethink the Self*, ed. Diana Meyers (Boulder, CO: Westview Press, 1996).

43   Steven A. Holmes, "People Can Claim One or More Races on Federal Forms," *New York Times*, p. A.1, col. 1, October 30, 1997. The year 2000 national census forms will permit respondents to identify themselves as belonging to one or more racial population groups, and then to indicate whether they are Hispanic. In the 1990 census, respondents were permitted to choose a single racial category, even if they were biracial or mixed race.

44   In this major Hollywood film, whose title reflects the premise of social segregation, a beautiful young white woman decides to marry a handsome black physician and springs him on her shocked upper-class

parents; the black doctor similarly surprises his parents. The film was released in 1967 and starred Katherine Hepburn, Spencer Tracy, and Sidney Poitier.

45 Cf. David Fowler, *Northern Attitudes Towards Interracial Marriage* (New York: Garland Press, 1987).

PART 3

New Directions

CHAPTER 9

Asian Women: Invisibility, Locations, and Claims to Philosophy

YOKO ARISAKA

Introduction

"Asian women" is an ambiguous category; it seems to indicate a racial as well as a cultural designation. The number of articles or books on "being Asian" or "Asian American" is on the rise in other disciplines, but in comparison to the material on black or Hispanic identities, Asians are largely missing from the field of philosophy of race. Things Asian in philosophy are generally reserved for those who study Asian philosophy or comparative philosophy, but that focus usually excludes reflections on Asian identities as such. This lack in the literature prompted me to start my own reflection with such questions as: Why do Asians not take an active interest in discourse on race? What does the category "Asian" designate? What contributes to their invisibility in general? Is this a stereotype? Are they simply "white-identified?" Are Asians responsible for their own invisibility, or is there some other factor? What is the relation between Asian philosophy and being Asian, if any? Is there any interesting connection between being Asian and being feminist? As a Japanese woman philosopher who is also interested in feminism, these questions seemed natural. This paper is an attempt to clarify some of these issues in the light of my experience working in the profession of academic philosophy.

I begin by analyzing the possible contributing factors of Asian invisibility as a cultural phenomenon, in the first three sections. In the first section, I dissect the category "Asian" and show that it cannot serve as a basis for an identity because of its inherently fragmented meaning. The first contributing factor to invisibility is thus the very category of "Asian" itself. However, beyond fragmentation, the term "Asian" does seem to indicate a set of certain cultural characteristics which is often stereotyped. Thus in the second section I focus on the the cultural elements within the Confucian tradition. I have chosen Confucianism not only because that is the tradition I am familiar with, but also because I believe that if anything is responsible for the *cultural* stereotype of being "Asian," Confucianism is. Confucianism contributes to it in a way that exacerbates the problem of invisibility, especially for women. The third section discusses the broader historical context of Eurocentrism and Orientalism which further contribute to the problem of invisibility. Both moves objectify the "Asian" as the "other," thereby rendering it inessential. Combined with the Confucian virtues which favor passivity, service, and harmony, Asian *women* are thus "doubly feminized."

Following these discussions on the various aspects of the problem of invisibility, in the fourth section I analyze how these ideas relate to the academic discipline of philosophy, in particular the claims regarding what counts as "real" philosophy, since it is in this context that the question of being Asian, or Asian philosophy, often becomes an issue. I analyze the rather common contradiction in the discipline between a broad self-conception ("metaphysics, ethics, epistemology, etc., are all proper philosophical inquiries") and the simultaneous exclusion of particular schools of thought (e.g., "Asian philosophy is not really philosophy"), even though these schools manifestly engage in the "proper" inquiries. I relate the possible grounds of such exclusionary claims to the positioning of Asian philosophy in the discipline. In the concluding section, I address the issue of "including Asian women" in the context of multiculturalism, feminism, and philosophy.

"Asian" as a Category?

Asia covers a vast geographical area encompassing the following: in the north and the north-east, Mongolia, parts of Russia, Korea, Japan, China, and Taiwan; in the south and the south-east, the Philippines, Malaysia, Thailand, Indonesia, Vietnam, Cambodia, Laos, Singapore, and Myanmar (Burma); and the Indian subcontinent and the surrounding countries of Sri Lanka, Bangladesh, Nepal, Bhutan, Tibet, Pakistan and Afghanistan.[1] It includes numerous languages, ethnic traditions, religious practices, and national historiographies. Some of these traditions share very little with one another, others have been in direct conflict for centuries. There are vast differences in the degree to which the regions are westernized or modernized. Sometimes the intra-Asian differences are greater than the so-called "East – West" differences.[2] Needless to say, there is little unity; the only thing which brings any of these cultural traditions together is the fact that they are located in certain parts of the Earth.

If by "Asian" we mean individuals from any of these regions or nations, then the use of the term is perhaps not too controversial as a description. However, that is usually not the sense in which the category is used or understood. "Asian" is supposed to be a racial, ethnic, or cultural category indicating in some vague sense "non-white." (The color of choice is yellow or brown, to which are added physical features involving short stature, slanted eyes, and straight, black hair.)[3] "Asian" is also "non-Christian," which may mean innocuously Buddhist or Hindu. But often, "Asian" means "heathen," "barbaric," or "evil." "Asian" is also "non-western," which is to say "eastern" or "oriental" (with the sense of distance, opacity, insignificance, or at best, exoticism). The connotations of the category "Asian" are often used in combination, and they are often problematic, especially when used in conjunction with "women."

When "Asian Americans" are classified together with those who are from Asia (the "first-generation Asians" or "Asian Asians") under the category of "Asian," then the term is used predominantly to indicate a racial grouping.[4] People are often classified in terms of racial appearance and grouped together by its perceived similarity. This is why, for instance, many people might assume at first sight that a first-generation white Argentinean immigrant is more "American" than a third-generation Chinese American, although the opposite is likely to be true. There might be nothing in common between a 19-year-old third-generation Korean-American woman growing up in the suburbs of Los Angeles listening to hip-hop and a 60-year-old Malaysian woman who has lived in the US for three months, but they are both "Asian females." Obviously, however, from the standpoint of culture, these women share little. Many Asian Americans speak only English, especially if they are third- or fourth-generations, and have little knowledge of Asia. They learn about Asia in the same way other American children learn about it. Those who come from Asia, on the other hand, learn English as a second language, experience "America" as a foreign country (often with the expectation that it is the "best in the West") and struggle to make sense of it as immigrants, long-term residents, or visitors. To this extent, "Asian" and "Asian American" are indeed distinct categories, although often they are conflated because of the supposed racial unity implied by the term.[5]

The sense of "Asian" as "non-Christian" is perhaps outdated today, but it is a part of racist cultural experience of the United States. For instance, Chandra Mohanty notes that during the era of "yellow peril," the "morality of Asian women" was used as a basis of exclusion under US immigration policies.[6] The ideology of "yellow peril" was of course used extensively during WWII, the Korean and Vietnam Wars, and in the 1970s in American relations with China before Nixon re-established diplomatic relations. The depiction of "sneaky, evil Orientals" in the early 1960s James Bond movies (*Dr. No*) portray them as immoral technocrats out to destroy the world.[7] Such a depiction preyed on xenophobia about "Godless" ones, and while it often targeted Communism, there was something especially menacing about the Asian version.

Asian women today continue to be stereotyped as "sex slaves," "man-pleasers" or "playthings," who are passive and lacking moral character. For many American servicemen who served in the Pacific War, Korean War, or in Vietnam, their first or only exposure to women in Asia was in the context of prostitution near overseas bases.[8] These associations of Asian women with sexual pleasure as "corrupt" or morally "dangerous" are often made by those who have puritan sensibilities.[9] The sense that Asia is definitely the uncivilized "other" is often rooted in the fact that except for the Philippines and to some extent Korea,[10] the dominant cultures in Asia are not Judaeo-Christian. That is a cause of suspicion in cultures which conflate moral sensibilities with religious beliefs.

When the term "Asian" is used in conjunction with a broader historical, cultural, or intellectual category, as in "Asian philosophy," "Asian religion," "Asian art," or "Asian food," then often "Asian" is supposed to indicate one of the "non-western" elements on the multicultural map; in this sense the connotation usually excludes "Asian American." At first sight this use of the term may appear rather neutral, as in the case of designating a geographical region, but it raises a threefold problem. First, when the term is combined with a further classification such as "philosophy," "religion," "art," or "food," then there are as many philosophies, religions, arts, and kinds of food as there are varied traditions and practices all over Asia, even within a seemingly unified region such as Japan. One really would have to specify a particular kind of philosophy, food, etc., and the general designation of "Asian" becomes rather empty. Second, be it literature, food, or religion, the broad category of "Asian," when displayed alongside other ethnic categories such as African, Hispanic, or Native American, gives people the false sense that they have understood something about Asia, when in fact no such category is adequate. This is a version of the trap which Stanley Fish calls "boutique multiculturalism."[11] Diversity is for the consumption of those who feel they should be knowledgeable about "other cultures" – though superficially – much as they enjoy ethnic restaurants. Third, and most seriously, the notion of "non-western" is often not neutral but heavily normative in a way that favors being "western" as the measure of legitimacy. So, if "Asian" is supposed to mean "non-western," then it is not an innocent designation. This is the problem of Eurocentrism, and it is this use of the term which becomes problematic in the understanding of "Asian philosophy." I will return to this point.

In sum, upon examination, the category of "Asian" is often either racist or it simply falls apart, much like other essentializing categories such as "woman," "Hispanic," or "poor people." "Asian" does not cover a politically unified racial platform, culture, linguistic group, class, or tradition. Most immigrants from Asia tend to identify themselves with particular national identities ("I am Taiwanese") or ethnic groups ("Hmongs" or "Sherpas"). Many Asian Americans claim a specific ethnic background to the exclusion of others ("I am *Chinese* American, not Japanese!"). Moreover, intra-Asia conflicts, such as between Korea and Japan, Tibet and China, or Indonesia and East Timor, are often so hostile that the idea of being put together in one group may be passionately resisted. This fragmentation results in the invisibility of the category of "Asian," especially among the immigrants. In fact, "Asian" is often not a category at all in the discourse on race, which is most visibly demarcated in terms of black and white.

Yet the term has practical or political applications, such as establishing academic departments (Asian Studies) and forming a group for strategic purposes such as economic empowerment (pan-Asian organizations) or fighting against racism. Moreover, most people, including people from Asia as well as Asian Americans, do have a sense that the term has some vaguely unified cultural meaning. But beyond vague generalizations, is there any recognizable content? And if so, how does it operate in our social consciousness?

Cultural Elements

The stereotype of Asians (in whichever sense one may take it) includes the idea that they are docile, withdrawn, and happily resigned to the status quo, never challenging or demanding anything. As a result, although racism against people of Asian descent is an unending reality, politically they are often either ignored, unrecognized, or worse, praised as the well-assimilating model minority. The so-called positive stereotyping of Asians exacerbates the problem; they are "studious," "smart," "cooperative," "hard-working," and therefore do not require protection. Many of them are middle-class, have access to education (sometimes better than that of whites) and are in other respects "privileged." They are perceived to be doing just fine without receiving special attention, just like all the other middle-class Americans. If they are assimilated, they are invisible as a group in the dominant culture as well as to the oppositional, "racial minority" cultures.

There are other cultural factors which contribute to invisibility. Some of these are psychological (or "internal") and these are especially pertinent to women. Others are sociological (or "external").[12] In addition to the complexity of being Asian, the category of "woman" or "women" has its own history of contested meanings. I need not review here the history of feminist thought, but there is one relevant way in which the category of "Asian women" is stereotyped, which is related to the connotation and use of the term "Asian" in general and contributes especially to the invisibility of Asian women.

Let me focus on the Confucian tradition to illustrate how it has helped form the Asian stereotype. This is the dominant cultural tradition in countries such as Korea, Japan, Taiwan, Singapore, and among Chinese immigrants who often become the dominant class in other parts of Asia and elsewhere. For both men and women, the ideals of Confucian virtue include "obeying authority," "yielding to others," "always making sure the others' needs are met first," "never calling attention to yourself," "one should always know one's place," and "he who speaks out destroys the harmony." In addition to these general human virtues of *jen*, or "humanity," Confucianism designates gendered virtues (such as a wife's duty to her husband, a son's duty to his parents) in explicitly patriarchal ways.[13] These ideals are very much a part of the culture in these countries, in the same sense that Christianity or individualism is a part of the culture in the US, permeating through gender, class, and race. For the sake of brevity and for my purposes, let me use the term "Asian" in the remainder of this section as designating "those whose living culture is based on the Confucian tradition."

The images of obedience, respect, and orderliness, when combined with women's position in the tradition, contribute to the stereotype of Asian women as docile, obedient, quiet, intuitive, or timid. The Asian female stereotype is either a character exhibiting passivity or the sexualized, exotic image (there is no middle ground). In other words, the designations of the traditional notions of femininity and Asianness more or less coincide; an outspoken, aggressive, independent Asian woman (or a man) is definitely seen as an unwelcome exception, so "un-Asian," even a threat or embarrassment, among many women themselves in Confucian Asia.[14]

For instance, for many women in Japan even today, maintaining Confucian virtues of "self-effacement," "harmony with others," and "enjoying the presence of silence and quietude" is an ethical as well as aesthetic way of life, often regarded even as an ideal in the sense used in virtue ethics.[15] It may be false consciousness (as I often try to point out), but the ideology nevertheless functions as a strong psychological component internally enforced by these women themselves.[16] In a culture where "repose" and "respect for others" amount to the same thing, the last thing they would want would be visibility, especially if it were perceived to come from their own agency; that is "too undignified" (as my aunt might point out). Note also that in a cultural setting where everyone speaks softly and pays much attention to others to begin with, one does not need to raise one's voice or act in such a way as to call attention to oneself. One is already visible enough.

The conflation of femininity and Asianness applies even for males in that "Asian male" remains a feminized category; even if they are martial arts experts (another stereotype) their "nimbleness" and "skillfulness" make them much more feminine than, say, an American football player, who is archtypically masculine. This is not to mention another stereotype of "those Asian engineer nerds" who will be good workers because they will "yield and obey orders." So the problem of the feminization of the non-western, so-called colonized peoples raised in the feminist literature[17] applies especially to the category of "Asian." It is not only a reality in the practical sense but also an explicit ideology of choice among those in the Confucian tradition themselves; *not* to have an independent or critical voice is not just a female virtue, but a virtue of cultivated personhood. In this context, it becomes almost impossible for a woman to speak up without feeling extremely awkward about her sense of place, and her own self-worth as a person of integrity and cultivation.[18] An Asian woman is in this way *doubly submissive* in western contexts, first as a woman, and second as an Asian.

Sociologically, the wholehearted drive to fit in and be a part of the whole is often closely associated with the phenomenon of Asian assimilation among immigrants from Asia into the dominant white middle-class American culture (especially into the value system of the puritan work ethic). The first thing many of the immigrant parents do is force their children to learn English, then to excel in school, and get a profession. This almost non-negotiable drive for upward mobility requires diligent assimilation. Self-pity, victim consciousness, and separationist self-consciousness are deadly to the process, a waste of time and energy, and therefore not allowed. As a result, many children of immigrant parents from Confucian Asia explicitly reject their own identity as Asian or Asian American, or member of a "minority culture," contributing further to the invisibility problem. In their view, in fact, invisibility is not a problem at all; if anything, it is a sign of success. Being "white-identified" is not a bad idea, if it leads to a more prosperous lifestyle. It is not unusual to see such assimilated Asians developing racism against blacks and Hispanics, adopting exactly the racism prevalent in white middle-class culture. The irony of course is that they are often targets of such racism themselves, yet they continue to think of themselves as being lucky that they are still "more white" than the other groups. They come to believe that what they have to do is to further separate themselves from other minority groups, as if they could be tainted by association with darker color. Here the invisibility problem takes a pernicious turn: the dominant discourse of racism has won all the way, obliterating the last remnants of resistance through assimilation.

Localizing the Asian: Modernity, Eurocentrism, and Orientalism

I would like to turn now to the issue of Asia in a broader historical context in order to examine the third contributing factor to invisibility. The assimilationist ideology of "white-identification" among Asians has another important source, and that is the problem of colonialism. In the nineteenth century European consciousness it was taken for granted that the West represented the "universal." For instance, European philosophers have always raised the question of "truth" about *the* human mind. As exemplified by Hegel, "history" was a linear temporal progress, from the premodern past to the modern present, culminating in the techno-scientific culture of Europe and America. Since both systematic philosophy and science developed primarily in Europe, the notions of "truth," "universality," "modernity," and "being western" came to be conflated in the minds of intellectuals. In this framework, thought that was "non-western" – a geopolitical designation – was either simply false or conceptualized as backwards in the temporal progression.[19] The assumption was that once "primitive" cultures developed, they would begin to manifest the European forms of culture and consciousness. The place of legitimate culture was Europe; and "exotic" Asia, Africa, South America, and anywhere else untouched by European modernity was culturally marginal and insignificant. It is worth noting, however, that this form of Eurocentrism was not so prevalent before the period of European expansion. Even in philosophy, Leibniz, for instance, studied Chinese thought and valued it highly.[20] The influence of Hinduism on Schopenhauer is also well documented.

The extent and type of the actual European colonization in Asia varied, but the idea that Europe was the center of modern civilization became a kind of pervasive cultural understanding in most of the Asian countries since the late nineteenth century. These cultures were colonized to the extent that the legitimate point of cultural reference was taken to be European civilization.[21] In Japan, for instance, the terms "westernization" and "modernization" were often used synonymously; for the past 100 years, viewing the world in terms of West vs. East, which amounts to "modern vs. traditional," became a cultural paradigm, affecting everything from politics, educational reform, fashion, and the idea of what should be valued. In this dualistic paradigm, the "West" represented what is new, advanced, and forward-looking; the "traditional," on the other hand, was old, backward, primitive.[22] Since the Europeans and Americans who came to Japan around the turn of the century were Caucasians, the perception of white people was associated with modern civilization. To be "modern," then, would be to act and "be" like white people: sit on a chair rather than a mat on the floor; use silver instead of chopsticks; wear blouses and skirts rather than kimonos; eat bread and meat instead of rice and fish;[23] don't get too much tan or else your skin will become dark. Although today the culture in Japan is a hybrid of Japanese, American, European, and other Asian influences; the "West vs. East" paradigm in which the "white West" symbolizes advancement is far from forgotten.

In this context, even within the consciousness of those in Asia, Asia became the "other" of Europe. This is the problem of self-alienation and internal oppression in colonized consciousness, but with respect to Asia, in particular, it is a part of the problem of Orientalism.[24] Since its publication in 1978, Edward Said's *Orientalism* profoundly changed the way in which the issues related to East and West are discussed.[25] Said's main thesis is that the very category of the "Orient," a sweeping category applied to all "Asiatic" cultures, was a European invention produced in order to contain difference in the era of colonial expansion. Either by way of rejection or exoticism, the category of the Orient served as a representational tool for Europeans to bring the unknown under control; it was by definition an aspect of European imperialism. The category of "Asia" or the "Far East" (east of Europe, of course) was a part of this orientalist discourse; the region was "so different," "mysteriously far," opaque and insubstantial. When such representations are adopted by those who are in the "Orient," they produce a self-alienated, colonized consciousness.

In India in the early part of this century, many Indians themselves came to believe that it was for their own good that the British ruled them, since modernity, the culture of the British, would ultimately liberate them from the pre-modern past.[26] Many Indians came to see their own culture as obscure and backwards, and the new and European lifestyle and values as better and more cosmopolitan. In reality, of course, despite its good intentions of modernizing India, the colonial administration systematically advanced a particular imperialist agenda. The real power of colonization is the ability to achieve this willing participation by transforming the colonized subjects' own point of reference from the native culture to the western one. The point of a postcolonial critique, as well as Said's idea of a solution, is to abandon the very categories of "Orient" and "Occident" altogether and to expose the inherent forms of domination and subjugation.

The ultimate irony is that the methodology of critique as well as the theories themselves are basically European in origin.[27] The very idea of theoretical empowerment for fighting oppression, which privileges knowledge, is often alien to the real victims of this whole process: women and ethnic minorities in these Asian countries who have virtually no access to education nor political power to begin with.[28] Those who can speak on their behalf are speaking, but the experience ultimately remains alienated and the promise of a good life seems unreal. In East Asia, moreover, the historical situation was complicated by the fact that the history of colonialism did not neatly fit into the Europe vs. Asia paradigm because Japan was itself a colonial power over Korea, China, the Philippines and parts of Indonesia.[29] The colonized women in Korea, for example, endured a three-fold oppression: Japanese imperialism, the West, and their own patriarchal system.[30] This history contributes to today's fragmentation of the category of "Asians," as mentioned above.

However, despite such complexity, to most of the European as well as American intellectuals Asia still remains one localized "other" in the Far East or on the other side of the Pacific. Despite the fact that in American academia the critique of Eurocentrism is by now a near-standard procedure and dominant discourse in some departments, Eurocentrism, or in the case of philosophy, Anglo-centrism, does remain a persistent reality, both in the US and elsewhere in the West as well as the non-West. As Dipesh Chakrabarty laments, "That Europe works as a silent referent in historical knowledge itself becomes obvious in a highly ordinary way ... Third-world historians feel a need to refer to works in European history; historians of Europe do not feel any need to reciprocate."[31] Needless to say, in philosophy the case is similar, if not worse. The study of philosophy usually excludes anything outside of western philosophy, and this is true even if one studies philosophy in Asia. In Japan, the academic discipline of philosophy (*tetsugaku*) generally does not include Japanese philosophy nor any other Asian thought; "philosophy" means, as a subject, the study of thought from the pre-Socratics, the Greeks, medieval thought, the modern period, the Enlightenment, eighteenth- and nineteenth-century European thought, then contemporary European philosophy including postmodernism, and analytic or Anglo-American philosophy.[32] In other words, in Japan the conception of "philosophy" is thoroughly Eurocentric; what is called "Asian philosophy" in the West is studied in Japan under "Eastern thought" (*toyo shiso*), often a separate discipline altogether.

Thus the problem of invisibility with respect to Asian thought is aggravated not only by the Eurocentrism and orientalism of most of the European and the majority of American intellectuals, but also by Asians themselves. In addition to the already-existing Confucian ideology of "fitting in" and "not making a case for oneself" – a particularly "feminine" mode of having a self – the Asian colonized consciousness which adopted Eurocentrism/orientalism as its own culture, compounds the problem further by identifying the point of legitimacy outside itself, thereby making itself even more invisible and *acknowledging* that invisibility is the way it ought to be.

In sum, Asians are invisible as a category because of the following reasons. First, upon close examination the category itself tends toward fragmentation rather than coherence. Second, the Confucian cultural influence, especially for women, promotes invisibility, as it is idealized as an ethical or aesthetic end. Third, Eurocentrism and orientalism contribute not only to the European or American ignorance toward Asia, but also produce a self-alienated colonized consciousness among Asians, which shifts the reference point of self-understanding to that of European consciousness. This self-alienation and assimilation render Asian self-consciousness invisible even to Asians themselves. I would like to turn now to some of the specific problems in philosophy as an academic discipline in the light of these contributing factors to invisibility.

Claims of Philosophy

The discipline of philosophy can itself be an object of critical analysis. What are its boundaries, and how should that understanding be reflected in the curriculum? Apart from politics and turf wars, there seems to me to be a variety of conceptions about what philosophers regard as the proper topic and method of philosophy as a discipline.

From broader to narrower conceptions, here are some of the ways in which philosophy seems to have been defined by academic philosophers:

(1) Philosophy as defined by the questions it asks, which are prompted by the nature of its various subdisciplines. Examples are: "What is a good life?" "What is reality?" "What is knowledge?" "What is the 'self?'" These are all "philosophical" questions to the extent that they are considered legitimate questions about basic human reality and beyond. This broad conception often includes the notion of philosophy as reflection and contemplation about, and analysis of, the "human condition."[33] Sometimes material from literature or other disciplines are used to articulate a point of view. Often introductory philosophy textbooks are organized around such questions and it is not unusual today to see the inclusion of some writings from other disciplines.

(2) Philosophy as a rational system of thought, as opposed to "mythic" storytelling or in contrast to other endeavors in the humanities or social sciences. Apart from literature, religion, psychology, sociology, anthropology, etc., philosophy in this sense takes a meta-position with respect to the production of knowledge itself and concerns itself with theory-building about the "fundamental questions" such as reality, justice, and personhood.

(3) Philosophy as the history of western philosophy. This is the conception mentioned above: the study of thought from the pre-Socratics to contemporary European or Anglo-American thought. By definition, anything outside of this tradition is not philosophy proper.

(4) Philosophy as a critical method of argumentation. In this conception philosophy is strictly about constructing sound arguments and effective counterarguments. The methodology adopts a scientific method of weeding out the propositions that can be falsified. This is often a presupposition in analytic philosophy. In this view contemporary European philosophy is not philosophy because it doesn't have arguments or because it contains propositions that can be neither true nor false. By the same token, any form of thought, if it does not have arguments of the kind studied by these philosophers, is not philosophy proper. At its narrowest conception, this approach may exclude not only contemporary European philosophy but also philosophies of any other tradition, ancient and medieval philosophy, feminism, environmental ethics, and many others which do not belong within the parameters of contemporary Anglo-American philosophy.

Often, Asian philosophy or comparative philosophy is included in the discipline under (1), the broadest conception. Many of the multicultural philosophy textbooks include not only Asian thought but the philosophies of other traditions. Certainly, all of these philosophical questions have been asked and analyzed in detail in Asia over the past 2,000 years, if not longer, and various systems or coherent schemes have been produced. Conception (2) could certainly include some Indian philosophical systems,[34] Buddhist metaphysics, or aspects of Japanese philosophy (e.g., Nishida's theory of place),[35] but perhaps not others, such as Taoist thought. Conception (3) excludes Asian philosophy because it is outside the western tradition. Conception (4) again should accept some forms of Indian metaphysics or Buddhist dialectic, such as the "Middle Way" of the Madhyamika school, which is highly technical in its logicism, but in common practice the particular conception of argumentation in question (and therefore the notion of philosophy) often must be based on the scientific method of the Anglo-American analytic tradition, so anything outside this tradition is excluded. Those who specialize in Asian philosophy, may be nervous at the prospect of having to justify the inclusion of Asian thought within philosophy to an often unsympathetic audience whose members agree with conceptions (3), (4) or even (2). This kind of experience is also all too familiar with anyone specializing in feminist thought in philosophy.

But in fact even those who narrowly conceive of philosophy as (2), (3), and (4) all *agree* that conception (1) is indeed a legitimate way to understand philosophy as a discipline. So yes, on the one hand, Asian philosophy belongs to philosophy to the extent that in it proper questions are being asked, but no, on the other hand, it's not really philosophy because the questions are not being analyzed or answered in the proper way. Often the inquisitor is unaware of the fact that he or she has switched meanings. But *if* one grants conception (1) as the legitimate subject-matter of philosophy, as most people in the field of philosophy indeed do, then endorsing (2), (3), and (4), while *at the same time* excluding Asian philosophy, requires a further justification. This is where the sticky questions of legitimacy, prejudice, exclusion, and power claims enter in.

One such prejudice is indeed Eurocentrism and the associated problems discussed above. For those who hold conception (3), it is a matter of definition that there is no such thing as a non-western philosophy. But if so, they must be claiming either that other traditions do not ask questions such as "what is a good life" or "what is reality," or that only the western versions of those questions and answers are legitimate. The former proposition is empirically false; the latter position is ethnocentric (in this case Eurocentric, but in essence no different from other cultures claiming that theirs is the measure of truth). Why should the philosophical answers arising out of a particular geopolitical history claim monopoly on the world's philosophical insights? Or on any group, including one's own, for that matter?

However, the source of Eurocentrism is deeper; it is not that Europe as such is privileged (ethnocentrism), but rather that this privilege is justified: that this intellectual history contains in itself something which is universal and "true," by which other traditions may be judged. This is what drives conceptions (2) and (4). The measure of truth is "scientific thinking" broadly conceived; it is an Enlightenment, "modern" methodology which employs critical thinking, verification and accurate abstraction, as opposed to simply relying on beliefs or authority, or pre-modern ways of thinking. It may be that European thought is just as contingently related to the "universal" as non-European thought, but it was nevertheless in Europe that science first flourished and technology was first developed on a large scale. This is why, so it is believed, Europe enjoys the culture of modernity, which is defined by the triumph of rationalism over mythic or religious beliefs, and universalistic thinking over local knowledge. So properly speaking, this form of Eurocentrism is a kind of scientism or modernism, and not only is this method used to critique non-European forms of thought, but even within Europe it is used in order to critique its own "dark ages," for instance.[36]

Subscribing to the belief that scientific modernism has merits is in itself not Eurocentric, nor is it automatically scientistic. The belief that Europeans are *superior* because they developed this culture is Eurocentrism, and the claim that anything that does not fit the criteria of scientific method is not knowledge or is false knowledge, is scientism. Asian philosophy is often excluded on both accounts, either because it is already deemed inferior or "too foreign," i.e., not made by Europeans, or because it is pre-judged as lacking the right criteria of knowledge. Exclusion based on Eurocentrism is prejudice, a version of orientalism. The scientism objection is trickier (apart from the bigger question of whether the very method of science is ethnocentric, universally justified, or "objective"). Even if one grants its framework, and the formal features of science or methods of critical thinking can be abstracted from European intellectual history, "scientific thinking" can still be employed to understand ideas from other cultures, or by people in such cultures themselves. If it is universal, then by definition it is not a "property" of Europe and there is no justification for exclusion *prior* to a scientific investigation of non-western thought.[37] So exclusion without serious investigation is also prejudice; as noted, there are systems in Asian thought which fit the description of "scientific" if one is patient enough to go through different modes of presentation (as in Indian or Buddhist metaphysical texts).[38] The critique of scientism itself is a separate discussion developed in post-modern literature and science studies. (I do not have the room to elaborate on it here.[39])

Including Asian Women

Finally, there is a more subtle form of exclusion that actually appears within the language of multicultural inclusion, and which is often known as "tokenizing"or "ghettoizing." This is where the stereotyping of Asian women becomes a practical issue. I grant that the language of multicultural inclusion is a big step in the right direction, but it still has a long way to go. Often scholars from India or China are proud of their own long tradition and philosophy and believe that they can make some contribution to philosophy in the West. However, much to their disappointment, they discover that their inclusion is not in itself a sign of *engagement* from outside their own group.[40] They are ghettoized, with no apparent connection to the rest of the academic community.[41] Often the only way the engagement might occur is if they conform to the methods of western philosophy, using European or Anglo philosophy as a framework to explain their own ideas, thereby reinforcing the Eurocentrism that discredits them in the first place.

Women and minorities are included for the sake of diversity, but anyone who is a woman or a minority philosopher knows very well the experience of finding that her ideas are not taken all that seriously or that her merit appears already to be in question. Because of the undiscriminating racial sense in which the term "Asian" is used, if one is from Asia or is an Asian American, almost without exception one is expected to know something about Asian thought and is thereby "given some authority." An Asian woman may feel especially that she should indeed study Asian philosophy, so as to be able to offer some kind of a bridge to the mainstream. Or she may assume that her outsider status is only "natural," that it is "her place" to be doing some non-mainstream philosophy, because of her colonized consciousness and her self-understanding that she should not be presumptuous. Yet at the same time she may feel disqualified because the whole field is marginalized. This is a case of triple-marginalization: being Asian, a woman, and teaching or doing research in a field that remains invisible.[42] Asians are in this way often relegated to "Asian philosophy" in the same way that women are somehow expected to include feminism as one of their areas of competence, only to find themselves located outside the mainstream.

An Asian woman may face a further obstacle. The particularly "feminine" characteristics of being an Asian woman may pose a problem within the feminist discourse itself, especially in the United States where the standard of respectability is strongly tied to autonomy and independence. Apart perhaps from feminist ethics, traditional feminist consciousness has focused predominantly on notions of oppression, subversion, and revolutionary change. Across the spectrum, the idea of oppositional "agency" (to patriarchy, capitalism, male-domination, injustice, disempowerment) is an essential component of the feminist movement.[43] This confrontational model is indeed quite alien to many of the women in Asia, especially among the strongly Confucian countries. An immigrant woman from Taiwan may feel that her cultural self is not only unappreciated, but even put in a negative light as a victim of false consciousness (and therefore patronized as being "in need of help").[44] Worse, she may be labeled "anti-feminist" to the extent that she may be perceived as actually willingly seeking the passive, dominated status. She may thus come to feel condemned and ashamed in the eyes of "liberated women," and that her own "backward" culture "denigrates women."[45] She may struggle to be "more liberated, more American" by forcing herself to be more aggressive, only to worsen the experience of self-alienation in the process of assimilation.[46] Yet an Asian woman also may be well aware of the fact that Confucian patriarchy has done much damage to the women in this culture and may wish for a change.[47] This is a catch-22, a doubly-alienated self-consciousness.

Further problems may include the fact that calling attention to his or her "Asianness" may be the last thing a particular person from Asia might want; a student from Asia may be seriously interested in studying Aristotle.[48] Or, the personal experience of "being Asian" may be quite alien to an assimilated fourth-generation Chinese-American person. The contradiction again is that, whether first- or fourth-generation, one is expected to express Asian ideas, but only through "legitimate" Anglo-American or European means and with the result of finding oneself thereby further alienated.

In addition, despite formal inclusion, the whole attempt at inclusion may have little to do with genuine interest; it may be for the sake of endorsing the political ideology of multiculturalism, which may be a very localized agenda of particular departments or individuals. Because the discourses of race and diversity are distinctly American, most scholars from abroad – even Europe – find foreign the very idea of politicizing academic discourse in that way. This is why many of the scholars from Asia either specialize in Confucianism, Indian philosophy, or comparative philosophy, with little political interest on race, or forgo any scholarship on culture or politics altogether and specialize narrowly in logic, epistemology, or metaphysics. If the former, then ghettoization is a problem. If the latter, then they are perceived to be assimilated and therefore invisible *qua* Asian. Granted, often the "privileged access" to the consciousness of women, minorities, immigrants, etc., is actually appreciated and the interest in this access is genuine, but one should be vigilant about the latent exclusionary move – the stamp of "otherness" which makes Asians, especially Asian women, invisible within the inclusive language itself.

If philosophy as practice has a role to play in this issue, it should, at a minimum, critique its own assumptions and methodology and eliminate claims which are unfounded – such as automatic prejudice against any non-western thought – so that a critical investigation and reflection on these issues can move forward and a path for real engagement and understanding can be articulated.[49]

What I hoped to accomplish in this paper was to provide one perspective on "being an Asian woman" in philosophy. In sum, the difficulties she may face are several. First, given the culture in which the norms of behavior does not particularly encourage visibility, oppositional agency, and subversive action, an Asian woman may miss the very vehicle which may be necessary for exposing injustice and creating change. Yet at the same time, even if she were to become conscious of the need for visibility and agency, the transformation of her own consciousness to such a stance may produce self-alienation. Second, if she were to become "visible," because of her perceived Asianness, she must then face the further problem of Eurocentrism or orientalism and the associated prejudice. Third, there is a doubling, tripling, or even quadrupling of the cultural negotiation problems in that an Asian woman faces not only the problem of "being a woman," but also the problem that the Asians are "feminized" to begin with. In addition, she may further face the problem of feeling internally compelled to take up the already-marginalized field of Asian philosophy (or feminism, or whatever else she may perceive as "more appropriate" in terms of the idea of service to the discipline) and she may face problems even within feminism, owing to the often negative connotation given to the "feminine." Including Asian women, then, involves a multi-layered task: one is called to be self-critical of one's possible prejudices against "Asians," "women," "non-European or American thought," and ways of being a woman other than those set by Euro-American standards.

In conclusion, let me say that I would, however, resist the categorization of philosophy as such as by definition Eurocentric and "white-male." Although these crude mind-sets do exist rather commonly and should be resisted, philosophy's critical method should not be abandoned because it is what makes critique possible in the first place. Resistance and vigilance should always be there to expose illegitimate grounds for dominance and marginalization, regardless of where it occurs. Claims to legitimacy must always involve a self-critique of its own foundation, and our inquiry must be guided by a genuine spirit of understanding.

Notes

1 The Association for Asian Studies (founded in 1941) established four elective area councils in 1970: South Asia, South-east Asia, China and Inner Asia, and North-east Asia, in order to guarantee each area constituency its own representation and a proportionate voice on the Board of Directors.

2 For a further analysis on the outdated duality of "East and West" in the reality of globalism, see David Loy, "Transcending East and West," *Man and World* 26/4 (1993), pp. 403–27.

3 By "race" I mean a socially constructed sense in which the term yields demarcations; I do not use it as a biological category. On the pragmatic significance of the category of race, see Naomi Zack, "Race and Philosophic Meaning," in Naomi Zack (ed.) *Race/Sex* (New York: Routledge, 1997), ch. 2.

4 David Kim offers a philosophical account of racial identity and the unity

and fragmentation within Asian-American identity in "Asian American Identities," in Linda Martín Alcoff (ed.) *Constellations* (forthcoming).

5   I wish to thank David Kim and Rebecca Chiyoko King for raising the following point: Politically speaking, "Asian Americans" came together as a group, not because of racial commonality but because they share the common experience of orientalist racism that has been endemic to American culture for centuries. Kim notes, borrowing from DuBois, that such a self-understanding has served as a basis for "Asian-American double consciousness."

6   One of the US Exclusion Acts in the late nineteenth century, "An Act to Prevent the Kidnapping and Importation of Mongolian, Chinese, and Japanese Females for Criminal and Demoralizing Purposes" (meaning prostitution) gave US immigration officers the power to determine whether the emigrating "oriental women" were "persons of correct habits and good character" (Chandra Mohanty, "Introduction: Cartographies of Struggle," in C. Mohanty, A. Russo, and L. Torres (eds) *Third World Women and the Politics of Feminism* (Bloomington: Indiana University Press, 1991), p. 25). This Act assumed a Judeo-Christian understanding of prostitution as *morally* corrupt on the part of the women involved, but this is not a presupposition shared by, for instance, many in Japan. The so called evilness of prostitution may be analyzed in terms of victimization, capitalism, or sexism, but such analyses may be distinct from a moral one in which the qualities of baseness and impurity are assigned to the women involved. For a cultural and historical comparison on prostitution, see Laurie Shrage, *Moral Dilemmas of Feminism: Prostitution, Adultery, and Abortion* (New York: Routledge, 1994), chs 5 and 6.

7   For an analysis of latent racism in 1960s dystopian science fiction and film, see Andrew Feenberg, *Alternative Modernity: The Technical Turn in Philosophy and Social Theory* (Berkeley: University of California Press, 1995), pp. 60–5.

8   When I lived near Camp Pendleton, a Marine base in northern San Diego, there were many occasions when people would ask me, "When and where did you meet your husband?" I was a student, neither married nor having anything to do with the base, but the assumption was that I came to the US because I married a serviceman abroad. The hidden purpose in the question often seemed to be to determine whether I worked in a bar near the base.

9   In this sense, Asian women are also the target of racialized sex objectification in the sense black and Hispanic women are sexualized. Unlike the "savage" image of black woman, however, the Asian woman is represented as "exotic," "super-feminine" and "hyper-hetero-sensual," to borrow Shrage's adjectives. See her discussion in *Moral Dilemmas*, pp. 151–8.

10 Nearly 25 percent of South Korean population is Protestant.

11 Stanley Fish, "Boutique Multiculturalism," in A. Melzer, J. Weinberger, and M. R. Zinman (eds) *Multiculturalism and American Democracy* (Lawrence: University of Kansas Press, 1998), ch. 4.

12 Esther Ngan-Ling Chow analyzes the cultural barriers Asian-American women face in their political activism and lists several "internal" and "external" barriers. See her essay, "The Feminist Movement: Where are All the Asian American Women?," in A. Jagger and P. Rothenberg (eds) *Feminist Frameworks: Alternative Theoretical Accounts of the Relations between Women and Men*, 3rd edn (New York: McGraw-Hill, 1993), pp. 212–19.

13 For an interesting essay on the negative views of women in Confucianism, see Julia Kristeva, *About Chinese Women* (New York: Marion Boyars Publishers, 1986), especially the chapter "Confucius – An Eater of Women," pp. 66–99.

14 Some of my relatives and personal friends in Japan, for instance, regard me with slight disdain because I have abandoned "high culture and grace" in the name of what they perceive as a "coarse" sensibility of American feminism. "Being Americanized" is a derogatory term indicating too much assertiveness, self-indulgence, and disruptive behavior, and as such, it directly contradicts what it means to be "feminine." I should add that the expectation of "assimilation" is strongly gendered. If the assimilation into the American culture is supposed to indicate "independence" and "self-confidence," then it is in general somewhat favored for males. But it is hardly ever the case that such assimilation is considered a good for females.

15 Such a depiction may be criticized as a stereotype and myth, and indeed, there are of course many powerful women (especially mothers) who do not fit these descriptions at all. However, it is nevertheless true that I do in fact have many friends who endorse and embody these almost mythically feminine qualities. For more details on the reality of Japanese women, the following books may be helpful: Anne Imamura (ed.) *Re-Imaging Japanese Women* (Berkeley: University of California Press,1996); Kumiko Fujimura-Fanselow and Atsuko Kameda (eds) *Japanese Women: New Feminist Perspectives on the Past, Present, and Future* (New York: Feminist Press, 1995); Takie Sugiyama Lebra, *Japanese Women: Constraint and Fulfillment* (Honolulu: University of Hawaii Press, 1984); and Sumiko Iwao, *The Japanese Woman: Traditional Image and Changing Reality* (Cambridge: Harvard University Press, 1993).

16 Although it was widely reported during 1998 and 1999 that Tokyo finally had a woman mayor (for the first time in history) and that women were demanding more political equality all over Japan, my perception is that many women, even the politically enlightened ones, still would

maintain that characteristics such as compassion, sympathy, and meeting others' needs are "feminine" virtues one should not abandon.

17 For instance, Sara Lucia Hoagland writes: "Colonizers depict the colonized as passive, as wanting and needing protection (domination), as being taken care of 'for their own good.' Anyone who resists domination will be sorted out as abnormal and attacked as a danger to society ('civilization') or called insane and put away in the name of protection (their own or society's)" ("Moral Revolution: From Antagonism to Cooperation," in Nancy Tuana and Rosemary Tong (eds) *Feminism and Philosophy: Essential Readings in Theory, Reinterpretation, and Application* (Boulder: Westview Press, 1995), p. 177).

18 This is a problem I often face in my dealings with international students from Asia, male or female; on the one hand, I would like them to participate actively in discussions, but on the other hand, I thoroughly understand the difficulty and dread they experience in any setting in which they are expected to speak up. The problem is not simply that they are "shy"; it has to do with a contradiction at the fundamental level of selfhood. However innocent, "speaking up" in itself produces the discomfort, albeit unwittingly, of exhibiting to others how uncultivated they themselves may be. If they speak up, then they often feel embarrassed and in other respects inadequate; if they don't speak up, then they feel like a failure in class.

19 I explore Japanese philosophy's reaction to this problem in "Beyond 'East and West': Nishida's Universalism and Postcolonial Critique," *The Review of Politics* 59/3 (1997), pp. 541–60.

20 Given their intellectual involvement with these materials, their interests seem more than a case of mere curiosity. See, for instance, G. W. Leibniz, *Writings on China*, trans D. Cook and H. Rosemont (Chicago: Open Court, 1994).

21 The contributing factors were often western medicine and technology, both practical applications of science; other factors, such as democracy and Christianity, were slower to be accepted.

22 One might argue that this dualism of "new vs. traditional" exists within the West itself, in terms of its own historical reflection (post-Enlightenment vs. the Middle Ages) or degrees of urbanization (city vs. the country). To this extent, it could be said that the West itself was colonized by its own notion of modernity and still continues to be under its grip, especially in terms of technological development.

23 Beef-eating, for instance, was officially approved; local authorities issued a public notice "recommending this unorthodox diet on the ground that it would create energy for the performance of patriotic duties and strengthen the national physique." This and other anecdotal accounts

are found in G. B. Samsom, *The Western World and Japan* (Tokyo: Charles Tuttle Co., 1984), p. 383.

24 The examination of the problem of colonized self-consciousness was made explicit in the late 1950s and early 1960s with Franz Fanon. The theoretical analyses of Asia, especially India, began fully around 1982 with a group of Indian intellectuals who established the journal, *Subaltern Studies*, and theorized their colonized consciousness *vis-à-vis* their colonizer, Great Britain. For a brief history of *Subaltern Studies*, see Dipesh Chakrabarty, "Postcoloniality and the Artifice of History: Who Speaks for 'Indian' Pasts?" *Representations* 37/25.

25 Edward Said, *Orientalism* (New York: Routledge, 1978), pp. 1–28. For a critique, see Aijaz Ahmad, *In Theory* (New York: Verso, 1992).

26 See Chakrabarty, "Postcoloniality" and also Gyan Prakash, "Writing Post-Colonialist Histories of the Third World: Perspectives from Indian Historiography," *Comparative Studies in Society and History* 32 (1990), pp. 383–408.

27 Postcolonial critique often borrows from poststructuralism, deconstruction, and from Foucault's analysis of power.

28 Similar points are discussed in Audre Lorde, "The Master's Tools Will Never Dismantle the Master's House," *Sister Outsider* (New York: The Crossing Press Feminist Series, 1984), pp. 110–13.

29 For a collection of essays on postcolonialism in East Asia, see Tani Barlow (ed.) *Formations of Colonial Modernity in East Asia* (Durham, NC, Duke University Press, 1997).

30 See Chungmoo Choi (ed.) *positions: east asia culture critique* 5/1 (1997), a special issue on "comfort women," for a collection of critical essays from a postcolonialist perspective. See also George L. Hicks, *The Comfort Women: Japan's Brutal Regime of Enforced Prostitution in the Second World War* (New York: Norton, 1997).

31 Chakrabarty, "Postcoloniality," p. 25.

32 The term *tetsugaku* ("philosophy") was coined in the early 1860s by two Japanese intellectuals, Amane Nishi and Mamichi Tsuda, who went to Holland and brought back Comte and Mill's utilitarianism.

33 For a wonderful example of a "philosophical reflection" in this vein, see Henry Bugbee, *The Inward Morning: A Philosophical Exploration in Journal Form* (Atlanta: University of Georgia Press, 1999).

34 For example, some of the classical or "orthodox" Hindu philosophical schools from the early centuries AD have been classified as "logical realism" (the Nyaya system), "realistic pluralism" (the Vaisesika system), and "evolutionary dualism" (the Samkhya system). For more discussions of Indian philosophy, see Stephen H. Philips, *Classical Indian Metaphysics* (Chicago: Open Court, 1995), and Sarvepalli Radhakrishnan and Charles

Moore, *A Sourcebook in Indian Philosophy* (Princeton: Princeton University Press, 1971).

35 For a discussion of Nishida's theory of "place," see Andrew Feenberg and Yoko Arisaka, "Experiential Ontology: The Origins of the Nishida Philosophy in the Doctrine of Pure Experience," *International Philosophical Quarterly* 30/2 (1990), pp. 173–205, and Masao Abe, "Nishida's Philosophy of 'Place,'" *International Philosophical Quarterly* 28/4 (1988), pp. 355–71.

36 Again, a parallel may be drawn here to a feminist critique of the "maleness" of rationality, mind, and universality against the "femaleness" of emotion, body, and particularity. See Nancy Tuana, *Woman and the History of Philosophy* (New York: Paragon Issues in Philosophy, 1992).

37 One might argue that my whole analysis is indeed "western" to the extent that I am using a critical method developed in western philosophy as opposed to some other method developed within Asia. But I am claiming that a critical method *per se* is not necessarily European, nor should it be monopolized by western philosophy. To judge other traditions as *inferior* because they lack critical thinking would be Eurocentric, but obviously that is not my position.

38 The modes of presentation from ancient India may indeed be quite alien to a modern reader, but it is perhaps no more alien than pre-Socratic or Greek philosophy. I am not saying that only the "scientific" kind of Asian writing should be considered worthwhile from the perspective of those who subscribe to scientism. There are of course rich traditions of what in the West would be called ethics, metaphysics, epistemology, and aesthetics in Asia and they should be appreciated in their content, regardless of form. However, this is still independent of whether one should apply some critical consciousness in assessing their content, and this is not in itself an "East–West" question.

39 For instance, for a feminist and postcolonialist critique, see Sandra Harding, *Is Science Multicultural?* (Bloomington: Indiana University Press, 1998). For a collection of essays in science studies, see P. Galison and D. Stump (eds) *The Disunity of Science: Boundaries, Contexts, and Power* (Stanford: Stanford University Press, 1996).

40 One obvious problem is a lack of translated material. However, even if there were many translations, it is not clear to me that the problem would then be solved.

41 For a philosophical as well as psychological analysis, see David Kim, "Contempt and Ordinary Inequality," in Susan Babbitt and Sue Campbell (eds) *Philosophy and Racism* (Ithaca: Cornell University Press, 1999).

42 I wish to thank Eileen Fung for this observation.

43 In this sense, Asian Americans too have generally adopted an explicit

self-consciousness of oppositional agency against racism; this is the "American" part of "Asian-American identity."

44 Resisting western imperialism, even in feminism, has become a standard procedure among Asian feminists: "Today, any attempt on the part of Western observers, including feminists, to impose ethnocentric notions of a 'superior' understanding or a better moral solution is increasingly rebuffed by Asian feminists, academics, and activists, who are battling not only their indigenous patriarchal institutions, but also the universalist assumptions of Western scholars claiming to represent women outside their own cultures" (Maria Jaschok and Suzanne Miers (eds) *Women and Chinese Patriarchy: Submission, Servitude and Escape* (London and New Jersey: Zed Books and Hong Kong University Press, 1994), p. 15).

45 Uma Narayan discusses the danger of hastily condemning another culture's unfamiliar customs as "anti-women." See her essay, "Cross-Cultural Connections, Border-Crossings, and 'Death by Culture,'" in *Dislocating Cultures: Identities, Traditions, and Third World Feminism* (New York: Routledge, 1997), pp. 81–117.

46 I was already quite independent by the time I came to the United States at age 19, but still it took me over ten years of conscious self-reflection and transformation to negotiate this kind of issue regarding feminist agency vs. the cultural self which may oppose it directly. I remain sympathetic to any woman who has to deal with this struggle. I have spoken with many international students from Japan who explicitly state that "trying to be more aggressive like an American woman" in fact produces *more* anxiety, confusion, and internal oppression than working with men in Japan, despite the patriarchal conditions which even these women regard as "oppressive." Even despite the less-than-ideal working conditions, they claim that at least they can relax more because they don't have to "act like someone else."

47 For critical essays on the oppression of women under the "contemporary legacy" of Confucian patriarchy, see Maria Jaschok and Suzanne Miers, *Women and Chinese Patriarchy*. Although the essays are not explicitly critiques of Confucianism, the general patriarchal culture first emerged in Confucianism and continued to thrive through neo-Confucian periods into the present. However, this is not to say that *all* oppressive practices against women in China are Confucian. Economic growth and colonialism are also heavily responsible for the degraded treatments of women.

48 Again how this tokenizing works becomes obvious in a rather ordinary way. Suppose there is an opening for a position in Kantian ethics, and there are Chinese-American candidates as well as others from the US or Germany. The perceived qualification immediately favors either the American or German candidates. Or suppose the opening is for Asian

philosophy; the Chinese American is perceived to fit the position better, even with weaker qualifications.

49 The engagement should be in the spirit of what Maria C. Lugones and Elizabeth V. Spelman call "friendship": such a stance "requires that you make a real space for our articulating, interpreting, theorizing, and reflecting about the connections among them – a real space must be a non-coerced space – and/or that you follow us into our world out of friendship" ("Have We Got a Theory for You! Feminist Theory, Cultural Imperialism and the Demand for 'The Woman's Voice,'" in Tuana and Tong, *Feminism and Philosophy*, p. 499.

I wish to thank Andrew Feenberg, Eileen Fung, David Kim, Rebecca Chiyoko King, Jeff Thompson, Rowena Tomaneng-Matsunari, Irene Wei, and Naomi Zack for their helpful comments and suggestions.

CHAPTER 10

On Judging Epistemic Credibility: Is Social Identity Relevant?

LINDA MARTÍN ALCOFF

The idea underlying this anthology appears to be that social identity is a relevant consideration even in the lofty realms of philosophy. Certainly there are many philosophers, in the Anglo-American tradition at least, who will wonder at this assumption. But these philosophers themselves assume that racial and ethnic identity markers should be tastefully ignored in the seminar rooms of philosophy departments. Philosophical disputation is a practice open to all, they might think, and social identity is properly an irrelevant consideration in determining either its participants or its outcomes.

Perhaps this idea needs scrutiny, and minimally needs to be argued for rather than merely assumed. In this paper, I want to question the assumption that social identity should be irrelevant in philosophy as well as in other endeavors involving knowledge. My question will be this: in assessing a claim or judgment, is it justifiable to take into account the social identity of the person who has made the claim? Does a claim or judgment gain or lose credibility in virtue of the claimant's social identity?

The political debate over this issue has primarily focused on jury diversity: if social identity is epistemically relevant, then it makes sense to require racial and gender diversity in juries. If social identity is not epistemically relevant, then diversity is not an issue of concern for jury selection. There may be other reasons given, of course, for diversity in jury selection, such as those involving the *perceived* legitimacy of the jury by diverse communities, or the argument that a jury of one's peers must include a representative sample of one's specific ethnic or racial community, especially if the society has had a history of prejudice against this particular group. But I want to set those sorts of arguments aside in order to focus on what is arguably a more defensible reason for jury diversity: that it will increase the likelihood of an epistemically better judgment. In the US court system, jury selection is driven by the concerns of competing attorneys to win their case, concerns that may only coincidentally conform with establishing the truth. But in the arena of legal theory, debates have arisen over whether random selection of jurors from among registered voters, for example, or from among homeowners, excludes populations that could be important in reaching the best decision of a case given the evidence. In particular, if the poor are systematically excluded by these methods, and yet it is the poor who make up a significant portion of defendants in criminal trials, might it be the case that the adequacy of jury decisions is adversely affected?

This question also taps into a much larger concern within epistemology, that of testimonial knowledge. Testimonial knowledge is, in fact, the primary form of knowledge in everyday life, far exceeding its relevance to the courtroom, and there seems to be a small but increasing recognition in epistemology of the important role testimonial knowledge plays in actual belief-forming practices.[1] Most of our knowledge is achieved on the basis of testimony from others, whether we hear them give eyewitness reports, make other sorts of claims, or we read knowledge claims in a less direct encounter. We obtain most of our knowledge by reading or hearing what other persons tell us to be the case in a variety of personal, direct and indirect media. Despite this obvious fact, for too long it has been the case that epistemology has based its analyses of knowledge on atypical scenarios of direct perception by an individual; whereas if one is aiming for a *general* account of knowledge one would think the more typical case of belief generation should be taken as the paradigm, that is, knowledge based in one form or another on the testimony of others.[2]

Feminist epistemologists such as Lorraine Code and Lynn Hankinson Nelson have argued that the importance of testimonial knowledge has implications for the stock issues epistemologists focus upon. Such knowledge raises different sorts of epistemological questions than direct perception, questions not about perceptual reliability or perceptual memory but about trust and the basis of interpersonal judgement, credibility and epistemic reliability. We cannot often directly assess the processes by which the other upon whom we are relying has obtained their knowledge; we cannot know with certainty *how* they obtained their knowledge nor do we necessarily have the expertise to know *what a reliable procedure would be* for obtaining certain kinds of knowledge. Therefore, we must assess the other person in a more general way before we can afford them an authority in any epistemic matters.

Thus, knowledge based on the testimony of others requires assessing the epistemic reliability of those offering the testimony. Keith Lehrer argues that epistemic reliability requires epistemic justification:

> When Ms. Oblate tells me that the sun is not round, then I must evaluate ... whether Ms. Oblate is trustworthy in what she thus conveys. As a result, I am completely justified in believing that the sun is not round only if I am completely justified in accepting that Ms. Oblate is completely trustworthy in what she conveyed. The latter is true only if Ms. Oblate is completely justified in accepting that the sun is not round. The knowledge we acquire by the transfer of information from others is, therefore, intrinsically dependent on the others being completely justified in accepting what they convey.[3]

Sosa argues, in my view rightly, that this requirement is too strong:

> The informant can be trustworthy in the way that a child or a recording device can be trustworthy, which suffices to make the informant a possible source of our own justification.[4]

And I would add that Lehrer's account actually gives no guidance about how to assess Ms. Oblate's trustworthiness. If I am required to assess every informant's own justification, then am I not simply achieving direct justification on my own?

I agree that *I* cannot be said to be justified in a belief simply because it came to me from another person's direct report: my own justification requires that I assess the reliability of the person or source from whom I hear the claim – just as I would distinguish between perceptions in the dark and perceptions in full light – even if it is merely to make a distinction between the *National Enquirer* and the *Washington Post*. I can only rarely assess with any adequacy my source's own epistemic justification. And, as Sosa argues, this is not even a necessary requirement for my own justification in believing the claim. Far more commonly, we make "ball-park" estimates of our source's trustworthiness: my uncle tells me the family can be traced directly back to Charlemagne, but given the fact that he previously claimed that we were related to Jimmy Carter on the basis of a single name in common – "Smith" – I take this new claim with a grain of salt. My neighbor gives me pruning advice and on the evidence of her rose-bushes, I take it. But what about the case where one of my students comes to report to me a case of sexual harassment, a case where there are no external witnesses; how am I to assess her trustworthiness?

In cases where my source is direct rather than indirect, that is, from the testimony of an individual rather than some form of news media, special forms of evaluation must be used. One is in effect assessing the person. But how does one make such an assessment, and how does one determine what aspects of persons are relevant to take into account?

Gadamer argues that one can make a rational assessment of authority. Against the mistaken Enlightenment belief that giving someone else epistemic authority is "diametrically opposed to reason and freedom," Gadamer argues that authority "properly understood, has nothing to do with blind obedience . . . Indeed, authority has to do not with obedience but with knowledge." One *grants* authority to another not arbitrarily but because one believes that he or she "has a wider view of things or is better informed . . . Thus acknowledging authority is always connected with the idea that what the authority says is not irrational and arbitrary but can, in principle, be discovered to be true."[5] In other words, conferring authority is not a contradiction of rational behavior but one form of it.

Lorraine Code argues further that an account of testimonial knowledge will have two specific effects in epistemology: the first is to motivate a revaluation of the traditional fallacy of the *ad hominem* argument. Considering the messenger of a claim and not just the claim itself is often epistemically necessary in order to judge the claim.[6] But this suggests, secondly, that interpersonal assessments need to be reflective about the moral implications of their assumptions. And this means that epistemological deliberations must be coupled with ethical deliberations. A project of what Code calls " 'everyday' or 'practical' epistemology" – that is, a development and evaluation of normative epistemic principles based not on ideal knowers but on "what real, variously situated knowers actually do" – makes ethical deliberation "*integral* to epistemic discussion."[7] Like virtue epistemologists, Code holds that a fully developed account of epistemic responsibility must consider the moral issues involved in the production and dissemination of knowledge.

But my focus is this: on what basis should we make an *epistemic* assessment of another's authority to impart knowledge? What features of the other are relevant for such an epistemic assessment? Some obvious and uncontroversial features would be: whether we have known this person in the past to be reliable and trustworthy; whether this person has the necessary perceptual capacities or relevant expertise in regard to the knowledge claim; whether we have any reason to believe that in this particular instance, whatever the past performance has been, this person may be unreliable. In some cases we have no prior experience on which to base our judgment and only the most rudimentary knowledge of the person's cognitive capacities. In cases where we lack any knowledge of these *obviously* relevant features, the question arises as to whether in some cases other features might be legitimate to take into account, such as appearance. Surely this is innocuous and straightforward some of the time. When someone young and muscular assures me that rollerblading is easy to learn, I respond, as we often do, "easy for you to say." Their appearance warns me that their judgments in physical matters may be skewed, at least in so far as my body type is concerned. Other times, assessing appearance might be more problematic. I was confused by the use of the term "FLK's" by a staff member of a campus rape crisis center some years ago, and I was disturbed to discover that the term meant "funny-looking kids" and was used as a shorthand among some members of the staff to distinguish credible students from those they thought lacked credibility (on the basis of the number of body piercings and the like). Judgments of appearance introduce social practices of interpretations, cultural meanings, and so forth, and may also operate as a covert means to take into account social identity, such as race or sex.

There are three sorts of questions that social identity raises for epistemological judgment: first, whether it is ever relevant to epistemic assessment, and second, if it is ever relevant, under what conditions is it relevant, and third, how much weight or significance should any such factors be given.

Although these issues are related, such that, for example, the answer to the second question will bear on the first, I would like to hold off as far as possible from approaching the second and especially the third question. I want to address the epistemological question of the relevance of identity without having them immediately to develop an account of its practical implications. In any case, this issue, it seems to me, would be better approached by moral and legal theorists. And I would deny that a "yes" answer to the first question – the question of relevance – entails any given answer to the third question – the question of weight or significance. Moreover, there may be other factors that are more critical in answering the third question, such as political considerations.

The first and second questions are less easy to separate: the first (the question of relevance) is probably impossible to answer without providing some answers to the second (under what conditions). But I want to focus on the question of relevance, without having to provide a fully adequate answer to the question of under what precise conditions such relevance may emerge. Often, in my experience, radical social criticisms are cut off at the gate in just this way, by demanding that the claimant provide both the necessary and sufficient conditions for identifying in every case the problem they claim to exist, as well as a fully worked out remedy. And more generally, as epistemologists enter the arena of social interaction, we need to be reflective about the appropriateness of various theatrical standards.

To return to the issue at hand, it is clear that social identity is not a legitimate feature to take into account in every case of assessing epistemic reliability; it would not be germane to a simple perceptual report, for example (unless someone is giving a simple perceptual report of a kicking fetus or some other forms of experience specific to certain body types, such as are mentioned above). However, there *are* instances where social identity might be deemed relevant, such as in determinations of criminal culpability where a relatively small amount of evidence is the only basis for the decision and where social prejudices can play a role in inductive reasoning. In this sort of case, social identities may be taken into account out of a desire to eliminate bias. Even here, the issue is controversial: biases may occur from all quarters and it cannot be assumed that any given group will be free from prejudicial reasoning. But the further question I want to raise is whether social identities are only ever relevant for the purposes of eliminating bias. Is there a more positive epistemic role that social identity can play in assessing epistemic reliability?

The case against taking social identity into account is strong. There are at least three main lines of objection. Why should socially prescribed identity categories – often having an arbitrary, culturally variable nature, especially in the case of racial identity – have a bearing on one's epistemic reliability? Social identities like race and sex are not in one's control; they make no reference to agency or subjectivity. Except perhaps for one's status as an adult, what can social identity have to do with perceptual ability, judgment, trustworthiness? These capacities are distributed throughout the population without correlation to social identity. Intellectual capacities of cognition and reasoning are universal across the species and thus not connected in any meaningful way to specific identities.

Moreover, the claim that epistemic reliability *is* correlated to social identity has been a key feature of discrimination. Particular groups have been held to have intrinsic tendencies and limited capacities with epistemic relevance, and have been excluded from juries and many other positions of judgment on that basis. In *Blyew* v. *U.S.*, the courts forbad testimony by a black witness against a white defendant. Through the first part of this century, black testimony in courts required independent corroboration from white witnesses, much as we often require today in the case of children's testimony.[8] Stephen Shapin has provided detailed historical accounts of ways in which epistemic credibility was correlated with rank and privilege in Europe.[9] Peasants, slaves, women, children, Jews and many other non-elites were said to be liars or simply incapable of distinguishing justified beliefs from falsehoods. Women were too irrational, peasants too ignorant, children too immature, and Jews too cunning. And slaves, as Aristotle famously argued, were so naturally prone to deceit that they had to be tortured to tell the truth. Surely now we must realize that social identity carries no intrinsic epistemic proclivities or necessary limitations on cognitive practice. Such a claim is tantamount to racism and sexism in whatever form it takes.

A third objection targets the very concept of identity itself, arguing that social identities based on racial and ethnic categories and concepts of gender mistakenly homogenize disparate experience. We neither can nor should assume a similarity of experience, outlook, or perspective among those who share only a socially recognized identity category, and in fact to do so is to continue rather than ameliorate oppression. It is true that individuals must interpret and respond to their inclusion within identity categories, and thus the ways they are identified and grouped are always important features of an individual's life. But there are too many variable responses that individuals can make to their identities for these to serve as useful predictors of individual outlook. Therefore, social identities cannot be taken as relevant aspects for judging epistemic reliability.

Against this last objection, I concede that identity categories group together individuals without a common essence or uniform outlook. Even a shared experience is likely to be interpreted in very different ways. Identities are always social constructions of one form or another, attempts to organize the diversity of human experience into categories with some practical relevance. Sociologist Manuel Castells explains identity as a generative source of meaning, necessarily collective rather than wholly individual, and useful not only as a source of agency but also as a meaningful narrative.[10] And Satya Mohanty makes strong arguments that identity constructions provide narratives that explain the links between group historical memory and individual contemporary experience, that they create unifying frames for rendering experience intelligible, and thus they help to map the social world.[11] To the extent that identities involve *meaning*-making, there will always be alternative interpretations of that meaning.

Of course, identities can be imposed on people from the outside. But that is more of a brand than a true identity, or more of an ascription than a meaningful characterization of self. Identities must resonate with and unify lived experience, and they must provide a meaning that has some purchase, however partial, on the subject's own daily reality. Anuradha Dingwaney and Lawrence Needham explain that lived experience "signifies affective, even intuitive, ways of being in, or inhabiting, specific cultures . . . it is perceived as experience that proceeds from identity that is given or inherited . . . but it is also, and more significantly, mediated by what Satya Mohanty calls 'social narratives, paradigms, even ideologies.' "[12] In other words, although experience is sometimes group-related (and thus identity-related), its meaning is not unambiguous. Dingwaney and Needham go on to say, following Stuart Hall, that:

> What we have are events, interactions, political and other identifica-
> tions, made available at certain historical conjunctures, that are then
> *worked through* in the process of constructing, and/or affiliating with,
> an identity. However, to say that identity is constructed is not to say
> that it is available to any and every person or group who wishes to
> inhabit it. The voluntarism that inheres in certain elaborations of the
> constructedness of identity ignores, as Hall also notes, "certain con-
> ditions of existence, real histories in the contemporary world, which are
> not exclusively psychical, not simply journeys of the mind"; thus it is

incumbent upon us to recognize that "every identity is placed, positioned, in a culture, a language, a history." It is for this reason that
claims about "lived experience" resonate with such force in conflicts
over what does or does not constitute an appropriate interpretation of
culturally different phenomena.[13] (emphasis in original)

Dingwaney and Needham (and Hall) emphasize the non-voluntary
character of location and experience because they want to insist that
identity makes a difference specifically for knowledges, especially those
knowledges involved in cultural interpretation. I agree with this claim,
and will argue for it further on, but here I have introduced it at this
point as an example of an account of identity that holds *both* that
identity makes an epistemic difference *and* that identity is the product
of a complex mediation involving individual agency in which its
meaning is produced rather than merely perceived or experienced. In
other words, identity is not merely that which is given to an individual
or group, but is also a way of inhabiting, interpreting, and working
through, both collectively and individually, how it is to be lived. There
are many ways in which the identity "woman" can be lived, many
interpretations of it as intersected by other types of identity. Yet every
woman must construct for herself an identity that grapples with this
culturally mediated concept, and even if that grappling is an attempt
at complete opposition, this is a struggle those identified as "men"
don't need to make. This account, then, answers the third objection
in so far as it takes identity to be epistemically salient even while it
would reject a notion of identity as a fully determined meaning
uniform across all the individuals of a given identity category.

On a hermeneutic account, identity is understood as constituted by
a horizon of foreknowledges within which experience is made meaningful and from which we perceive the world and act within it.
Identities are thus not opposed but incorporate individual agency.
Foreknowledges, or horizons, are not, however, so easily interchange-
able, nor are they completely different for every individual. Horizons
can be usefully grouped. For example, there is the horizon from which
some individuals perceive the United States primarily as a nation that
was created through stealing the lands of one's ancestors. There is the
horizon from which one's ancestors came here for freedom and
economic opportunity. I am picking out historical narratives as key to
these horizons, as containing collective memories that provide contexts within which individuals make their lives meaningful.

Thus I would agree that identities cannot be taken as indications of a uniform outlook or any shared set of beliefs. Rather, identities mark the background for one's outlook, and these backgrounds themselves can be usefully grouped. This should afford at least prima facie grounds for holding that social identities may have epistemic relevance. I have not established that identities produce shared views or outlooks, but that there is something homogeneous between specified identities nonetheless: a relation to a historical narrative, a location on the map of cultural symbols, a figuration in dominant representations as purported threat, and so on.

In regard to the second objection, that holding social identities to be epistemically relevant carries the danger of discrimination, I will not argue that such danger does not exist. But I do maintain that this possibility in itself cannot determine the answer to the question of epistemic relevance. That is, if social identities can be used against individuals, as a means to discriminate or repress, this in itself does not establish whether or not social identity is a relevant consideration in assessing epistemic credibility. It may certainly affect what we decide to do with this information, or with the moral implications of considering social identity in epistemic judgments, but it does not determine the epistemic relevance in and of itself.

Moreover, the danger of discrimination goes both ways. That is, not taking social identity into account can also lead to discrimination. I will give an example of such a case that builds on Patricia Williams's work in legal theory.[14] Williams's writing is particularly abundant in concrete examples of how social identity makes epistemic differences in what is noticed, understood, meant, and thus, known.

Having discovered Patricia Williams's work, I ask a white male in-law, a civil rights lawyer with whom I often share political agreement, if he has read her work, expecting him to be as excited as I am by it. He is not. "I don't really see why I have to read a description of what she's wearing," he says, evincing an impatience with the informal, narrative, personal style in which Williams writes legal theory. It is true that her writing is not linear, spare, or "objective." We find out about her family life, her feelings, and, yes, the condition of her bathrobe. My relative finds her writing chatty, cute, indulgent. I find it well-organized, scholarly, and intellectually powerful. Her narratives richly portray concrete contexts within which her conclusions then make sense and their plausibility is made clear. Explaining her choice of writing style, Williams writes: "much of what is spoken in so-called objective, unmediated voices is in fact mired in hidden subjectivities and unexamined claims."[15] The informal style she uses is entirely deliberate, she tells us: since there is no norm for black women's legal writing – no space, discursive or social, where such a thing has been possible until very recently – she will try to create one, to write fully as herself rather than aiming toward mastering current white male norms. The inclusion of personal information is likewise motivated; she says "I leave no part of myself out, for that is how much I want readers to connect with me. I want them to wonder about, and to think about some of the things that trouble me."[16] Like any good teacher, she knows that the most important thing to impart is a sensibility to discern and be engaged by important questions, and not simply the ability to remember the received answers.

All of these arguments might be taken to be beside the point of the topic of social identity's epistemic relevance. That is, Williams's work is a sustained argument toward the redesign of legal education based on her claim that knowledge is not as the current norms in law school understand it to be. Thus Williams's claim, and her aim, is universal rather than particular. If "much of what is spoken in so-called objective unmediated voices is in fact mired in hidden subjectivities and unexamined claims," then no one escapes the personal or the narrative that her work makes explicit. Her informal style also works to underscore this point: informality in this context is a form of irreverence toward the shibboleths of academic convention. This is not a relativism about procedures of inquiry but an attack on one set of claims and a defense of another. Thus, so one might argue, Williams's work canot be taken as an argument for the epistemic relevance of social identity but as an argument for a reconfigured account of knowledge and legal judgment, one that can accommodate the ineliminability of context and narrative.

I concede that Patricia Williams is no relativist, gladly. But her arguments strike me as supporting two points: (1) that certain dominant epistemological assumptions in legal theory, those concerning objectivity, transparency of meaning, decontextualized judgment, and so on, are wrong, and will be so in any sphere of discourse; but also (2) that knowledge is dependent on subjectivity, identity, and experience, at least in some important cases. Point (1) is supported directly by point (2), not in contradiction to it. Because knowledge cannot be completely disentangled from social location and experience the pretension to abstraction only conceals the relevant context, preventing the productive dialogue between contexts that is the only means by which true agreement and understanding might emerge.

One of the examples Williams uses is related to a recent conversation I had with friends at my own institution. We were sharing experiences of sexism and racism in the classroom, and of the combined sexism and racism some of us experienced from students. Thankfully, most of our students are not problems in this way, though each of us that evening told a story of a class whose dynamic became difficult because it contained too many such students, a critical mass if not a majority. And for everyone in that conversation, the examples revealed were unmistakable: we knew what certain student behaviour was about, as clearly as we knew whether it was raining. There are students who, when we introduce topics about race or gender identity in the classroom, close their faces up, avert their eyes, and pack their minds away, just like those who always pack their books up ten minutes before class is over. There are students who have decided that they know why we are introducing such material, what we think about it, and what we want them to think about it, before they have endeavoured to study the material or hear what is being said. We also heard stories about students who are inordinately presumptious, who inquire about our qualifications, who are overly (sometimes way overly) casual and physically impertinent. One white male student in a seminar I taught sat next to me, moving closer and closer during my opening remarks, practically leaning against my shoulder to read the notes I was using. When I asked him what he was doing, he reacted with mock innocence and surprise at the question, but five minutes later was at it again until I had him change his seat. Another student had a habit of prefacing his disagreements with my interpretations with the phrase "What Hegel is really saying is that . . ." I have had other white male students persist in interrupting me in class or making sexual remarks in loud whispers until I had to take disciplinary measures. And I remember so well a 19-year-old telling me how proud she was of my accomplishments, and that I should be proud as well. Excuse me?, I wanted to say, who are you to take pride in my accomplishments, my mother?

In philosophy classrooms, we provoke student resistance, we rejoice over persistent questioning, and we like, and often learn from, students who share with us and the class their different interpretations or insights. And in my classroom, I encourage a fair amount of informality and democracy. This is not what I am talking about. In the majority of cases, I can tell full well when a student is attempting to be a true philosopher or simply being playful and when they are simply being a pain in the ass. I could not explain this difference by setting out a set of criteria, e.g., how many questions per class period asked, but I will assert unequivocal knowledge nonetheless, at least in regard to the unambiguous cases of which there are unfortunately too many. My knowlege received confirmation in the conversation that evening from colleagues who have similar identities and had experienced similar treatment, and who understood completely what I was talking about when I began to describe some difficult situation.

This is a problem well known, I would venture, especially among women of color teaching in any white-dominant institution of higher learning today. Equally well known is the absence of assistance, and the lack of sympathy to be expected from white or male colleagues (though, thank goodness, not all are this clueless!). After raising the issue of racism among her students at a faculty meeting, Williams reports: "I was told by a white professor that 'we' should be able to 'break the anxiety by just laughing about it.' Another nodded in agreement and added that 'the key is not to take this thing too seriously.'"[17] But how can they possibly know just how serious the problem is? If they cannot presume to know the scope of the problem, how can they presume to toss off its (easy) solution? Williams's colleagues counseled her to "not give the voices of racism 'so much power.'"[18] Thus they blamed her for the degree of power racism had in her classroom, and accorded her the individual, unsupported ability to disempower it. Like Williams, I will not accept that such problems are my fault, or that if I had a better style of teaching I could forestall such problems; I have won teaching awards, I have great teaching relationships with students most of the time, I know I can teach well, and so, though I sometimes bungle it, I am not responsible for "giving power" to the problem.

This problem of the inability for almost anyone but women or people of color to recognize the special pedagogical difficulties we sometimes face has much more serious consequences than simply our being misunderstood or not believed. An untenured faculty friend of mine, a Chicana who teaches at a nearby university, was demoted because of this very problem. Her contract was not renewed in the usual way but reduced in length and made contingent on the condition that she prove herself a better teacher. A white male graduate teaching assistant, a new student in the department, had complained about her to the chair just as her third year review was approaching. My friend believed the student to be groundless in his complaints, and that they were actually grounded in his discomfort in the position of teaching assistant to a Chicana. Against her account, and without speaking to anyone but the disgruntled student, the department majority formed the opinion that my friend was not a good teacher. This opinion perhaps confirmed their own lack of comfort with her, her "different" style of speaking, interacting, socializing, which she had sensed on many occasions. But this was a young professor who had student evaluations that were numerically consistently above the average of the college faculty as a whole. This was a young untenured faculty member who acted as the beloved advisor of the Latina student group, who cooked for her students every semester, who had many great student – teacher relationships, and who had already published one book and received a major grant to write her second. Yet she enjoyed not the slightest presumption of credibility with much of her department when it came to problems of discrimination in the class-room. They assumed that they, a white-only amalgam of faculty, could assess the situation.

Within a year, that same complaining graduate student developed problems with another member of the department, a senior white male. This senior professor then concluded that the student didn't really have a problem with my friend, but with authority in any form. And the rest of her colleagues then changed their view of her and made an effort to accept her back into the fold. But the real problem was never owned by the department chair or her colleagues. They never considered the possibility that her concern about discrimination was accurate, even if the student also had problems with other faculty. She suffered two years of anguish and self-doubt because of this roadblock in her career. And the university ultimately lost her to another institution.

What should have happened in this situation? The chair should have doubted his own ability to judge the case, given the fact that he had never himself experienced teaching a woman of color, nor seen a woman of color alone in a classroom full of white students. On this basis, the chair should have had more consultation, with other students certainly, but also with those at the institution that would be in a better position to evaluate the conflicting claims. I actually spoke to him on the telephone before the department meeting at which her contract renewal was decided, urging him to consult with such people, and suggested who they might be. He would have none of it, rejecting out of hand the possibility that cultural difference played any role in this. Although I found this hubris frustrating, I sensed that his motivations were at least partly the desire to treat my friend fairly, but to him this meant treating her as an individual without social identity and resisting the possibility that such facts might be relevant unless he himself could see without a doubt that they were so. In my view, his refusal to consider the possibility that social identity might be relevant, that my own motivations, for example, could be based in shared knowledge and not simply in friendship, or that her knowledge of discrimination could be accurate and based on experience, resulted in very unfair treatment. Such is the everyday life of institutional racism and sexism.

This example suggests that not taking social identity into account in some cases can lead to discrimination, and thus that the argument that we should ignore social identity, because to do so may often lead to discrimination, is not persuasive. There are certainly dangers on both sides, and serious ones. But it is simply a mistake to continue to hold that social identity cannot be relevant to epistemic judgments because epistemic reliability is equally distributed throughout the population. It has long been accepted that perception is an interpretive exercise; whenever a human being sees something *as* some thing, delimited and identified, that person is bringing specific (and alterable) ontological commitments to bear. Both Kant and Nietzsche believed such commitments to be universal to the human species as such, though Nietzsche believed them to be alterable and Kant did not. The world is a giant Rorschach test, we might imagine, with multiple frames of intelligibility by which a picture can come into relief.

The hypothesis being considered here, however, is that such perceptual framing occurs not only at the species level but also at the level of social identity. The difference between frames in this latter case need not be as drastic as the difference between the epochs that mark human cognitive transformations, and there is likely to be vast agreement with only a small disagreement. Moreover, there is nothing in this hypothesis that commits me to hold that the different perceptions associated with social identity cannot change, or be learned by others, or even disintegrate. These possibilities should, in fact, be considered necessarily the case given that what we are discussing here are *social* identities, subject to all the plasticity and dynamism of the social domain. However, any difference between what we will for now call frames of intelligibility will count, as long as it is correlated to social identity and it is relevant to knowledge. But anything having to do with perception is, of course, relevant to knowledge.

This must raise the specter of standpoint epistemologies. Am I then defending a version of a standpoint theory, which holds that group identity acts as a standpoint from which knowledge claims are made?

Sandra Harding, the most influential standpoint epistemologist, has held at different times two versions of the standpoint theory. In her early version, standpoints were conceptualized as something like perspectives, yielding fully formed articulations of experience and judgment.[19] This is too easily defeasible by the objection that no such social group is homogeneous enough to have such a shared perspective. The notion of a "woman's standpoint" was either so thin as to be epistemically irrelevant or it was implausibly thick.

Harding then modified her position to hold, following Dorothy Smith, that standpoints yield questions rather than answers. In particular, she argued that the social positions of marginalized people give rise to new questions concerning dominant points of view that members of dominant groups are not likely to consider otherwise. If a scientific research community, for example, is homogeneous enough to share common assumptions and methodological approaches, these shared assumptions and approaches may well be invisible, since there are no contrary assumptions present by which they come into relief. Marginalized social groups, then, entering this community, may well not share all of these assumptions, and may find some of them implausible, thus yielding new and potentially fruitful questions for research.[20]

This notion of social identity leading to new questions is a feasible account, in my view, but it leads to fairly narrow conclusions. It counsels us to work for diversity in research communities, but it does not establish any correlation between social identity and epistemic credibility.

Mohanty suggests just such a correlation: "social locations facilitate or inhibit knowledge by predisposing us to register and interpret information in certain ways. Our relation to social power produces forms of blindness just as it enables degrees of lucidity."[21] On this account, identity does not determine one's interpretation of the facts, nor does it constitute fully formed perspectives, but it yields more than mere questions. Mohanty's idea strikes me as something like this: identities operate as horizons from which certain aspects or layers of reality can be made visible. In stratified societies, differently identified individuals do not always have the same access to points of view or perceptual planes of observation. Two individuals may participate in the same event, but they may have access to different aspects of that event. Social identity operates then as a rough and fallible but useful indicator of differences in perceptual access.

This argument does not rely on a uniformity of opinion within an identity group but on a claim about what aspects of reality are accessible to an identity group. As such, it does rely on a certain amount of uniformity of experience within an identity group, though only in regard to a more or less small sector of their experience, for example, that sector involving being treated in the society as a certain identity, or having a common relationship to social power. On this account, social identity is relevant to epistemic judgment not because identity determines judgment but because identity can in some instances yield access to perceptual facts that themselves may be relevant to the formulation of various knowledge claims. As Mohanty and others have also argued, social location can be correlated with certain highly specific forms of blindness as well as lucidity. This would make sense if we interpret his account as correlating social identity to a kind of access to perceptual facts: to claim that some perceptual facts are visible from some locations is correlatively to claim that they are invisible to others.

Such an account of the relevance of social identity to epistemic judgment needs to be supported by a theory of perception within which it would make sense. Two such views of perception present themselves as providing such support, those of Merleau-Ponty and Foucault; they describe perception not as simple and immediate but as a historically and culturally variable learned practice and as the foundation of consciousness. Merleau-Ponty says of perception:

> Perception is not a science of the world, it is not even an act, a deliberate taking up of a position; it is the background from which all acts stand out, and is presupposed by them. The world is not an object such that I have in my possession the law of its making; it is the natural setting of, and field for, all my thoughts and all my explicit perceptions . . .[22]

Merleau-Ponty follows Husserlian phenomenology, not in its focus on the immediacy of perception, or in the belief in a reduction whereby meanings can be bracketed off from perceptual experience, but in according a centrality to perceptual experience as the key constitutive feature of human existence. The centrality that Merleau-Ponty accords to perceptual experience in no way leads him toward positivist conclusions. Because the cogito is founded on the percipio, it is both undetachable from bodily experience and *incapable* of achieving absoluteness or permanence. In other words, because knowledge is based in bodily perceptual experience, cognition is incapable of total closure or complete comprehensiveness precisely because of our concrete, situated, and dynamic embodiment. It is only because being is always being in the world, and not apart or over the world, that we can know the world. But it is also because being is always being in the world that our knowledge is forever partial, revisable, incomplete.[23] On Merleau-Ponty's view, bringing bodily experience into the center of epistemology has the precise effect of dislodging any hope of certainty or an indubitable foundation.

For Merleau-Ponty, the meaning of an experience is produced within an embodied synthesis of consciousness in the world. Meaning exists in the interworld of history, and thus refers to a world which is always already there before me and yet a world whose meaning is always a meaning for-me (and thus whose meaning necessarily includes values).

> We therefore recognize, around our initiatives and around that strictly individual project which is oneself, a zone of generalized existence and of projects already formed, significances which trail between ourselves and things and which confer upon us the quality of man, bourgeois or worker. Already generality intervenes, already our presence to ourselves is mediated by it and we cease to be pure consciousness, as soon as the natural or social constellation ceases to be an unformulated *this* and crystallizes into a situation, as soon as it has a meaning – in short, as soon as we exist.[24]

Thus the world is not an object at a distance from me, nor something I construct or form, but rather, as Merleau-Ponty said in the previous passage, "it is the background from which all acts stand out ... the natural setting of, and field for, all my thoughts and all my explicit perceptions."[25] As Iris Young explains, for Merleau-Ponty:

> Consciousness has a foundation in perception, the lived body's feeling and moving among things, with an active purposive orientation. Unlike

a Cartesian materialist body, the lived body has culture and meaning inscribed in its habits, in its specific forms of perception and comportment. Description of this embodied existence is important because, while laden with culture and significance, the meaning embodied in habit, feeling, and perceptual orientation is usually nondiscursive.[26]

Thus experience is never capable of being understood or represented as if prior to specific cultural and historical locations. It is clear today that Merleau-Ponty did not fully grasp all of the implications of this analysis, particularly as these impacted his own "generic" descriptions of bodily comportment, as if such descriptions could be given without taking into account gender and other differences. Nonetheless, his most general characterizations of experience reiterate their constitutive relationship to the specificity of social location.

If racial and gendered identities, among others, help to structure our contemporary perception, then they help constitute the necessary background from which I know the world. Racial and sexual difference is manifest precisely in bodily comportment, in habit, feeling and perceptual orientation. These then make up a part of what appears to me as the natural setting of all my thoughts. Perceptual practices are tacit, almost hidden from view, and thus almost immune from critical reflection. Merleau-Ponty says that, "—perception is, not presumed true, but defined as access to truth."[27] Inside such a system, the specificity of perceptual practices disappears. And moreover, because they are nondiscursive, perceptual backgrounds, are incapable of easy description or justification.

Although perception is embodied, it is also learned and capable of variation. The realm of the visible, or what is taken as self-evidently visible (which is how the ideology of social identities naturalizes their specific designations), is argued by Foucault to be the product of a specific form of perceptual practice, rather than the natural result of human sight. Thus he claimed that:

the object [of discourse] does not await in limbo the order that will free it and enable it to become embodied in a visible and prolix objectivity; it does not preexist itself, held back by some obstacle at the first edges of light. It exists under the positive conditions of a complex group of relations.[28]

His central thesis in *The Birth of the Clinic* is that the gaze, though hailed as pure and pre-conceptual, can only function successfully as a source of cognition when it is connected to a system of understanding which dictates its use and interprets its results.

> What defines the act of medical knowledge in its concrete form is not . . . the encounter between doctor and patient, nor is it the confrontation between a body of knowledge and a perception; it is the systematic intersection of two series of information . . . whose intersection reveals, in its isolable dependence, the *individual* fact.[29]

On this account, which is hardly unique to Foucault, visibility itself cannot serve as the explanatory cause of perceptual outcomes. Thus Foucault shares the view now commonly held by philosophers of science that a "pure" observation is not an observation at all, in the sense that to count as an observation it must be able to serve as a support for a theory or diagnosis. It will not become an observation until and unless it can be deployed within a relevant theoretical context.

> The smallest possible observable segment . . . is the singular impression one receives of a patient, or, rather, of a symptom of that patient; it signifies nothing in itself, but assumes meaning and value and begins to speak if it blends with other elements . . .[30]

What Merleau-Ponty and Foucault's work helps us to understand is that perception is not the mere reportage of objects and their features, but serves as an orientation to the world, a background of experience that constitutes one's capacities of discernment and observation.[31] Moreover, it is itself historically situated within particular discursive formations – as Foucault would have it – that structure the possibilities for delimiting objects, concepts and subject-positions, or legitimate viewpoints to be taken up by knowing subjects. Foucault famously makes knowing practices – that is, justificatory practices – internal to a discourse, or discursive formation, rather than essentially (or potentially) unchanged across historical and cultural difference.

These accounts do not provide standard sorts of empirical evidence for their claims, although both Merleau-Ponty and Foucault had direct clinical experience out of which they formulated their views. Providing such evidence would seem to be necessary for establishing the validity of such views, although these views will have an impact on how "evidence" is understood and evaluated. But this is certainly beyond the scope of this paper as well as beyond what philosophy can contribute. What I have tried to provide here is a coherent story about how this claim – that social identity is sometimes epistemically salient – might make sense, to unpack its presuppositions and to assess its intuitive plausibility. The only remaining thing needing to be done is to show the link between such accounts of perception and social identity.

Identity's epistemic relevance follows primarily from its relation to experience, since identity serves as a shorthand marker for experience. We assume that identities are correlated with particular experiences, of oppression, of privilege, a particular history, etc., and though this correlation is often more complicated in reality than a shorthand can express, and sometimes in fact the correlation is nonexistent, there persists a utility, however fallible and sometimes misleading, in making a connection between identity and experience. Thus, the utility of identity categories significantly hinges on the issue of the cognitive significance of experience.[32]

In his essay "Identity, Multiculturalism, Justice," Satya Mohanty argues that experience refers to a process in which human beings make sense of information, or stimuli, and that it is through this process that a substantive self is developed.[33] This process always involves a kind of mediation or interpretation. That is, an event of which I am a part conveys meaning to me through a mediation I perform. In the phenomenological tradition, starting with Dilthey, experience (*erlebnis*) is an event involving simultaneously the immediacy of perception *and* a meaning attribution. The meaningfulness of an experience is not understood as attached to the event, after the fact, but as emerging in the event itself. Thus, the conceptual separation between "raw stimuli" and the attributions of meaning are only a useful cognitive division that we as theorists make to understand the nature of experience: the separation is not a part of the phenomenology of the experience itself. Hans-Georg Gadamer explains this view as follows:

> units of experience are themselves units of meaning . . . The unit of experience is not understood as a piece of the actual flow of experience of an "I," but as an intentional relation . . . Everything that is experienced is experienced by oneself, and part of its meaning is that it belongs to the unity of this self and thus contains an unmistakable and irreplaceable relation to the whole of this one life.[34]

The intrinsic intentionality of experience is the key to understanding its cognitive content. Because experience is an event involving intentionality – involving the "whole of this one life" – a similar event may be experienced very differently by different persons. The interpretive process itself is both individual and social: the effort to establish meaning is performed by the individual, and subject to modification upon her critical reflectiveness, but it is always also conditioned by the concepts, narratives, values, and meanings that are available in her social and discursive context.

Social identities are relevant variables by which available interpretive processes are grouped and distinguished. This is not of course to say that differently identified individuals live in different worlds, or experience globally different perceptions, but that prevalent narratives and concepts are often correlated to specific social identities.

Charles Mills argues in his essay "Non-Cartesian Sums: Philosophy and the African American Experience" that the concept of "sub-personhood," or of the *Untermensch*, is a central way to understand "the defining feature of the African-American experience under conditions of white supremacy (both slavery and its aftermath)."[35] By this concept, which he develops through a contrast drawn between the Cartesian sum and Ralph Ellison's invisible man, Mills elucidates the comprehensive ramifications that white racism had on "every sphere of black life – juridical standing, moral status, personal/racial identity, epistemic reliability, existential plight, political inclusion, social metaphysics, sexual relations, aesthetic worth."[36]

To be a sub-person is not to be a non-person, or an object without any moral status whatsoever. Rather, Mills explains,

> the peculiar status of a sub-person is that it is an entity which, because of phenotype, seems (from, of course, the perspective of the categorizer) human in some respects but not in others. It is a human (or, if this seems normatively loaded, a humanoid) who, though adult, is not fully a person . . . [and] whose moral status was tugged in different directions by the dehumanizing requirements of slavery on the one hand and the (grudging and sporadic) white recognition of the objective properties blacks possessed on the other, generating an insidious array of cognitive and moral schizophrenias in both blacks and whites.[37]

On the basis of this, Mills suggests that the racial identity of philosophers affects the "array of concepts found useful, the set of paradigmatic dilemmas, the range of concerns" with which they each must grapple. He also suggests that the perspective one takes on specific theories and positions will be affected by one's identity, as in the following passage:

> The impatience, or indifference, that I have sometimes detected in black students [taking an ethics course] derives in part, I suggest, from their sense that there is something strange, for example, in spending a whole course describing the logic of different moral ideals without ever talking about how *all of them* were systematically violated for blacks.[38]

This results from an understanding that black lived experience "is not subsumed under these philosophical abstractions, despite their putative generality."[39] It seems eminently plausible that such a point of view taken in regard to the general ethics curriculum has a strong correlation to social identity. From the perspective of those at the "underside of history" and the underside of European modernism in particular, the modernist debates over moral systems may well appear unintelligibly silent about the simultaneous and systematic patterns of colonialism and enslavement.[40]

Mills develops this argument further in *The Racial Contract*, in which he claims that racist social systems must develop corresponding moral epistemologies and norms of epistemic judgement. "There is agreement about what counts as a correct, objective interpretation of the world, and for agreeing to this view, one is . . . granted full cognitive standing in the polity, the official epistemic community."[41] This merely describes normal science, or any discursive community, but Mills further argues that

> on matters related to race, the Racial Contract prescribed for its signatories an inverted epistemology, an epistemology of ignorance, a particular pattern of localized and global cognitive dysfunctions (which are psychologically and socially functional), producing the ironic outcome that whites will in general be unable to understand the world they themselves have made. . . . One could say then, as a general rule, that white misunderstanding, misrepresentation, evasion, and self-deception on matters related to race are among the most pervasive mental phenomena of the past few hundred years, a cognitive and moral economy psychically required for conquest, colonization, and enslavement.[42]

These are strong claims. Mills neither naturalizes nor universalizes them; that is, he neither sees these cognitive dysfunctions as natural to whites nor universal among whites, and he sees whiteness itself with its concomitant perspective as socially constructed. Nonetheless, if his description of cognition at least with respect to racial matters holds true, then there is indeed a strong correlation between social identity and epistemic ability at least in regard to certain kinds of issues.

Social identity matters because experience and perception matter for the possibility of knowledge. No individual is capable of knowing every experiential location, and in our present culture, our social identities are in some cases relevant to our experiential locations, though these are certainly not the most or only relevant feature. The accounts of perception given in much of contemporary phenomenology as well as in analyses of the relation between perception and discourse (or theory), as I have related here through the work of Merleau-Ponty and Foucault, show that perception is a kind of social practice: learned, interpretive, and an index of culture. But the fact that our culture is far from homogeneous must suggest that basic level perception of events and of people, perception which surmises identity, credibility, salient evidence, probable causal relations, plausible explanations, and other important epistemic judgements, can vary across social identities. This variability pertains not only to factual description but also to evaluation and moral assessment. Thus, like Code, I believe that we need to re-evaluate the status of *ad hominem* arguments. Code says that "Prohibitions against appeals to ad hominem evidence derive their persuasiveness from a tacit endorsement of the interchangeableness model of epistemic agency . . . These prohibitions assume that the truth merely passes . . . through the cognitive (= observational) processes of the knowing subject."[43] I have tried to offer accounts of perception that would show that identity differences can effect interchangeableness. Social identities are differentiated by perceptual orientations, which involves bodily comportments that serve as the background for knowledge, learned practices of perception, and narratives of meaning within which new observations become incorporated.

If this account is right, what follows for jury selection or for the judgment of epistemic credibility generally? A mechanistic quota system on juries would seem inadequate to the complexities and constructedness of social identity. But the substantial difficulties in formulating responsible epistemic procedures given the non-inter-changeableness of knowers does not justify simply ignoring the epistemic salience of social identity. The correlation between social identity and some types of knowledge does not confer absolute status on anyone's knowledge claims, to authorize or disauthorize merely on the basis on identity. It does not establish a uniformity of knowledge within a specified group, given the active, mediated nature of experience. And it certainly does not establish that social identity is always epistemically relevant in judging credibility (or even most of the time). Identity and experience remain dynamic, complex, never transparent. And yet, to retreat to an epistemic individualism in the face of these complexities is to negate the patterns that can be seen over the long haul, through a wide lens. It is no accident that new forms of scholarship have emerged from the academy since its democratization with the GI Bill, the passing of civil rights legislation, and affirmative action. All I have argued for is that it is not irrational to consider social identity as a contributing factor in some cases toward establishing the credibility of others' testimony.

Notes

I would like to thank Leslie Bender, Nancy Tuana, Sandra Morgen, and Pablo De Greiff for their help with this paper.
1   See e.g. Keith Lehrer, "Personal and Social Knowledge," *Synthese* 73 (1987), pp. 87–107; Ernest Sosa, *Knowledge in Perspective: Selected Essays in Epistemology* (New York: Cambridge University Press, 1991), ch. 12; James Ross, "Testimonial Evidence," in Keith Lehrer (ed.) *Analysis and Metaphysics: Essays in Honor of R. M. Chisholm* (Dordrecht: Reidel, 1975); H. H. Price, *Belief* (New York: Humanities Press, 1969); John Hardwig, "Epistemic Dependence," *Journal of Philosophy* 82 (1985), pp. 335–50; Catherine Elgin, *Considered Judgement* (Princeton: Princeton University Press, 1996); Frederick Schmitt, "Justification, Sociality, and Autonomy," *Synthese* 73 (1987), pp. 43–86.
2   In the history of philosophy, there is surprisingly scant discussion of this issue. Sosa cites the following: Gottfried Wilhelm Leibniz, *New Essays on Human Understanding*, trans. and ed. P. Remnant and J. Bennett (New York: Cambridge University Press, 1981), bk. IV, ch. xv, sec. 4; David Hume, *An Inquiry Concerning Human Understanding*, ed. Charles W. Hendel (Indianapolis: Library of Liberal Arts Press, 1955); and Thomas Reid, *Inquiry and Essays*, ed. R. E. Beanblossom and K. Lehrer (Indianap-

olis: Hackett, 1983). But in each of these works, there are only a few pages on questions of testimony. Introductory textbooks on epistemology have little if any discussion of this issue, and none that I have seen devote an entire chapter to it as they do to perception, memory, induction, a priori knowledge, and so on. The burgeoning field of social epistemology is beginning to consider issues involved in testimony, though much of social epistemology works instead on questions related to collective knowing, such as in scientific research teams. The questions involved in assessing testimony are different in important respects from epistemic questions concerning collective processes of knowledge acquisition, which concern, for example, rule-governedness, the justifiability of paradigms, and problems around consensus. Frederick Schmitt provides an overview of possible positions on testimony in the introduction of his edited collection *Socializing Epistemology: The Social Dimensions of Knowledge* (Lanham, MD: Rowman and Littlefield, 1994), but he admits that "we" (meaning Anglo-American philosophers) "do not even have a detailed version of weak individualism, even though it is the historically dominant view of testimony" (p. 17). And it is telling that the view he claims to be dominant, what he names "weak individualism," itself works to reduce the importance of testimony from others, by holding that the only source that can justify testimonial beliefs will be non-testimonial beliefs (p. 5).

3   Lehrer, "Personal and Social Knowledge," pp. 96–7; quoted in Sosa, *Knowledge in Perspective*, p. 216.
4   Sosa, *Knowledge in Perspective*, p. 216.
5   Hans-Georg Gadamer, *Truth and Method*, trans. Joel Weinsheimer and Donald G. Marshall, 2nd rev. edn (New York: Crossroad, 1989), pp. 279–80.
6   Lorraine Code, *Rhetorical Spaces: Essays on Gendered Locations* (New York: Routledge, 1995), pp. 70–1.
7   Ibid., pp. xi–xii.
8   See Patricia Williams, *Seeing a Color-Blind-Future: The Paradox of Race* (New York: Noonday Press, 1997), p. 47.
9   Steven Shapin, *A Social History of Truth: Civility and Science in Seventeenth Century England* (Chicago: University of Chicago Press, 1994).
10   Manuel Castells, *The Power of Identity* (Cambridge, MA: Blackwell Publishers, 1997), p. 7.
11   Satya Mohanty, *Literary Theory and the Claims of History: Postmodernism, Objectivity, Multicultural Politics* (Ithaca, NY: Cornell University Press, 1997).
12   Anuradha Dingwaney and Lawrence Needham, "The Difference that Difference Makes," *Socialist Review* 26. 3 & 4 (1996), p. 21.
13   Ibid., pp. 20–1. The passage quoted is from Stuart Hall, "Minimal

Selves," in *Identity*, ed. Lisa Appignanesi (London: ICA, Document 6, 1987), pp. 44–5.
14 Patricia Williams, *The Alchemy of Race and Rights* (Cambridge, MA: Harvard University Press, 1991).
15 Ibid., p. 11.
16 Ibid., p. 92.
17 Ibid., p. 166.
18 Ibid., p. 167.
19 See e.g. *The Science Question in Feminism* (Ithaca, NY: Cornell University Press, 1986).
20 See *Whose Science? Whose Knowledge?* (Ithaca, NY: Cornell University Press, 1991; and "Rethinking Standpoint Epistemology," in L. Alcoff and E. Potter (eds) *Feminist Epistemologies*, (Ithaca, NY: Cornell University Press, 1993). My dissatisfaction with Harding's arguments on these specific points holds against a background of profound agreement I have with her overall epistemic claims. Moreover, Harding more than anyone else deserves credit for creating a space for thinking about social issues in relation to epistemology, and insisting on the necessity of doing so, a credit she never gets in the malestream social epistemology literature.
21 Satya Mohanty, *Literary Theory*, p. 234.
22 Maurice Merleau-Ponty, *The Phenomenology of Perception*, trans. Colin Smith (Atlantic Highlands, NJ: Humanities Press), p. xi.
23 Ibid., p. xiv.
24 Ibid., p. 450.
25 Ibid., p. xi.
26 Iris Young, *Throwing Like a Girl* (Bloomington: Indiana University Press, 1990), p. 14.
27 Merleau-Ponty, *Phenomenology of Perception*, p. xvi.
28 Michel Foucault, *The Archaeology of Knowledge*, trans. A. M. Sheridan Smith (New York: Pantheon, 1982), p. 45.
29 Michel Foucault, *The Birth of the Clinic: An Archaeology of Medical Perception*, trans. A. M. Sheridan Smith (New York: Vintage Books, 1975), p. 30.
30 Foucault, *Birth of the Clinic*, p. 118.
31 Similar accounts of perception have been developed by Kuhn, Nietzsche, and others, though I think Merleau-Ponty and Foucault offer more detailed and illuminating descriptions.
32 This explains the interest in "authenticity," especially in terms of racial and ethnic identity. I am not referring here to the existential concept of authenticity, as in accepting one's freedom, but to the more everyday meaning of the term, as in "authentic creole cooking." There have been numerous and compelling criticisms of the concern with authenticity made since the 1960s. One criticism is that it is used as a test to discredit

persons in a reductive manner, where someone's political position may
be rejected on the grounds of their purported lack of an authentic
identity from which to speak. It also assumes a homogeneity across a
specified group and seems to make all-important a criterion that should
not even be relevant in assessing a person's claims. And it sets up a
pecking order among the oppressed concerning who is more "street,"
who has suffered more, creating divisiveness instead of solidarity. While
all of these criticisms have merit, the kernel of truth in the interest in
authenticity is rooted in an epistemic concern that reveals the link
between identity and experience: Is the person's testimony reliable, e.g.
about the effect that expecting to go to jail has on a boy growing up?
This legitimate epistemic concern does not erase all the negative effects
of the "authenticity test" as described above, but it suggests that we
need to acknowledge that the grounds of the concern over authenticity
is not mere opportunism or the desire for a simplified evaluative process.
In other words, in critiquing the concern for authenticity as reductive,
we should also avoid making a reductive characterization of authenticity
itself.

33 Mohanty, *Literary Theory*, pp. 198–253.
34 Gadamer, *Truth and Method*, pp. 65–7.
35 Charles Mills, "Non-Cartesian Sums: Philosophy and the African-Ameri-
    can Experience," *Teaching Philosophy* 17/3 October 1994), p. 228. Also
    in Charles Mills, *Blackness Visible: Essays on Philosophy and Race* (Ithaca,
    NY: Cornell University Press, 1998).
36 Mills, Non-Cartesian Sums, p. 228.
37 Ibid., p. 228.
38 Ibid., p. 226.
39 Ibid., p. 225.
40 On this point, see also Enrique Dussel, *The Underside of Modernity*, trans.
    and ed. Eduardo Mendieta (Atlantic Highlands, NJ: Humanities Press,
    1996) and *The Invention of the Americas: Eclipse of "the Other" and the
    Myth of Modernity*, trans. Michael Barber (New York: Continuum, 1995).
41 Charles Mills, *The Racial Contract* (Ithaca, NY: Cornell University Press,
    1997), p. 18.
42 Mills, *Racial Contract*, pp. 17–19.
43 Code, *Rhetorical Spaces*, p. 70.

CHAPTER 11

Cognitive Science and the Quest for a Theory of Properties

DASIEA CAVERS-HUFF

Preliminaries

As this is a volume representing women of color who are engaged in the practice of academic philosophy, I think some discussion of how I arrived at this metaphysical perspective is in order. I was immediately fascinated by traditional problems in metaphysics and in the philosophy of psychology. However, with my mother's dictum that I had to be twice as good as anyone else to make it in the "white man's world" ringing in my ears, I decided to make myself even more marketable by studying the physical sciences as well as psychology, along with philosophy. Recently, with the advent of the cognitive studies specialization, this interdisciplinary approach has become much more common.

Through the study of perceptual and cognitive psychology and biology I learned about the array of adaptations that develop because of environmental contingencies. As this newly acquired knowledge helped me to gain what I took to be a more satisfactory hold on some of the philosophical problems I was working on, it also gave me a way to think about some of the adjustment issues I was facing in studying and working in an almost entirely white, overwhelmingly male sub-specialty within philosophy. Our ways of experiencing the world are shaped by our cultural, perceptual, and even linguistic background. The way I perceived the world and the way some of my colleagues perceived the world seemed as different in some respects as human perception and bee perception.

However, that was not as great a revelation as was the fact that this is entirely acceptable. In the framework of realism, there is only one world, and one correct way of perceiving it, as in Keith Campbell's "full, genuine, literal, and metaphysical interpretation." That was the point at which I was stumped. I thought it had to be my way, "they" thought it had to be "their" way. However, my research has taught me that there are many "ways," all equally coherent and equally valid. Many metaphysicians fear reductionism because they fear that there is only one way to reduce. The historical name for the central problem of this paper is the problem of "one over many."

In 1987 Alvin Goldman presented a paper to the Eastern Division of the American Philosophical Association, which was titled "Cognitive Science and Metaphysics."[1] This paper was the first attempt, that I am aware of, to explore the ramifications of work in the cognitive sciences for traditional problems in metaphysics. In it Goldman explored the implications of Gestalt psychology for our object unification schema.

I propose to extend this idea – the application of principles derived from the cognitive sciences – to another long-standing problem in metaphysics: the theory of properties. The discussion will proceed in four distinct stages; first I will explain the need for a theory of properties. Second, I will explain why I take traditional realist doctrines, and nominalism with respect to properties, to be inadequate responses. Third, I will sketch the way in which the cognitive sciences can help to provide the framework for a theory of properties which is consistent with the goals of philosophical naturalism. Fourth, I will address the most formidable objection to this account.

The Need for a Theory of Properties

An observation that leads one to postulate properties as part of the ontology is that it is difficult to give an account of similarities between objects without a theory of properties. This may be referred to as the problem of resemblance and qualitative recurrence. When one claims that two objects are similar in a respect this may plausibly be construed as meaning that two objects are similar in that they possess the same property.

W. V. Quine and Nelson Goodman develop a nominalism that attempts to do away with properties and abstract entities.[2] A clear statement of this thesis is given by Quine (1980):

One may admit that there are red houses, roses, and sunsets, but deny, except as a popular and misleading manner of speaking, that they have anything in common. The words 'houses', 'roses', and 'sunsets' are true of sundry individual entities which are houses, roses and sunsets . . . but there is not, in addition, any entity whatever, individual or otherwise, which is named by the word 'redness', nor for that matter, by the word 'househood', 'rosehood', 'sunsethood'. That the houses and roses and sunsets are all of them red may be taken as ultimate and irreducible, and it may be held that McX is no better off, in point of real explanatory power, for all the occult entities he posits under such names as 'redness'. (p. 10)

It is a striking phenomenon that unlimited numbers of things appear to share the same (or similar) characteristics. It is not entirely satisfying to say that the similarities are ultimate and irreducible. This may ultimately be the case, but the fact that the available theories that attempt to account for the phenomenon are problematic is not a reason, in and of itself, to reject properties out of hand, especially if they serve a necessary explanatory function.

Also, our ability to recognize and classify new things along with other things that we are familiar with is best explained by the hypothesis that the things share common properties. The ability to classify things is the ability to sort things and group them according to qualitative similarities. One way to construe qualitative similarities is in terms of shared properties.

Another complex issue involving properties is providing the truth-conditions for statements that make reference to properties. There are many statements that appear to be straightforward quantifications over properties. It is impossible to paraphrase these statements in such a way that the reference to properties is eliminated. Statements of this type seem to require, for their semantics, a theory of properties. For example, consider sentences such as:

1   Redness resembles orangeness more than it does blueness.
2   Red is a color.

If we paraphrase these statements in a way in which the quantifiers range over ordinary concrete objects, we get something like the following sentence:

1'   Red objects resemble orange objects more than they do blue ones.

If the objects referred to in (1′) are red lollipops, orange birds, and blue lollipops, then where (1) appears, *prima facie*, to be true, (1′) is plainly false. It is impossible to come up with paraphrases for sentences like (1) and (2) that don't contain an ineliminable reference to properties.[3]

It does not matter whether one is a Platonic realist about universals or whether one has a different view of what properties are, properties serve a useful function as a semantic device. They can serve as the values of the quantificational variables in sentences that quantify over properties. It is not necessary to be a Platonic realist about universals, but some theory of properties is needed to provide a semantics for such sentences.

The Big Three: Platonism, Aristotelian Realism, and Nominalism

In the philosophical literature concerning the theory of properties, the name "realism" has been given to a doctrine whose roots are generally traced back to Plato. The most common application of the term is to those theories that hold that properties consist in a type of object, called a universal. However, there are a number of distinct doctrines which fall under the category of realism. Two of the most influential of these theories are Platonic (universal) realism and Aristotelian realism.[4]

Platonic realism

For the Platonic realist, each property, relation, action, and kind presuppose a multiply instantiable entity. If two things are both red, the Platonic realist believes that there is literally some one thing, redness, which is shared by the two objects. If two couples are both married couples, the *same* relation, marriage, binds each of the couples. If two people cough, these are two instances of the *same* action. Platonic universals are interesting entities. Whenever an object exemplifies a universal, the universal is wholly and completely present in it. What distinguishes universals from particulars is that, in the case of universals, one and the same entity is present in many different objects. This is what is meant by saying that universals are multiply instantiable or multiply exemplifiable. Because it is impossible for one and the same physical object to occupy different regions of space-time, the Platonic realist postulates an independent realm of existence for the universal, outside time and space.

The two most vexing of the legendary problems raised by Platonic realism are those of ontological economy and of explaining the relation obtaining between universals and particulars. Adherence to the doctrine of Platonic universals entails positing a "transcendent" realm, outside time and space, in which the universals exist. Also, there is the issue of getting a conceptual grasp on what exactly a "universal" is. Adherents of philosophical naturalism balk at positing transcendent realms and countenancing "abstract" entities. Concerning the difficulty in explaining the relation between universals and particulars, there is the infamous "third man" regress. Also, discussions of the relations of "sharing," "participation," and "imitation" never quite descend from the level of the metaphorical. There is textual evidence that even Plato himself was never fully satisfied with his attempts to explain the relation.[5] There are no absolutely decisive arguments against the existence of transcendent universals, as there have never been concerning the existence of nonphysical minds. However, if one is a philosophical naturalist, the problems are an incentive to find an account of properties that avoids the problems raised by postulating transcendent universals.

Aristotelian realism

In the *Categories*, Aristotle states that there are things that are both *in* and *said of* substances. The particular example that Aristotle uses is that of knowledge. The type-token distinction, the distinction between particular instances (tokens) and general categories under which these particular instances fall (types) may help to explain Aristotle's distinction. Knowledge is *in* the mind (tokens). Knowledge may be *said of* subjects, such as grammatical knowledge (type).[6] One way of interpreting this section of the *Categories* is that the modern term "property" contains a systematic ambiguity. On the one hand, there is Aristotle's notion of property as "non-substantial individuals."[7] These are the properties possessed by the "primary substances" or objects. Any one of them is an individual, because my knowledge of grammar belongs to me, not to anyone else. This knowledge is numerically distinct from all the other bits of grammatical knowledge possessed by anyone else. It is not a substance because it would not exist if I (or at least my mind) did not exist. In the sense that knowledge is a type, it is a universal, a category. You can use knowledge as the grammatical subject of a sentence – Knowledge is never wasted. Bits of knowledge that are possessed by individuals are the non-substantial (knowledge) individuals, and the general category of knowledge is the universal.

For many theorists, Aristotelian realism is particularly appealing because it brings properties into time and space, as opposed to standing apart in some transcendent realm.[8] However, explaining the relation of "inherence" or "instantiation" – the tie that binds non-substantial individuals and particulars – poses a problem for the Aristotelian realist as it does for her Platonic counterpart. One answer is to say that this is just the way things are, that the world consists of particulars instantiating properties, and that this is a basic fact that cannot be analyzed any further.[9] But any attempt to analyze the concept of instantiation leads to the same type of regress that plagues Platonic realism.

There is also a further line of criticism. If properties are "non-substantial individuals" that are possessed by objects, there is a sense in which objects possessing the same property should have an exactly resembling aspect, or, in other words a common physical structure. I will refer to this as the "common physical structure thesis." Larry Hardin, in *Color for Philosophers*, identifies a list of at least fifteen distinct physical causes of things appearing blue to us.[10] This and other examples strongly suggest that there is no common component that all things which appear to possess the same property share.

Nominalism

Nominalism, with respect to properties, is a doctrine which has also enjoyed a long history. The philosophers most commonly associated with nominalism in the twentieth century are W. V. Quine and Nelson Goodman. The nominalist denies the existence of properties, relations, classes, and other abstract entities. In a jointly-authored essay, Quine and Goodman state their position:

> We do not believe in abstract entities. No one supposes that abstract entities – classes, relations, properties, etc. – exist in spacetime; but we mean more than this. We renounce them altogether. We shall not forego all use of predicates and other words that are often taken to name abstract objects. We may still write "x is a dog," or "x is between

y and z"; for here "is a dog," and "is between … and …" can be construed as syncategorematic: significant in context but naming nothing … Any system that countenances abstract entities we deem unsatisfactory as a final philosophy.[11]

The nominalist position is quite difficult to get a clear grasp on. Nominalists say that there are no such things as properties. We use terms that refer to properties meaningfully, but here Goodman and Quine state that they actually name nothing. In other places, it seems as if nominalists such as Quine are actually realists about classes.[12]

I believe that for most authors, nominalism is not a well-developed theory, in and of itself, but a reaction to the excesses of Platonic realism.[13] In a number of different places, including the passage quoted above, it is clear that the modern nominalist equates property realism with Platonic universal realism: "No one supposes that abstract entities exist in spacetime." If the nominalist thinks that Platonic realism is the only realist game in town, she has set a false dilemma for herself. There may be explanations of qualitative recurrence other than either postulating it as basic and unanalyzable, or countenancing Platonic transcendent universals. There are several problems that cry out for an explanation:

1   How to provide a coherent semantics for statements that refer to properties;
2   How to explain resemblance and qualitative recurrence;
3   How to arrive at our schemes of categorization and classification.

The fact that nominalism fails to answer any of these questions is a compelling reason to continue to search for alternative accounts of what it is to be a property. In all likelihood, this theory will be quite complex. In the proposal that follows, it will involve many disciplines outside the province of traditional metaphysics.

Cognitive Science and Metaphysics Revisited: Toward a Theory of Properties

The theory that I will sketch is not a new one. Aspects of it are to be found in Kant's distinction between the phenomenal and the noumenal. It is also not unlike Descartes' and Locke's theories of secondary qualities. What is new, however, is that the sciences of cognitive and perceptual psychology, psychophysics, evolutionary psychology, and ethology, allow us to give these ideas an empirical grounding that was not available to Descartes, Locke, or Kant.

I construe our attributions of properties to objects to consist of complex relations between perceivers, environments, and objects. To say that an object is red is to use a shorthand way of referring to the very complex relation between the visual system of a chromat (an organism with color vision), the ambient environment, and some object. To stress the centrality of the perceptual and cognitive mechanisms of organisms to the attribution of properties to objects is not to deny some minimal form of realism.

In order to illustrate this point, we shall consider color. "Colored" light does not exist. What exists is electromagnetic radiation of certain wavelengths. Only a certain portion of the entire spectrum of wavelengths is visible to humans. These particular wavelengths are interpreted as color by the human visual system. There are other organisms whose visual systems are able to interpret as colors, electromagnetic radiation that lies outside the human visible spectrum. Thus, there are colors which, although visible to these other organisms, will never be known by humans. For instance, bees, can see color far into the ultraviolet range. Such light lies outside the human visual spectrum.[14]

Color, then, is an essentially visual phenomenon. If there were no observers, there would be no colors. There would be no reason for there to be colors. Color is an invaluable stimulus dimension for organisms. It enables them to localize and identify target objects in the environment. Color vision is crucial to the survival of some organisms, such as humans and bees. It may well mean the difference between life and death for bees that they are able to identify the hint of color that indicates the presence of nectar-bearing flowers hidden among bushes, grasses, and leaves.

To argue in this fashion is not to deny that there is a dimension of color that is independent of the perceptual and cognitive mechanisms of organisms. There is the pigment contained within the object's surface which selectively absorbs and reflects light. The pigment is not to be identified with the color, however. There are pigments which absorb and reflect different wavelengths that give rise to the same apparent color. This is the phenomenon of metameric matches: two different wavelengths of light, which are interpreted by the visual system as the same color. Another phenomenon is that of surface colors. In the case of metallic colors, such as gold and silver, the apparent colors are not due to pigments. The appearance is due to the way in which the surface reflects the light, and that reflected light is interpreted by the visual system as color. With the phenomena of pigments, metameric pairs, and surface colors, there is no thing possessed by the object that can be equated with the color, but there are objective features of objects which are implicated as part of the color phenomenon.[15] Thus, while there is something about the structure of the object which is involved in an essential way with the attribution of properties to objects, the involvement of the perceptual and cognitive mechanisms of organisms is just as important. A human scientist, and if they existed, scientists among dogs and bees, would attribute properties to objects in very different ways. All organisms capable of perception are limited by their particular perceptual and cognitive structures, which are crucially involved in determining what the world is like for them. They are every bit as important as what objects are like in themselves (if there is such a thing). There is no view from nowhere.

Color is not the only object property that can be analyzed in this way. Apparent size, shape, and brightness are all influenced by cognitive mechanisms. A strict perceptual realist, who may be roughly characterized as holding the view that the perceived properties of objects correspond, in a rather precise way, to the physical stimuli which give rise to our perceptions of those properties, would be confounded by the number and variety of cognitive mechanisms that go into our perception of objects. One psychophysicist states:

> The perception of many aspects of the environment is due not only to the biophysical character of the incoming stimulation and the appropriate sensory receptor mechanisms, but is also due to certain dispositions and existing intentions within the perceiver. There are psychological processes . . . that play a role in organizing incoming stimulation into a meaningful percept.[16]

The constancies

I will now briefly summarize some of the cognitive mechanisms which are active in shaping our perception of object properties. The constancies account for the stability of our perceptual experience throughout myriad changes which take place in the physical environment. The eye is in a state of continual movement, executing between two to four movements per second. Also we are constantly moving from environments with greater and lesser amounts of illumination, and we rapidly approach and retreat from objects in the environment. The reason we do not get the visual sensation of watching a damaged videotape, the sensation of familiar objects magically "changing" color as we move from areas with more or less light, or of objects growing and shrinking as we approach or retreat, as they would if our perceptions exactly matched the retinal image that objects cast, is due to the action of the constancies.

We utilize a number of different cues in conjunction with physical stimuli in order to generate a percept. Some of these cues are physiological. The visual system is "aware" of the functioning of its different elements. The lens of the eye accommodates, or changes shape when the distance fixated upon changes. And in binocular vision the eyes converge in order to focus on near objects, and they diverge when focusing on things further away. The visual system takes into account these accommodation changes in determining the distance of the object being viewed, and incorporates this information into perception. There are also neural inhibitory changes that take place to keep colors and illuminance (brightness) constant as we move through different levels of ambient illumination.[17]

Knowledge and experience are also important factors in the effect of the constancies. For instance, researchers studied two groups of students, college students from Pennsylvania and students matched for age and educational level from Guam. All the students viewed a scene which exemplified the Ponzo illusion, where, if two logs of the same size are placed between and parallel to apparently converging parallel lines, such as train tracks, the furthest log appears larger than the near one, although they are the same size. The Pennsylvania students overestimated the size of the second and more distant log significantly more than did the students from Guam. This is probably due to the fact that there are no railroads on Guam, and the vistas are quite short, owing to hills and tropical plant growth. The type of distance viewing possible in Pennsylvania is not possible in Guam, and the students from Guam have not learned to take into account the distance cues, and thus do not experience the Ponzo illusion to the same extent as the Pennsylvania students.[18] Experiments like this one demonstrate the role of experience in perception. Knowledge, such as the knowledge that objects closer to a light source will have more available light to reflect, will cause objects closer to the light source to appear brighter than those more distant from the source, even in cases where the more distant ones are actually reflecting more light to the retina of the eye.[19]

Memory color

There is a classic experiment in perceptual psychology to determine the effect of memory on perceived color. Cut-outs of a donkey and a leaf are presented to subjects. These forms are bathed in a spectrally pure red light. Under these viewing conditions the cut-outs should both appear to be a neutral grey color. But subjects routinely report that the apparent color of the leaf is "greener" than that of the donkey.[20]

It is impossible to link the apparent color difference between the leaf and donkey cut-outs to the light reflected by the object and transmitted to the eye, because in both cases, this reflected light is the same. The only plausible explanation for the reported color difference is the knowledge that donkeys are typically grey and leaves are usually green. Thus, experience, recorded in memory, is imported into perception. These experimental results have been frequently replicated. When subjects are asked to match color chips with the remembered colors of familiar objects, the color chip selected for grass is greener than actual grass, the chip selected to match the color of an apple is a truer red than actual apples, and that chosen to match "memory" bananas is yellower.[21]

Any current perceptual experience consists of a complex evaluation of the significance of stimuli reaching our receptors. Through our life experience we learn that certain objects or conditions have a high probability of being related to each other. On this basis we make our best bet as to what we are viewing. Perception is more of an active construction as opposed to the passive reception of external stimuli. Contextual effects derived from past experiences are a large part of our ability to construct our viewpoint.

There are many culturally relative psychological effects in perception. One example is the viewing of pictures. When three-dimensional scenes are represented in pictures, cues such as depth cues, determine which objects appear closer and allow the viewer to interpret the action in the picture. Isolated observers who are not very familiar with pictorial representation have great difficulty utilizing depth cues in pictures. There is a vast difference in the ability to utilize pictorial depth cues between these isolated subjects relative to more urbanized subjects familiar with pictorial representation.[22]

The examples provided here provide support for understanding some of the diverse factors that take us from sensory stimulation to a full-blown conception of objects in the physical world. In some respects, what contemporary perceptual psychology suggests concerning metaphysics is reminiscent of the Kantian perspective, in that there is a split between the world of our perception and the "real" world. There is now a wealth of experimental data which supports the conclusion that many aspects of our experience consist of a construction or a projection. Our experiences of the world go far beyond what is given in sensation. In some cases the mechanisms active in perception appear to be "hard wired," in that there are distinctive ways that humans with normally functioning perceptual apparatuses will perceive objects in the environment, e.g., as colored. There are numerous other factors important to perception that must be learned, for instance, our spatial perception ability, language, and context effects upon perception. Thus many of the properties attributed to objects in the environment must be explained in terms of complex relations between perceivers, environments, and of course, the objects themselves.

An Objection and a Reply

One objection to my approach here is that the properties of objects *seem* to us to be located *in* the object. For example, the shirt is red, the wastebasket is rectangular. It is not the observer, the environment, and the shirt or basket together that, to us, is red or rectangular. There is something oddly unsatisfying and counterintuitive to us about an account that proposes such a thing. Traditional realist accounts and trope theory, which locate properties entirely within objects, are much more satisfying in this respect. One noted author in the area of metaphysics states:

> Subjectivism comes in at least three forms, all of which must be, in one way or another, projectivist. It is the essence of every subjectivism to hold that whatever does literally bear the colour properties, it is not the

bodies (or the surfaces, or the light sources) that seem to. So, appearances must deceive; anyone who thinks that grass is green – in the full, genuine, literal and metaphysical interpretation of that proposition – must be making a mistake. Every projection theory is an error theory. They all hold that because grass acts on us so that it looks green, we wrongly suppose that it is green. We project greenness onto the cause of looking green, and so fall into error. All subjectivisms are projectivist, so they are all error theories.

That by itself is not fatal. But error theories are fall-back positions. They do not recommend themselves as inherently plausible; they are positions to which one is forced, reluctantly, by the untenability of the alternatives. This is true of error theories in general – in ethics, for example. And it is true for colour. Indeed error theory about colour is not just a fall-back option; it is a desperation option.[23]

Theorists such as Campbell criticize projectivist accounts as proposing that there is something faulty about our perception of the world. However, in the last section I was discussing normal perception. If normal perception diverges so sharply from the way "the world" actually *is*, there is perhaps some reasonable explanation for it.

This brings us to a very important point. A distinction needs to be drawn between the explanation of what a property *is* (an ontological issue) and the explanation of *why* we attribute the properties that we do, or why we attribute them at all (a functional/teleological issue). This propensity of ours to locate properties *in* objects is very relevant to it. However, with respect to the ontological issue, the matter may be summed up by a quote from cognitive scientist Alexander Rosenberg: "The mere fact that one explanation allays feelings of curiosity better than another cannot be a basis for saying that it is more correct, complete or otherwise superior to a subjectively less satisfying explanation."[24]

Our lack of appreciation of the science of an adequate ontology of properties suggests a couple of analogies. We are not conscious of the vast amount of metabolic activity occurring in our bodies as we sit still in our chairs. In fact, it took many thousand years to come to a scientific understanding of the inner workings of our bodies; the research is ongoing, and will be for a very long time to come. Even those of us who are well versed in human physiology have no awareness of most of our bodily functioning. The same goes, for the most part, for both mechanically and non-mechanically inclined drivers of cars. If this were not the case, then sophisticated computerized diagnostic analyses of the automobile's functioning by the mechanically inclined would not be needed. Thus it is not surprising that the details of the ontology of the properties that we attribute to objects are not given in our experience of those objects.

Georges Rey, commenting on consciousness, states that "people regularly express surprisingly strong (often conflicting) opinions about the mental lives of many things around them – ants, rats, chimps, infant humans – opinions that bear almost no relation to any serious examination of those things."[25] According to commentators such as Rosenberg and Rey, the fact that the account under consideration is counterintuitive does not necessarily count against it. Even if it did, the theory I am proposing is in no worse shape than either traditional realism and nominalism.

Fortunately, there are some explanatory resources to draw on in making the conclusion that our phenomenal experience is at best illusory, somewhat more palatable. The hypothesis is this: the functional/teleological explanation for our perceiving objects as having the properties that we experience is that it confers advantages upon us, *qua* organisms. The attributions might not be literally correct, but they are useful from a functional/teleological standpoint. The ability to attribute phenomenal properties to objects has arisen through the process of natural selection.

These abilities have been selected for because making such attributions confers an adaptive advantage on those organisms who can do so. Attributing properties to objects confers a survival advantage. Red fruit is ripe, and therefore good to eat. A recent study reported in a book on sex differences suggests that individuals whose scents are most sexually appealing to us are generally quite genetically different from us, therefore decreasing the chance of certain inherited genetic defects in our offspring.[26]

Natural selection is the best scientific explanation of adaptive complexity. Adaptive complexity describes any system composed of many interacting parts where the details of the parts' structure and arrangement suggest design to fulfill some function.[27] The engineering elegance of the mechanisms which play an integral part in the attribution of phenomenal properties to objects constitutes strong evidence that they evolved as a result of serving some useful function. Adaptationist explanations are appropriate when we are confronted with a complex design which carries out some reproductively significant function.

Some of the most striking examples of such structures are in the area of perception. The human eye, for instance, to use an oft-cited example, is a highly complex arrangement of specialized features that obviously do some very useful things for us. It is even more striking, when we consider the differences in perceptual structures, across species. These structures vary in quite predictable ways which suit the environments that these species inhabit.

For example, the retinas of frogs contain "bug detectors": neural receptors that fire at an optimal rate in the presence of bugs. However, the retinal bug detectors in the frog respond not only to bugs, but also to any object that is perceptually similar – small and black and moving in a certain trajectory. The rabbit retina also has a variety of specialized devices not found in human retinas, including a "hawk detector." There are numerous sensory mechanisms possessed by organisms that are elegant solutions to the special adaptive problems posed by the environments they inhabit. Examples could be given endlessly: pit organs in snakes, electric charges from fish, and the bat's echo-location system.

All of the sensory mechanisms found in organisms solve some adaptive problem. The issue is not to accurately represent the world as the realist would prefer. The point is survival – feeding, fleeing, fighting, (and you know the other "f" word). The ripe fruit might not literally be red, but it is certainly efficacious to perceive it as being so. Thus, while the attribution of phenomenal properties to objects does not yield literal truth, it demonstrably confers a great benefit upon those who are able to do so.

Notes

1   Alvin Goldman, "Cognitive Science and Metaphysics," *Journal of Philosophy* 84 (1987), pp. 537–54.
2   W. V. Quine, "On What There Is," in *From a Logical Point of View* (Cambridge: Harvard University Press, 1980). Nelson Goodman and W. V. Quine, "Steps Toward a Constructive Nominalism," in N. Goodman, *Problems and Projects* (Indianapolis: Bobbs-Merrill, 1972).
3   For an extended discussion of the problems raised by the semantics of statements which refer to properties, see D. M. Armstrong, *Universals and Scientific Realism*, vol. I (Cambridge: Cambridge University Press, 1978), especially ch. 6.
4   There is another major realist contender: trope theory, the doctrine of

278   Dasiea Cavers-Huff

abstract particulars. This doctrine is expounded by D. C. Williams in "On the Elements of Being I and II," *Review of Metaphysics* 6 (1953), p. 6, and more recently in Keith Campbell's *Abstract Particulars* (Oxford: Blackwell Publishers, 1990). However, limitations of time and space prevent me from giving it the discussion that it deserves. Aristotelian realism may be interpreted as a type of trope theory, so the criticisms of that doctrine apply more or less to canonical trope theory as presented by Williams and Campbell.

5   Hilary Staniland, *Universals* (New York: Anchor Books, 1972). See ch. 1, especially pp. 4–5.

6   Aristotle, *Categories*, in R. McKeon (ed.) *The Basic Works of Aristotle* (New York: Random House, 1941), 1a29–1b2.

7   For discussions of the concept of non-substantial individuals in the *Categories*, see R. Heinaman, "Non-substantial Individuals in the *Categories*," *Phronesis* 26/3 (1981), pp. 295–307; J. Annas, "Individuals in Aristotle's *Categories*: Two Queries," *Phronesis* 10/1 (1965), pp. 97–105; and R. E. Allen, "Individual Properties in Aristotle's *Categories*," *Phronesis* 14/1 (1969), pp. 31–9.

8   D. M. Armstrong classifies his version of property realism, which is set forth in *Universals and Scientific Realism*, as an "Aristotelian realism."

9   Armstrong uses Scotus' analogy of the simultaneous unity and distinguishability of the members of the Holy Trinity as an example of the type of "tie" between the universal and particular he envisions. This discussion takes place in vol. I, pp. 109–11.

10 C. L. Hardin, *Color for Philosophers* (Indianapolis: Hackett, 1988), pp. 2–6. In this section Hardin explains that the blue of the sky, the blue of bodies of water, the blue of eyes, the blue of sapphires, and the blue of lapis lazuli, to mention only a few, arise through the action of quite distinct physical processes.

11 Goodman and Quine, "Steps Toward a Constructive Nominalism," p. 173.

12 W. V. Quine, "New Foundations for Mathematical Logic," in *From a Logical Point of View*, pp. 80–101.

13 Rudolf Carnap, *The Logical Structure of the World* (London: Routledge, 1967); John Searle, *Speech Acts* (Cambridge: Cambridge University Press, 1969), especially p. 105; Quine, "On What There Is," p. 14.

14 The visual system of bees, along with the comparative perceptual psychology of numerous species is presented in a very elegant fashion in Diana Ackerman's *A Natural History of the Senses* (New York: Vintage Books, 1990).

15 On the topics of metameric matches and surface colors, see Hardin, *Color for Philosophers*, ch. 1.

16 H. R. Schiffman, *Sensation and Perception* (New York: Wiley, 1976), p. 253.
17 The neural inhibitory factors involved in the constancies are discussed in detail in the classic text on visual perception, T. N. Cornsweet's *Visual Perception* (New York: Academic Press, 1970).
18 H. W. Leibowitz, R. Brislin, L. Perlmutter, and R. Hennessy, "Ponzo Illusion as a Manifestation of Space Perception," *Science* 166 (1969), pp. 1174–6.
19 J. Beck, "Apparent Spatial Position and the Perception of Lightness," *Journal of Experimental Psychology*, 69 (1965), pp. 170–9.
20 K. Duncker, "The Influence of Past Experience upon Perceptual Properties," *American Journal of Psychology*, 52 (1939), pp. 255–65.
21 J. L. Delk and S. Fillenbaum, "Difference in Perceived Color as a Function of Characteristic Color," *American Journal of Psychology* 78 (1965), pp. 290–3.
22 On the subject of cultural factors involved in the perception of pictures, see J. B. Deregowski, "Illusion and Culture," in R. L. Gregory and E. H. Gombrich (eds) *Illusion in Nature and Art* (New York: Scribner, 1973), pp. 161–92; G. Jahoda and H. Mc Gurk, "Pictorial Depth and Perception: A Developmental Study," *British Journal of Psychology* 65 (1974), pp. 141–9; P. L. Kilbride and M. Robbins, "Linear Perspective and Pictorial Depth Perception and Education Among the Baganda," *Perceptual and Motor Skills* 27 (1968), pp. 601–2, H. F. Duncan, N. Gourlay, and W. Hudson, *A Study of Pictorial Representation among the Bantu and White Primary School Children in South Africa* (Johannesburg: Whitwatersrand University Press, 1973).
23 Keith Campbell, "David Armstrong and Realism about Colour," in J. Bacon, K. Campbell, and L. Reinhardt (eds) *Ontology, Causality, and Mind: Essays in Honour of D. M. Armstrong* (Cambridge: Cambridge University Press, 1993), p. 265.
24 Alexander Rosenberg, "Why DNA Contains Thymine and Why Humanists Should Care," Distinguished Faculty Lecture, University of California Riverside, Spring 1995, p. 3.
25 Georges Rey, "Towards a Projectivist Account of Conscious Experience," in T. Metzinger (ed.) *Conscious Experience* (Schoningh: Imprint Academic, 1995), pp. 123–42.
26 Deborah Blum, *Sex on the Brain: The Biological Differences Between Men and Women* (New York: Penguin Books, 1998), pp. 14–15.
27 S. Pinker and P. Bloom, "Natural Language and Natural Selection," *Behavioral and Brain Sciences* 13 (1990), pp. 707–84.

CHAPTER 12

Descartes' Realist Awake–Asleep Distinction, and Naturalism

NAOMI ZACK

Prologue

My ultimate perspective on philosophy is architectonic. Since college, I have been interested in the shapes of ideas, in how blocks of knowledge from different areas of study are related to one another. My philosophical training at Columbia University in the late 1960s had, to the best of my knowledge, nothing to do with race, insofar as I understood both race and philosophy at that time. Since 1990, when I returned to academic philosophy after a long absence, I have pursued work on racial categories and, collaterally, built on my interests in the history of philosophy.

I have always liked Descartes as a philosopher because of the way he develops abstract intellectual inquiry in a writing style that personalizes his thought. I cannot form an idea of what Descartes might have said about race, as we now understand it, because the modern biological idea of race was not in existence when he wrote and he made no direct contributions to its development. I do know that Descartes thought that philosophy was, in principle, as accessible to women as men.[1]

My discussion of Descartes' distinction between being asleep and awake is primarily a textual interpretation. I am fascinated that the most rationalist of rationalists was in a fundamental sense, a realist. I am some species of realist, myself. My work on the false biological categories of race presupposes that something must be real, as an object of science. If nothing were real, there would not be much importance in showing that race is unreal in the ways in which people (falsely) assume that it has a foundation in the biological sciences.[2]

The connection of reality to waking experience that I ascribe to Descartes, below, has existential and social, as well as epistemic implications. For instance, when Martin Buber contrasted a spiritual emphasis on social interaction with a practice of isolated withdrawal from the world, he evoked Heracleitus of Ephesus. Heracleitus related the experience of cosmic order to activity undertaken by human beings in common, while awake.

> "Not as men asleep," says Heracleitus, "must we act and speak." For in sleep appearance reigns, but reality exists only in waking and, in fact, only to the degree of our working together.[3]

Descartes' vision of the experience of cosmic order, or of science, was tied to indubitable first principles that were made up of clear and distinct ideas. Clear and distinct ideas were experienced in the first person by individuals. Therefore, Descartes did not fully recognize the social, or interhuman, dimension of scientific objectivity. Nonetheless, he did fully recognize that it is better for the accumulation of knowledge if knowers are awake, than if they are dreaming. And, as did Heracleitus (according to Buber's interpretation of Heracleitus), Descartes appreciated the association of reality with wakefulness.

Descartes' Realist Awake–Asleep Distinction, and Naturalism

Descartes' claim in the Sixth Meditation that the *coherence* of awake experience distinguishes it from sleep experience has always been difficult to defend. In this paper,[4] I argue that the debate about the coherence account does not do justice to Descartes' realist distinction between being awake and asleep. Besides his Sixth Meditation phenomenological account of the coherence of first-person awake experience, Descartes' realist awake–asleep distinction rests on the existence of a mind-independent world which is perspicuously present to an awake person but not to a dreamer. Descartes' rationalism, however, requires that his distinction be restricted to ordinary sensory experience, so as to preserve the awake–asleep neutrality of first principles. With that restriction, I offer an interpretation of Descartes' awake–asleep distinction that is consistent with ordinary intuition, as well as with theories of sleep in contemporary neuroscience. The defensible Cartesian awake–asleep distinction is also compatible with the existence of non-sensory mentation in sleep, which is in principle no different from such mentation in awake states.

Part 1 is an examination of the failure of the coherence account of awake experience as it is traditionally ascribed to Descartes. Part 2 is an exploration of Descartes' realism about awake experience and an examination of its tensions with his rationalism. In part 3, Descartes' realist awake–asleep distinction, and his claim for the sleep-invariant knowledge of first principles, are compared with conclusions from findings in contemporary neuroscience.

First, a note on the distinction between dreaming and non-dreaming sleep. Descartes once claimed to have interpreted a dream in his sleep, which shows that he was aware of that distinction.[5] Nevertheless, he usually wrote as though to sleep were automatically to dream and since the sleep – dreaming distinction is not important for parts 1 and 2 of this paper, I am going to follow Descartes in the conflation until the distinction does become important, in part 3. I am also going to ignore the cases in which sleep seems to occur without any kind of mentation, again following Descartes (although not because his awake–asleep distinction requires continuous mentation in creatures with souls.)

1 The Failure of the Coherence Criterion for Being Awake

Assumptions behind the coherence criterion

The necessity for a criterion that will determine wakefulness with certainty seems partly to be based on an assumption that sleep episodes are inherently biased toward giving the sleeper the false impression of being awake. As Descartes put it, "there is apparently no mark by which [we] can with certainty distinguish sleep from the waking state."[6] This casts doubt on each single instance, taken separately, in which we think that we are awake; although, as Bernard Williams has shown, it does not imply that all of our awake experience is suspect.[7]

There is a second assumption that it is better to be awake than asleep for epistemic purposes. In the *Discourse on Method*, Descartes associates truth in general with wakefulness:

> Reason tells us that since our thoughts cannot possibly be all true, because we are not altogether perfect, that which they have of truth must infallibly be met with in our waking experience rather than in that of our dreams.[8]

This epistemic superiority of wakefulness over sleep is a motive for taking seriously doubt that one is awake. As a result, the question, "Am I really awake?" takes precedence over the question, "Am I really asleep?" However, if there were a criterion for wakefulness as distinct from dreaming, it should be possible to apply that criterion while dreaming and conclude that one is not-awake, or dreaming. In fact, some of the contemporary research on *lucid dreaming* indicates that dreamers can learn to determine that they are dreaming, while they are dreaming.[9] And, even without specialized introspection, we may sometimes be sure we are dreaming, while dreaming. There are also bad dreams and unwanted awake experiences for which the supposition that we are or have been dreaming is welcome because the experience can then be dismissed as unreal.[10] Therefore, although philosophical "dream skepticism" is skepticism about being awake, doubts about dreaming while dreaming are not insignificant and their neglect in the Cartesian dream literature emphasizes the aim to secure foundations and criteria for reliable knowledge that can be acquired and used while awake. Indeed, most philosophers in both the rationalist and empiricist traditions would dismiss out of hand the idea of knowledge that can be acquired and used while asleep. However, the privileged status of wakefulness is often taken for granted in the literature on dream skepticism, so that the requirement of a criterion for being awake which is neutral as to the state of awareness in which the criterion is applied, is obscured. Thus, the assumption that it is better to be awake supports an assumption that it is normal to be awake, which in turn supports an acceptance of a criterion for being awake that can be applied only when one is awake.

The coherence criterion

Descartes introduces the coherence account at the end of the Sixth Meditation and offers three main characteristics of the coherence of awake experience: (1) different events are connected through memory; (2) events are connected in ways that conform to known laws of causation, motion, identity, change, appearance, and the like; and (3) memory, sense experience and thought have results consistent with one another.[11] Descartes does not provide details about how we ought to resolve conflicts among (1) to (3) and he does not say whether part or all of conditions (1)to (3) are necessary, sufficient or both. He signals the awake-dependent nature of coherence as a criterion, by parenthetically remarking that perceptual images that violated coherence would be judged "similar to those which I form in sleep."[12]

If coherence is a criterion for being awake, then it ought to be possible to apply it without an antecedent requirement that one be awake, simply because it should be possible for the criterion not to be satisfied. Hobbes objected that if one could dream that he doubted "whether he dreams or no," he could also dream that an event were connected with past events.[13] It seems odd that Hobbes locates the doubt about "whether he dreams or no" in the state of dreaming, because Descartes always raises the question of "whether he dreams or no" in the context of awake experience. But, if the answer to the question of "whether he dreams or no" is "he dreams" – which is a possible answer whenever the doubt is possible – then there is no reason why the question cannot arise in sleep. That is, whenever we doubt that we are awake, it could be the case that we are asleep and entertaining that doubt in sleep. In moving doubt to a sleep state, Hobbes implicitly emphasizes the requirement that the awake–asleep criterion be neutral as to one's state of being either awake or asleep when the criterion is applied. In his reply to Hobbes, Descartes conceded that the satisfaction of the criterion could be dreamed ("For who denies that in his sleep a man may be deceived?") but asserted that such deception could be corrected when the sleeper has awakened.[14] Descartes thereby shifted the discussion back to the epistemically privileged and normal state of wakefulness.

Williams defends Descartes' response by claiming that the coherence criterion must be applied in awake experience only, because we can explain dreams from the standpoint of being awake but not the other way around. Williams insists that since we cannot rationally "tell" anything while we are dreaming, the criterion has to be a way of telling that we are awake when we are awake.[15] If Descartes and Williams are correct, it reinforces the non-neutrality of the coherence criterion. If they are not correct, Hobbes' objection holds and the coherence criterion fails for the simple reason that the coherence of wakeful experience can be dreamed. Hobbes said that if one could dream being awake then one could dream coherence but it is also true that if one could dream coherence, this would, on the acceptance of the coherence criterion, entail that one could dream being awake.

For someone, S, to apply the coherence criterion with success, S would not merely have to be awake, but know it. If S did not know S was awake and applied the criterion in a non-optimal awake state, such as fatigue or disorientation, S might incorrectly conclude that S were dreaming, because S's state could make otherwise coherent experience seem incoherent.[16] But, when S applies the coherence criterion in an awake state, with the knowledge that S is awake, the criterion does not yield any new knowledge about S's state, or tell S anything that S does not already know about S's state.

Thus far, the problem with coherence as a criterion is that the criterion has to be positively met before it can be applied, because it can be applied successfully only if one is awake. Since, as Hobbes indicated, one could always dream that *any* criterion for being awake had been satisfied, the only way to exclude that possibility is to make sure, beforehand, that one is not dreaming. Nonetheless, this is not yet a problem with the nature of coherence itself, but with its role as a criterion.

Objective coherence

Robert Hanna suggests that coherence is not a criterion but an ontological aspect of the difference between being awake and asleep. On Hanna's interpretation of Descartes, awake experience *is* coherent and dreaming is not.[17] If Hanna is right, the question is no longer whether coherence is an adequate epistemological criterion for being awake but whether coherence provides an adequate description of the awake–asleep difference. That is, it could be that awake experience is coherent, sleep experience is not coherent and that most of the time we do know whether we are awake or asleep but that we do not always know if this is based on our experience of the coherence of awake experience. Awake experience might be coherent and it still might not be possible to construct an adequate epistemological account of how we use coherence to distinguish wakefulness from sleep.

The problem with Hanna's interpretation is the assumption that awake experience is coherent and sleep is not. For the assumption to support an awake–asleep distinction, awake experience would have to be coherent all the time. If awake experience is not always coherent, then either Descartes was mistaken or Hanna has misinterpreted him. On the face of it, it is not true that awake experience is always coherent according to Descartes' conditions. These conditions do not apply if (1) memory fails; (2) faulty memory, confusion, fatigue, chemical impairment and insanity, etc., result in disconnected experience, and unforeseen or inexplicable events and poor perceptual conditions disrupt customary connections; and (3) different combinations of distortions in the perceiver and unusual events cause discrepancies between memory, sense experience, and thought.

Furthermore, not all sleep experience is incoherent. Recurrent dreams contain memories of earlier dream experience; also, dream experiences that are bizarre from an awake perspective may make sense to the dreamer while dreaming. Indeed, current hypotheses of the *grammar of dream mentation* are attempts to formalize impressions that dreamers often have of the meaningful order or normality of dream events.[18] From an awake perspective, bizarre and delusive dreams can yield important insights about awake experience, through dream interpretation, which is one way in which dreams can be used by non-dreamers to explain awake experience. But if an insight about awake experience is clear to a dreamer while dreaming, then awake experience may be directly explained in dreams.

The content of dreams may also be causally connected with events in the dreamers' recent awake experience, with physiological events in the dreamer while dreaming (such as digestive processes), and with events that awake observers, including the erstwhile dreamer, can identify as raw material for the fabrication of dream events, given people's systemic propensity to "guard" sleep (that is, subconsciously to prevent external distractions waking them).[19] Rational thought processes in non-dreaming sleep also connect sleep experience with awake experience. Our ability in some dreams to wonder if we are dreaming suggests that there is an awareness of an awake–asleep distinction, in sleep, and that we can ask things in dreams, perhaps because (contra Williams) we can also tell things in dreams. In sum, many dreams are coherent to the dreamer while dreaming – in ways that suggest sense, as well as order – or to the erstwhile dreamer or someone else in an awake state.

A defender of coherence might point out that the paradigm case of a bizarre, delusive dream does lack coherence according to the conditions specified by Descartes at the end of the Sixth Meditation, and that the paradigm case of awake experience under "ideal conditions" is coherent. However, and this is the main problem with the coherence account, the concept of coherence does not do justice to the distinctive value of awake experience as opposed to dreaming. It could be the case that our awake experience were generally haphazard, jumbled and confused and that all of our rational and reasonable experience of a lawlike universe took place in sleep. That is, Nietzsche's assignment of an Apollonian worldview to dreaming could be an accurate depiction of the human condition.[20] But even in that case, awake experience would still have greater value – to most of us, including Nietzsche – because only it would be real. And, if both awake and asleep experience were coherent or both were incoherent, many of us would still value the state of wakefulness over dreaming, on the basis of the same attachment to reality. When Descartes raised the possibility that all of our awake experience were a dream, on his malicious-demon level of doubt, he cashed in on this realistic value of wakefulness over dreaming. The prospect that we may always be dreaming when we think we are awake, is alarming, not only because of the enormity of the intellectual error it portends but because the external world has incommensurable value in comparison to the stuff of which dreams are made.

2 Descartes' Realism and the Awake–Asleep Distinction

The realist distinction

The failure of coherence as an epistemological criterion for being awake does not disturb Descartes' Sixth Meditation observation that awake experience usually is coherent from a first-person perspective, when it is contrasted with dreaming experience. Neither does the failure of the coherence account to yield a rigorous awake–asleep ontological distinction present an ontological problem with Descartes' awake–asleep distinction, because he did not draw the ontological distinction in terms of coherence but on the basis of his claim that when we are awake, the objects of our perceptions exist. As he said to Frans Burman, "in perception the images are imprinted by external objects which are actually present."[21] For Descartes, on the ontological level in which awake states are distinguished from sleep states, perception is caused by objects that exist and perception takes place only in awake states. Thus, for Descartes, the awake–asleep distinction amounts to this:

(D₁) When we are awake, we are able to perceive objects that exist and when we are asleep we lack this ability.

This formulation of Descartes' awake–asleep distinction sheds light on Descartes' frequent use of the possibility that one may be dreaming, as grounds for doubting the existence of external objects.[22]

However, D_1 is a simplification of the difference between awake and asleep experience, in the following way. When S is dreaming and it seems to S that external objects are present, they are not always present in the way in which they seem to S to be present because they, or more likely, other external objects, may be present in some other non-apparent way. For example, the noise caused by a lawn mower may be accompanied by a dream about a war zone. In such cases, perception may be deluded, as well as distorted, but it is still caused by an external object. Thus, Descartes' awake–asleep difference, as formulated in D_1, requires the perceptual perspicuity of awake states. The precise awake–asleep distinction lies in the nature of the seeming, in the connection between what seems to be the case when S is awake or asleep, and what is the case.

This perspicuity of wakefulness would be twofold for Descartes. First, the state of being awake is in some way given to us while we are awake. Even if we are not constantly aware of being awake while we are awake, we take our being awake for granted, while we are awake. If someone were to ask S who is awake if S is awake, besides answering Yes, S would wonder why the question had been posed. This obviousness about being awake is a result of the perspicuity of wakefulness. Wakefulness seems to be what it is and it is what it seems to be. Second, being awake is perspicuous in that the existence of the external objects of our awake perceptual experience is also taken for granted. This form of perspicuity is what Descartes must have had in mind when he claimed that the perception of an object entails the existence of that object and its presence to the perceiver.

The two kinds of perspicuity, of state of awareness and of the existence of objects of awareness, stem from Descartes' causal theory of perception: objects that exist cause the perceptions we have of them when we are awake and they cause them in ways closely resembling how they seem to cause them; other objects that exist cause our perceptions in sleep but not as those perceptions seem to the sleeper to be caused, especially when the sleeper seems to be perceiving an object that is entirely different from the object that is causing the perception. Accordingly, the Cartesian awake–asleep distinction becomes:

> (D₂) When we are awake, we are able to accurately perceive objects that exist and when we are asleep we lack this ability.

In the Sixth Meditation, Descartes mentions our God-given nature to perceive the world as it more or less is, with enough accuracy to protect us from harm.[23] And in the *Principles* (xliii), he anticipates Locke's humility in accepting perceptual limitations:

> [S]ince God is no deceiver, the faculty of Knowledge that He has given us cannot be fallacious, nor can the faculty of will so long as we do not extend it beyond those things that we clearly perceive.[24]

However, the perspicuity of normal awake experience, like its coherence, is a contingent matter, which in Descartes' terms cannot be rationally demonstrated.[25] God might have constructed us so that our ordinary wakeful experience were always deceptive, even though objects existed.

Alternatively, we might have been constructed with accurate wakeful experience that did not seem to be accurate. Thus, when Descartes says we cannot doubt our clear perceptions, he does not mean that they are indubitable according to his method or that they are metaphysically certain. Rather, he means that we, as we have been constructed by God, are constitutionally reluctant to doubt them. The psychological confidance in our perceptions is neither an epistemological certainty nor an ontological justification of our perceptions, unless the premise is added that God constructed our psychology to yield perceptions that corresponded to the objects perceived. Descartes stopped short of that premise because he did not rely on human psychology to guarantee knowledge.

Rationalism and the realist awake–asleep distinction

Descartes' epistemology of science undermines the realism of D_2 if the distinction is applied to knowledge of first principles. This problem results from Descartes' demarcation between common sense and rationalist science and his demarcation between the first principles of science and empirical truth.

According to Descartes, science was a radical, indubitable departure from ordinary common sense perception. He claims in the beginning of the *Principles* that perception is a poor source of knowledge because many of our judgments about perception were formed in childhood, before the use of reason (I)[26] and we know more about our minds than our bodies (XI).[27] Those who have not "studied philosophy in an orderly way" do not distinguish their minds from their bodies and falsely believe that they perceive with parts of their bodies instead of with their minds (XII).[28]

The inadequacy of perception without a criterion for clear and distinct ideas is a well-known theme of Descartes. But even when our ideas of the external world are clear and distinct, they cannot yield the principles for knowledge or science, according to Descartes. He maintains that perceptual knowledge is adequate for the conduct of life while we deliberately doubt in the search for truth.[29] And once it is proved that God is not a deceiver, our natural perceptual perspicuity is of course acceptable.[30] But it does not follow from this that sensory perception is the basis of certainty and nowhere in the progression to knowledge does Descartes incorporate sensory perceptual truth as a foundation for knowledge. Descartes did recognize the importance for science of empirical investigation that would have depended on sensory observation and he conducted many such observations himself.[31] However, the immediate results of investigative empiricism would not have been scientific knowledge for him because these results were at best highly probable or *morally certain* – they could be doubted. In that sense, when compared to Locke, Boyle, Gassendi, or to his friend and colleague Mersenne, Descartes was not an empiricist because he was not content with anything less than certainty for scientific knowledge.[32]

Descartes contrasts the dubitability of sensory perception with the indubitability of first principles, and the preferred indubitability of first principles is so strong that it resists the epistemic distortions of sleep. There are passages throughout Descartes' work where he says that whether he is asleep or awake he knows he exists and that mathematical principles are true. Although he makes this claim in order to deal with the possibility that any episode of awareness that seems to be an awake state could be a delusive episode of sleep, the effect of the claim is that it does not matter if he is asleep or awake when it comes to the truth of first principles. He seems to be saying not merely that first principles are true in all possible worlds, which would trivially include a world in which he, or all of us slept all the time, but that the epistemic or justificatory connection of a knower or believer to such first principles can take place while dreaming, as well as while awake. Descartes first indicates this indifference in the *Discourse on Method*:

> For even if in sleep we had some very distinct idea such as a geometrician might have who discovered some new demonstration, the fact of being asleep would not militate against its truth.[33]

In the Second Meditation, after discovering that the certainty of his own existence cannot be doubted, he asks rhetorically,

> Is there nothing at all in this which is as true as it is certain that I exist, even though I should always sleep and though he who has given me being employed all his ingenuity in deceiving me?[34]

The sleep-resistant nature of first principles is offered again, as a safety net for lingering doubts about the knowledge Descartes has proved by the end of Meditation Five, namely:

> But even though I slept the case would be the same, for all that is clearly present to my mind is absolutely true.[35]

Descartes' implied indifference of being asleep or awake, for the truth of first principles, is problematic for the realist awake–asleep distinction. In terms of sleep, the indifference suggests that such truth is detached from reality, because first principles can be experienced in sleep, and reality is something that can be experienced only while awake. In terms of awake experience, insofar as awake experience is distinguished from sleep experience by the objective existence of what the experience is about, knowledge or true belief ought to be restricted to awake experience.

However, these reality dilemmas can be solved by further qualifying the realist awake–asleep distinction. If we can have knowledge of our own existence in sleep, there is no problem with the reality content of that knowledge because we exist while we are sleeping. If mathematical principles are about mathematical objects only, there is no reason to believe that mathematical objects could not cause one's beliefs about them in sleep, in the same way as they do in awake states. And if, as Henry Frankfurt interprets Descartes, mathematical principles are always true because they are true of everything that exists, then mathematical principles entertained in sleep are about objects that exist, in the same way that they are about existent objects in awake states.[36] Awake or asleep, in entertaining a mathematical principle, we could not be aware of the full subject domain of that principle if it were true of everything that existed. The objective existence during sleep of the self and of the mathematical objects, together with our inability to apprehend all existent objects while awake or asleep, entails that the realist awake–asleep distinction does not hold for knowledge of first principles. Therefore, Descartes' distinction between being awake and asleep needs to be restricted to sensory experience, as follows:

(D₃) When we are awake, we are able to accurately perceive sensory objects that exist and when we are asleep we lack this ability.

Descartes' metaphysics of science requires that the realist awake–asleep distinction be further restricted to common sense or pre-scientific sensory experience. According to Descartes, sensory perception is not most importantly sensory, and sensory objects do not exist as we perceive them. The best knowledge of perceptible objects, namely knowledge about their extension and mathematical properties, is arrived at through the mind, not through the senses. The first principles of science are based on the knowledge that objects exist, not as sensible objects given in pre-scientific perspicuous perception, but as objects with abstract properties.

After he resolves his *Meditation* doubts to his own satisfaction, Descartes does not retract the position of the Second Meditation on primary and secondary qualities: what he knows about the fresh wax that melts in his fire is not its changing qualities that affect his senses, but its extended attributes that are the subjects of the judgments he makes about the wax in his mind.[37] In the *Principles* (LXIX and LXX), the distinction between primary and secondary qualities is drawn more sharply: it is only primary qualities, which are not directly perceptible but abstracted from sensory perception by thought, that can be clearly known or even properly said to be perceived.[38] Here, Descartes' reasoning appears to be that since primary, mathematical qualities exist in objects, while colors and sounds, for example, do not, we do not really perceive colors and sounds because if we perceive something it must exist. Thus, our perceptual knowledge, insofar as it can be a foundation for science, is not knowledge based on sense, but knowledge based on the workings of the intellect.

If we do not really perceive colors and sounds and all of the other secondary qualities of objects even while we are awake – for the simple reason that those objects of apparent perception do not exist – then the realist distinction between being awake and asleep dissolves from a metaphysical scientific perspective. If there were more agreement among the apparent sensory perceptions of dreamers and it were possible to develop a precise science of the causes of the perception of secondary qualities in dreams, there would be no difference in principle between secondary sensory perception while awake, or while dreaming.

However, the delusive aspect of secondary sensory perception in awake experience appears only from a metaphysical scientific perspective. The assumed and verifiable existence of the objects of secondary sensory perception in ordinary, non-scientific awake experience is not disturbed by the (real) non-existence of these objects in metaphysical scientific terms. And it is on the ordinary ground that Descartes' realist distinction between being awake and dreaming holds. The defensible Cartesian difference between being awake and dreaming is now this:

(D₄) When we are awake, we are able to accurately perceive sensory objects that seem to exist in the world of common sense and when we are asleep we lack this ability.

3 Descartes' Awake–Asleep Distinction and Naturalism

In order to relate Descartes' thought on dreams to contemporary naturalism, some description of naturalism, even if it is partly stipulative (and incomplete for other purposes), should first be offered. A naturalistic perspective presupposes the ability to distinguish between being awake and asleep and the construction of knowledge from that perspective is assumed to take place among awake thinkers and sensory observers. Ordinary knowledge and observation, which is the starting point for empirical science, is undertaken on a broad assumption that there is a world external to knowers and observers, which in varied ways, is independent of their minds and senses. In studies of human phenomenological or subjective, first-person events, such as dreams as they appear to the dreamer, a naturalistic perspective is distinguished by its third-person standpoint on such events. Thus, any science of sleep would be a study of the physiological and phenomenological aspects of sleep, undertaken by awake thinkers and observers. As Owen Flanagan suggests, a naturalistic methodology in the science of sleep could also include psychological, biographical, evolutionary, and cultural aspects of sleep and dreams.[39] However, since the awake states of the scientists of sleep is presupposed, philosophical skepticism about being awake does not arise from the naturalistic perspective. The scientists of sleep do not second-guess their findings by wondering if they have been dreaming during their observations, any more than physicists or chemists do. Not only is their own awake state presupposed, but so is their ability to determine whether the subjects of their studies are awake or asleep, taxonomies of the complex stages of sleep not withstanding.

Naturalism and Descartes' own dream accounts

Overall, throughout his writings on sleep and dreams, with the exception of the problems raised by the inability to prove wakefulness in any one given instance, Descartes worked from such a naturalistic perspective. His reply to Hobbes that the errors of sleep can be corrected when one is awake, is presented in a way that assumes the epistemic superiority of wakefulness to sleep, as well as the ease of knowing that one is awake when one is.

Descartes also had a naturalistic perspective on his three dreams of the night of November 10,1616. According to George Stebba's reconstruction of Descartes' account of these dreams, after his second dream, Descartes awoke with a start because of a perceptual experience that the objects in his room were emitting sparks. He was frightened that this might be a supernatural occurrence, a sign that God was punishing him for his thoughts in his first dream. But he calmed himself and decided to apply scientific methodology. He then opened and closed his eyes in order to determine whether the sparks were an optical illusion, in which case they would persist with his eyes closed, or a real external event that would not have been perceptible with his eyes closed. Satisfied that the appearance of the sparks had been generated by optical events originating in him, he categorized the experience as a dream, instead of an unwelcome vision, and went back to sleep.

Shortly thereafter, Descartes had a third dream, which he wanted to make sure had been a dream. He made the determination without waking up, and then went on to interpret that dream in his sleep.[40] Descartes clearly did not question his ability to tell the difference between his own dreams and waking experience, on the basis of a realist distinction. He was also confidant that he could tell the difference between dream and non-dream sleep mentation (even in his sleep). And, it apparently never occurred to him that he might have been dreaming when he made either of the distinctions. He made his distinctions and then proceeded with his real task concerning his dreams, namely their interpretation in terms of his life and work. And despite subsequent differences about how Descartes' dreams of that night might best be interpreted, almost everyone writing on the subject accepts Descartes' distinctions between his own dreams and awake experience.[41]

Descartes' dream theories and contemporary neuroscience

From a contemporary naturalistic perspective, Descartes was largely right about the sensory difference between being awake and asleep. Descartes took a physiological approach to the delusive nature of sensory experience in dreams. He assumed that we are generally unable to have clear and distinct sensory ideas while dreaming and he basically described sensory perceptions in dreams as the effect of "brain traces."[42] He hypothesized that dreams contained sensory perceptions that were caused by the body, without dependence on the relevant nerves that were connected to external sensory receptors. Unlike imaginings, dreams are unwilled, so that,

> they cannot be numbered among the actions of the soul, for they arise simply from the fact that the spirits, being agitated in various different ways and coming upon the traces of various impressions which have

preceded them in the brain, make their way by chance through certain pores rather than others. (*Passions of the Soul*, no. 21)[43]

Contemporary neuroscientists attribute more dynamic and complex mechanisms in the brain to dreams, but Descartes' hypothesis located the physiological aspect of dreams in the same kind of events and in the same location as is done today. Sensory experiences in dreams are now widely held to be accompanied by the self-stimulation of the neural systems of different sensory modalities.[44]

Descartes was also correct about the sensory shutdown that takes place during sleep. Indeed, sleep is now empirically distinguished from wakefulness largely on the basis of that shutdown: as the hypothalamus, an area of the brain connected with thermoregulation and hormone manufacture, initiates the physiological process of sleep, sensory perception becomes dull or absent in NREM (non-rapid-eye-movement) sleep and then becomes internally generated in REM (rapid-eye-movement) sleep, the sleep phase in which sleeping subjects report bizarre and delusive dreams, when awakened.[45]

Finally, in the context of contemporary neuroscience and sleep, Descartes seems to have been partly right about the invariance to sleep and wakefulness of first principles. His claim that awake or asleep I can still have knowledge of my own existence is supported by recent neurological findings that neuronal oscillation patterns of a certain range (40Hz) are linked to awake subjective awareness and also to REM sleep.[46] Thus, in addition to the philosophical realist claim that my existence "causes" my subjective knowledge that I exist, there is empirical evidence that the physiological accompaniment to my subjective awareness is present in delusive dream sleep, as well as awake states. Although mere subjective awareness is not equivalent to a *cogito*, subjective awareness is necessary for a *cogito*.

At last, we come to Descartes' claim that knowledge of mathematical truths is possible in sleep. Flanagan wagers that while the neurochemical restorative functions of sleep may have to occur in order for mathematical mentation to occur, such mentation is unlikely to take place in sleep. Flanagan's bet is based on the fact that the neurons which release the neurochemicals involved in attention, memory, and learning slow down in NREM sleep and turn off during REM sleep.[47] This suggests that contrary to Descartes' example, it is unlikely that a geometrician could discover some new demonstration in sleep. We seem to need information from our senses in order to think about things that are not directly related to sensory input while we are thinking about them. But it is imprecise to fault Descartes for his claim about the sleep–awake neutrality of mathematical principles on these grounds. In his reply to the seventh set of Objections, Descartes rebuked Bourdin for treating "doubtfulness and certainty not as relations of our thought to objects but as properties of the objects and as inhering in them eternally."[48] If doubt and certainty are relations to objects, this suggests that mathematical principles ought not to be true to someone who sleeps because it would be difficult if not impossible to justify the truth of such principles in sleep. However, what Descartes said was that "even if" we were asleep when we had a distinct idea such as a demonstration in geometry, being asleep would not "militate against" its truth. A demonstration would seem to be on the side of the relation of thought to an object, in this case perhaps a proof of a theorem, rather than knowledge of the theorem alone. Thus, Descartes should be read as claiming that if justification for a first principle could be found in sleep that this would not count against it. He is not claiming that such justification is found in sleep, or that first principles are best learned in sleep.

Conclusion

Scholars of Descartes ascribe to him the claim that the coherence of awake experience distinguishes it from sleep experience, both epistemologically and ontologically. In the Sixth Meditation, Descartes offers the apparent coherence of awake experience as an account of the phenomenology of being awake, in contrast to dreaming, but he does not claim that coherence can be used to distinguish between wakefulness and dreaming in a rigorous epistemological sense. Coherence fails as an epistemological criterion because it requires antecedent wakefulness, and it fails as an ontological distinction because there are too many exceptions to the general rule that awake experience is coherent while sleep experience is not. Descartes' fundamental awake–asleep distinction rests on the real existence of the objects of awake sensory experience. This distinction is echoed in contemporary neuroscientific theories of sleep.

The realist interpretation I have offered of Descartes' awake–asleep distinction has two interesting consequences. The first is the strange but not impossible conclusion that there is in principle no difference between non-sensory mentation during awake and sleep states. The second consequence is that for Descartes, an epistemological criterion for being awake as opposed to being asleep would be identical to an epistemological criterion for the mind-independent existence of objects of sensory perception. That is, questions such as, Am I awake now? Was I awake in the past? and Have I been awake most of my life? would reduce to questions such as, Do the objects of my present perception exist? Did the objects of my past perceptions exist? and Have I perceived objects that exist most of my life?

Notes

1   Naomi Zack, *Bachelors of Science: Seventeenth Century Identity, Then and Now* (Philadelphia: Temple University Press, 1996), pp. 23–4.

2   See: Naomi Zack, *Race and Mixed Race* (Philadelphia: Temple University Press, 1993); Zack, "Race and Philosophic Meaning," in Zack (ed) *RACE/ SEX: Their Sameness, Difference and Interplay* (New York: Routledge, 1997); Zack, "Philosophy and Racial Paradigms," *Journal of Value Inquiry*, forthcoming.

3   Martin Buber, *The Knowledge of Man*, ed. Maurice Friedman (Atlantic Highlands, NJ: Humanities Press, 1988), p. 95.

4   I have been thinking about the material in this paper for five or six years. I am grateful to my colleagues in the Philosophy Department at the University at Albany for feedback when I read an earlier version of these ideas at a colloquium in October 1995.

5   Stebba reconstructs and interprets Baillet's account, which was based on Descartes' journal, which itself was later lost; see Gregor Stebba, *The Dream of Descartes*, ed. Richard A. Watson (Carbondale and Edwardsville: Southern Illinois University Press, 1987). The reference to Descartes' claim to have interpreted a dream while sleeping is on p. 30.

6   René Descartes, *Principles of Philosophy*, Part I, art. iv, in *Philosophical Works of Descartes*, trans. E. S. Haldane and G. R. T. Ross (Cambridge: Cambridge University Press, 1973) (hereafter HR), p. 220.

7   Bernard Williams, *Descartes: The Project of Pure Inquiry* (New York: Penguin Books, 1978), pp. 50–3.

8   Descartes, *Discourse on the Method of Rightly Conducting the Reason*, part IV, in HR I, p. 106.

9   Stephen LaBerge, *Lucid Dreaming* (New York: Burges, 1990), pp. 1–77.

10   See Zack, *Bachelors of Science*.

11   Descartes, Meditation VI, *Meditations on First Philosophy*, in HR I, pp. 198–9.

12   Ibid.

13 Thomas Hobbes, "Third Set of Objections and Author's Reply," in HR II, p. 78.

14 Ibid.

15 Williams, *Descartes*, Appendix 3, pp. 212–13.

16 See Robert Hanna, "Descartes and Dream Skepticism Revisted," *Journal of the History of Philosophy* 30 (July 1992), p. 387, n.18, p. 390.

17 Ibid., pp. 388–98.

18 Thus, for example, as Owen Flanagan summarizes the work of J. Allen Hobson's research group, there are "narrative, scriptlike structures" that dream material is sorted into: locations change rapidly and characters and objects gradually. See R. Stickgold, C. D. Rittenhouse and J. Allen Hobson, "Constraint on the Transformation of Characters, Objects and Settings in Dream Reports," and "Dream Splicing: A New Technique for Assessing Thematic Coherence in Subjective Reports of Mental Activity," both in *Consciousness and Cognition* 3 (1994), pp. 100–13 and 114–28, cited by Flanagan in "Deconstructing Dreams: The Spandrels of Sleep," *Journal of Philosophy* 92.1 (January 1995), p. 25.

19 Flanagan, "Deconstructing Dreams," p. 24.

20 Friedrich Nietzsche, *The Birth of Tragedy*, in *Basic Writings of Nietzsche*, trans. and ed. Walter Kaufmann (New York: Modern Library, 1968), pp. 2–146. (Nietzsche thought that, according to the genius of ancient Greek tragedians, it was our dream experience that was coherent, our awake experience incoherent.)

21 *Descartes' Conversation with Burman*, trans. John Cottingham (Oxford: Clarendon Press, 1976), [42], p. 27.

22 For examples see: *Discourse*, in HR I, part IV, p. 101; *Meditations*, II, in HR I, pp. 152–3; Meditation III, in HR I, p. 161; Meditation VI, in HR I, p. 189; *Principles*, Part I, art. iv, in HR, I, p. 220; *The Search After Truth*, in HR I, p. 321.

23 Meditations, VI, in HR, I, pp. 195–7.

24 *Principles*, Part I, art xliii, in HR I, p. 236.

25 Ibid.

26 *Principles*, Part I, art. i, HR I, p. 219.

27 Ibid. art. xi, p. 223.

28 Ibid., art. xii, p. 223.

29 Ibid., art. i, p. 219.

30 See Nietzsche, *Birth of Tragedy*.

31 For discussion of the relations between his experiments and his philosophy see: Stephen Gaukroger, *Descartes: An Intellectual Biography* (Oxford: Clarendon Press, 1995), pp. 270–90; Norman Kemp Smith (ed.) *Descartes' Philosophical Writings* (New York: Random House, 1958), editor's intro., pp. vii–xxviii.

32 Descartes expressed his ideal of providing certain first principles for

empirical science throughout his writings. For instance, in the First Meditation he begins by stating the goal of establishing "firm and permanent structure in the sciences" (Meditation I, in HR I, p. 144). About fifteen years earlier, in 1628, he had made a public announcement of his ability to secure such certainty at a meeting attended by the papal nuncio (Gaukroger, *Descartes*, p. 183).

33 *Discourse*, part IV, in HR I, p. 105.

34 Meditation II, in *Meditations*, HR I, p. 153.

35 Meditation V, in HR I, pp. 184–5.

36 This conception of mathematics as general principles of existing particulars refers to Descartes' First Meditation account of mathematics and not to mathematics as understood to be separated from the existence of particular objects. See H. G. Frankfurt, *Demons, Dreamers and Madmen: the Defense of Reason in Descartes' Meditations* (New York: Bobbs-Merrill, 1970), pp. 73–6.

37 Meditation II, in HR I, pp. 154–5.

38 *Principles*, Part I, art. lxix, lxx, in HR I, pp. 248–9.

39 Flanagan, "Deconstructing Dreams," pp. 5–8.

40 Stebba, *Dream of Descartes*, pp. 18–24.

41 One exception is George Stebba who thinks that the second dream of November 19th was not a dream at all but a *myoclonic start*. See *Dream of Descartes*, pp. 20–3.

42 For Descartes' belief that dreams were caused by "traces in the brain" that were the result of memories, or physiological processes occuring while dreaming, see: *The Philosophical Writings of Descartes*, trans. John Cottingham, Robert Stoothoff, Dugald Murdock, and Anthony Kenny (Cambridge: Cambridge University Press, 1991), vol. III, *The Correspondence*: to Merseene, 28 January, 1641, pp. 170–1; to Hyperaspistes, August, 1641, p. 196; to Princess Elizabeth, 1 September, 1645, p. 263.

43 Descartes, *Passions of the Soul*, XXI, in HR I, p. 341.

44 Flanagan, "Deconstructing Dreams," pp. 12–16.

45 Ibid., p. 15.

46 Ibid., pp. 9–10, n. 10. In keeping with a justificatory epistemic approach to certainty, Frankfurt argues that conditions for the certainty of *sum*, and not the proof of the entire *cogito*, were Descartes' primary concern in the *Meditations* (*Demons*, pp. 92–103). On this account, one would have to say that if my existence causes my knowledge of it when I am asleep, this does not mean that this knowledge is epistemically justified in sleep. Descartes' point would then have to be that if it were justified in sleep in that way, being asleep would not count against the justification any more than it "militates against" a geometrician's demonstration in sleep. See the conclusion, below.

47 Flanagan, "Deconstructing Dreams," pp. 14–15, 23–4.

48 Descartes, "Seventh Set of Objections with the Author's Annotations Thereon," in HR II, pp. 276–7. See also Frankfurt, *Demons*, pp. 92–103. Jeffry Tlumak develops a general account of how certainty for Descartes is "a relation between a person or persons, a proposition or set of propositions, and a time or set of times." See "Certainty and Cartesian Method," in Michael Hooker (ed.) *Descartes: Critical and Interpretive Essays* (Baltimore: Johns Hopkins University Press,1978), pp. 40–73.

Select Bibliography

Abe, Masao (1988) "Nishida's Philosophy of 'Place,'" *International Philosophical Quarterly* 28/4.

Aijaz, Ahmad (1992) *In Theory*, New York: Verso.

Alcoff, Linda and Potter, Elizabeth (eds) (1993) *Feminist Epistemologies*, New York: Routledge.

Allen, Anita L. (1996) "Forgetting Yourself," in Diana Meyers (ed.) *Feminists Rethink the Self*, Boulder: Westview Press.

Anzaldúa, Gloria (1987) *Borderlands/La frontera: The New Mestiza*, San Francisco: Aunt Lute Books.

Appiah, Anthony and Gutman, Amy (1996) *Color Conscious: The Political Morality of Race*, Princeton: Princeton University Press.

Arisaka, Yoko (1997) "Beyond 'East and West': Nishida's Universalism and Postcolonial Critique," *The Review of Politics* 59/3.

Aristotle (1941) *Physica*, in Richard McKeon (ed.) *The Basic Works of Aristotle*, New York: Random House.

Armstrong, D. M. (1978) *Universals and Scientific Realism*, vols I and II, Cambridge: Cambridge University Press.

Augustine (1991) *Confessions*, ed. and with intro. by Henry Chadwick, New York: Oxford University Press.

Baier, Annette (1994) *Moral Prejudices*, Cambridge, MA: Harvard University Press.

Barlow, Tani (ed.) (1997) *Formations of Colonial Modernity in East Asia*, Durham: Duke University Press.

Beauvoir, Simone de (1952) *The Second Sex*, New York: Vintage.

Beverley, John, Oviedo, José, and Aronna, Michael (eds) (1995) *The Postmodernism Debate in Latin America*, Durham: Duke University Press.

Bhabha, Homi K. (1994) *The Location of Culture*, London: Routledge.

Blum, Deborah (1998) *Sex on the Brain: The Biological Differences Between Men and Women*, Harmondsworth: Penguin Books.

Blum, Lawrence (1980) *Friendship, Altruism and Morality*, Boston: Routledge and Kegan Paul.

Bugbee, Henry (1999) *The Inward Morning: A Philosophical Exploration in Journal Form*, Atlanta: University of Georgia Press.

Bury, J. B. (1987) *The Idea of Progress*, New York: Dover Publications.

Campbell, Keith (1990) *Abstract Particulars*, Cambridge, MA and Oxford: Blackwell Publishers.

——(1993) "David Armstrong and Realism about Colour," in J. Bacon, K. Campbell, and L. Reinhardt (eds) *Ontology, Causality, and Mind: Essays in Honour of D. M. Armstrong*, Cambridge: Cambridge University Press.

Castells, Manuel (1997) *The Power of Identity*, Cambridge, MA: Blackwell Publishers.

Chakrabarty, Dipesh (1992) "Postcoloniality and the Artifice of History: Who Speaks for 'Indian' Pasts?," *Representations* 37/25.

Choi, Chungmoo (ed.) (1997) *positions: east asia culture critique* 5/1.

Chow, Esther Ngan-Ling (1993) "The Feminist Movement: Where are All the Asian American Women?," in A. Jagger and P. Rothengberg (eds) *Feminist Frameworks: Alternative Theoretical Accounts of the Relations between Women and Men*, 3rd edn, New York: McCraw-Hill.

Churchill, Ward (1997) *A Little Matter of Genocide: Holocaust and Denial in the Americas, 1492 to the Present*, San Francisco: City Lights Books.

Code, Lorraine (1995) *Rhetorical Spaces: Essays on Gendered Locations*, New York: Routledge.

Cornford, F. M. (1991) *From Religion to Philosophy*, Princeton: Princeton University Press.

Davis, Angela (1974) *Angela Davis: An Autobiography*, New York: International Publishers.

——(1981) *Women, Race and Class*, New York: Random House.

——(1989) *Women, Culture and Politics*, New York: Random House.

——(1998) *Blues Legacies and Black Feminism: Gertrude "Ma" Rainey, Bessie Smith and Billie Holiday*, New York: Pantheon Books.

Davis, F. James (1991) *Who is Black?*, University Park, PA: Pennsylvania State University.

Deloria, Vine, Jr. (1997) *Red Earth, White Lies: Native American and the Myth of Scientific Fact*, Golden, CO: Fulcrum Publishing.

Descartes, René (1973) *Philosophical Works of Descartes*, trans. E. S. Haldane and G. R. T. Ross, 2 vols, Cambridge: Cambridge University Press.

——(1991) *The Philosophical Writings of Descartes*, trans. John Cottingham, Robert Stoothoff, Dugald Murdock, and Anthony Kenny, 3 vols, Cambridge: Cambridge University Press.

DuBois, W. E. B. (1995) *The Souls of Black Folk*, New York: Signet Classic/ Penguin Books.

Dussel, Enrique (1995) *The Invention of the Americas: Eclipse of "the Other" and the Myth of Modernity*, trans. Michael Barber, New York: Continuum.

——(1996) *The Underside of Modernity*, trans. and ed. Eduardo Mendieta, Atlantic Highlands, NJ: Humanities Press.

Elgin, Catherine (1996) *Considered Judgement*, Princeton: Princeton University Press.

Elster, Jon (1998) *Deliberative Democracy*, Cambrige: Cambridge University Press.

Epictetus (1956) *Enchiridion*, trans. George Long, Chicago: Henry Regnery.

——(1966) *Enchiridion*, trans. P. E. Matheson, in Jason L. Saunders (ed.) *Greek and Roman Philosophy after Aristotle*, New York: Free Press.

Eskridge, William (1996) *The Case for Same-Sex Marriage*, New York: Free Press.

Fanon, Frantz (1963) *Black Skins, White Masks*, New York: Grove.

Feenberg, Andrew (1995) *Alternative Modernity: The Technical Turn in Philosophy and Social Theory*, Berkeley: University of California Press.

Feenberg, Andrew and Arisaka, Yoko (1990) "Experiential Ontology: The Origins of the Nishida Philosophy in the Doctrine of Pure Experience," *International Philosophical Quarterly* 30/2.

Feinberg, Joel (1984) *Harm to Others*, New York: Oxford University Press.

Fernández Retamar, Roberto (1989) *Caliban and Other Essays*, Minneapolis: University of Minnesota Press.

Fish, Stanley (1998) "Boutique Multiculturalism," in A. Melzer, J. Weinberger, and M. R. Zinman (eds), *Multiculturalism and American Democracy*, Lawrence: University of Kansas Press.

Flanagan, Owen (1995) "Deconstructing Dreams: The Spandrels of Sleep," *Journal of Philosophy* 92/1 (January).

Foucault, Michel (1975) *The Birth of the Clinic: An Archaeology of Medical Perception*, trans. A. M. Sheridan Smith, New York: Vintage Books.

——(1982) *The Archaeology of Knowledge*, trans. A. M. Sheridan Smith, New York: Pantheon.

Fowler, David (1987) *Northern Attitudes Towards Interracial Marriage*, New York: Garland Press.

Frankfort, H. G. (1970) *Demons, Dreamers and Madmen: The Defense of Reason in Descartes' Meditations*, New York: Bobbs-Merrill.

Fujimura-Fanselow, K. and Kameda, A. (eds) (1995) *Japanese Women: New Feminist Perspectives on the Past, Present, and Future*, New York: Feminist Press.

Gadamer, Hans-Georg (1989) *Truth and Method*, trans. Joel Weinsheimer and Donald G. Marshall, 2nd rev. edn, New York: Crossroad.

Galison, P. and Stump, D. (eds) (1996) *The Disunity of Science: Boundaries, Contexts, and Power*, Stanford: Stanford University Press.

García Canclini, Néstor (1995) *Hybrid Cultures: Strategies for Entering and Leaving Modernity*, trans. Christopher L. Chiappari and Silvia L. López, Minneapolis: University of Minnesota Press.

Goldman, Alvin (1987) "Cognitive Science and Metaphysics," *Journal of Philosophy* 84.

Goodman, Nelson and Quine, W. V. (1972) "Steps Toward a Constructive Nominalism," in N. Goodman, *Problems and Projects*, Indianapolis: Bobbs-Merrill.

Graham, Lawrence Otis (1999) *Our Kind of People: Inside America's Black Upper Class*, New York: Harper Collins.

Grewal, Inderpal, and Kaplan, Caren (eds) (1994) *Scattered Hegemonies: Postmodernity and Transnational Feminist Practices*, Minneapolis: University of Minnesota Press.

Grinde, Donald A. and Johansen, Bruce E. (1995) *Ecocide of Native America: Environmental Destruction of Indian Lands and Peoples*, Santa Fe: Clear Light Publishers.

Gutman, Amy and Thompson, Dennis (1996) *Democracy and Disagreement*, Cambridge, MA.: Harvard University Press.

Hampshire, Stuart (1987) "Liberator, Up to a Point," *New York Review of Books* 34/5 (March).

Hanna, Robert (1992) "Descartes and Dream Skepticism Revisited," *Journal of the History of Philosophy* 30 (July).

Hardin, C. L. (1988) *Color for Philosophers*, Indianapolis: Hackett.

Harding, Sandra (1986) *The Science Question in Feminism*, Ithaca: Cornell University Press.

——(1991) *Whose Science? Whose Knowledge?* Ithaca: Cornell University Press.

——(1998) *Is Science Multicultural?*, Bloomington: Indiana University Press.

Hart, H. L. A. (1968) *Punishment and Responsibility*, New York: Oxford University Press.

Haygood, Wil (1998) "Keeping the Faith," *American Legacy* 3/4 (Winter).

Hicks, George (1997) *The Comfort Women: Japan's Brutal Regime of Enforced Prostitution in the Second World War*, New York: W. W. Norton.

Higginbotham, A. Leon (1978) *In the Matter of Color: Race and the American Legal Process*, New York: Oxford University Press.

Hoagland, Sarah Lucia (1995) "Moral Revolution: From Antagonism to Cooperation," in Nancy Tuana and Rosemary Tong (eds) *Feminism and Philosophy: Essential Readings in Theory, Reinterpretation, and Application*, Boulder: Westview Press.

Hobbes, Thomas (1977) *Leviathan*, ed. Michael Oakeshott, New York: Collier.

Hooker, Michael (ed.) (1978) *Descartes: Critical and Interpretive Essays*, Baltimore: Johns Hopkins University Press.

hooks, bell (1984) *Feminist Theory: From Margin to Center*, Boston: South End Press.

Hume, David (1955) *An Inquiry Concerning Human Understanding*, ed. Charles W. Hendel, Indianapolis: Library of Liberal Arts Press.
——(1978) *A Treatise of Human Nature*, ed. L. A. Selby-Bigge, Oxford: Clarendon Press.
——(1984) *An Enquiry Concerning Human Understanding*, ed. Eric Steinberg, Indianapolis: Hackett.
Hutcheson, Francis (1971) *Illustrations of the Moral Sense*, Cambridge, MA.: Harvard University Press.
Imamura, Anne (ed.) (1996) *Re-Imaging Japanese Women*, Berkeley: University of California Press.
Irigaray, Luce (1993) *An Ethics of Sexual Difference*, Ithaca: Cornell University Press.
Iwao, Sumiko (1993) *The Japanese Woman: Traditional Image and Changing Reality*, Cambridge, MA.: Harvard University Press.
Jaimes, M. Annette (ed.) (1992) *The State of Native America: Genocide, Colonization, and Resistance*, Boston: South End Press.
Jaschok, Maria and Miers, Susanne (eds) (1994) *Women and Chinese Patriarchy: Submission, Servitude and Escape*, New York: Zed Books and Hong Kong University Press.
Keynes, John Maynard (1949) "My Early Beliefs," in *Two Memoirs*, New York: Augustus M. Kelley.
Kim, David (1999) "Contempt and Ordinary Inequality," in Susan Babbitt and Sue Campbell (eds) *Philosophy and Racism*, Ithaca: Cornell University Press.
——(forthcoming) "Asian American Identities," in Linda Martín Alcoff (ed.) *Constellations*.
Kristeva, Julia (1986) *About Chinese Women*, New York: Marion Boyars.
——(1986) "Women's Time," in Toril Moi (ed.) *The Kristeva Reader*, New York: Columbia University Press.
——(1991) *Strangers to Ourselves*, trans. Leon S. Roudiez, New York: Columbia University Press.
Kymlica, Will (1995) *Multicultural Citizenship*, New York: Oxford University Press.
LaBerge, Stephen (1990) *Lucid Dreaming*, New York: Burges.
Leibniz, G. W. (1981) *New Essays on Human Understanding*, trans. and ed. P. Remnant and J. Bennett, New York: Cambridge University Press.
——(1994) *Writings on China*, trans. D. Cook and H. Rosemont, Chicago: Open Court.
Levinas, Emmanuel (1979) *Totality and Infinity*, Boston: Martinus Nijhoff.
Lorde, Audre (1984) "The Master's Tools Will Never Dismantle the Master's House," *Sister Outsider*, New York: Crossing Press Feminist Series.
Lott, Tommy L. (1997) "DuBois on the Invention of Race," in John P. Pittman

(ed.) *African-American Perspectives and Philosophical Traditions*, New York: Routledge.

Loy, David (1993) "Transcending East and West," *Man and World* 26/4.

Lugones, Maria and Spelman, Elizabeth (1995) "Have We Got a Theory for You! Feminist Theory, Cultural Imperialism and the Demand for 'The Woman's Voice,'" in Nancy Tuana and Rosemary Tong (eds) *Feminism and Philosophy: Essential Readings in Theory, Reinterpretation, and Application*, Boulder: Westview Press.

Lyotard, Jean François (1984) *The Postmodern Condition: A Report on Knowledge*, trans. Geoff Bennington and Brian Massumi, Minneapolis: University of Minnesota Press.

Mihesuah, Devon A. (1996) *American Indians: Stereotypes and Realities*, Atlanta: Clarity Press.

Mills, Charles (1997) *The Racial Contract*, Ithaca: Cornell University Press.

——(1998) *Blackness Visible: Essays on Philosophy and Race*, Ithaca: Cornell University Press.

Minh-ha, Trinh T. (1989) *Woman, Native, Other: Writing Postcoloniality and Feminism*, Bloomington: Indiana University Press.

Mohanty, Chandra (1991) "Introduction: Cartographies of Struggle," in C. Mohanty, A. Russo, and L. Torres (eds) *Third World Women and the Politics of Feminism*, Bloomington: Indiana University Press.

Mohanty, Satya (1997) *Literary Theory and the Claims of History: Postmodernism, Objectivity, Multicultural Politics*, Ithaca: Cornell University Press.

Montaigne, Michel de (no date) *Essays*, trans. Charles Cotton, London: A. L. Burt Co.

Nagel, Thomas (1975) *The Possibility of Altruism*, Oxford: Oxford University Press.

Narayan, Uma (1997) *Dislocating Cultures: Identities, Traditions, and Third World Feminism*, New York: Routledge.

Olea, Raquel (1995) "Feminism: Modern or Postmodern?," in John Beverley et al. (eds) *The Postmodern Debate in Latin America*, Durham: Duke University Press.

Ortega y Gasset, José (1932) *The Revolt of the Masses*, New York: W. W. Norton.

Peterson, Robert (1970) *Only the Ball was White: A History of Legendary Black Players and All Black Professional Teams*, New York: Oxford University Press.

Philips, Stephen (1995) *Classical Indian Metaphysics*, Chicago: Open Court.

Pinker, Stephen and Bloom, Paul (1990) "Natural Language and Natural Selection," *Behavioral and Brain Sciences* 13.

Plato (1959) *Timaeus*, trans. Francis M. Cornford, New York: Bobbs-Merrill.

Prakash, Gyan (1990) "Writing Post-colonialist Histories of the Third World: Perspectives from Indian Historiography," *Comparative Studies in Society and History* 32.

Price, H. H. (1969) *Belief*, New York: Humanities Press.

Quine, W. V. (1980) "On What There Is," in *From a Logical Point of View*, Cambridge, MA: Harvard University Press.

Radhakrishnan, Sarvepalli and Moore, Charles (1971) *A Sourcebook in Indian Philosophy*, Princeton: Princeton University Press.

Ragland-Sullivan, Ellie (1987) *Jacques Lacan and the Philosophy of Psychoanalysis*, Urbana, IL: University of Illinois Press.

Rajchman, John (ed.) (1995) *The Identity in Question*, New York: Routledge.

Reid, Thomas (1983) *Inquiry and Essays*, ed. R. E. Beanblossom and K. Lehrer, Indianapolis: Hackett.

Rey, Georges (1995) "Towards a Projectivist Account of Conscious Experience," in T. Metzinger (ed.) *Conscious Experience*, Imprint Academic, Paderborn, Germany: Schoningh.

Rhodes, Robert W. (1994) *Nurturing Learning in Native American Students*, Hotevilla: Sonwai Books.

Richard, Nelly (1993) "The Latin American Problematic of Theoretical-Cultural Transference: Postmodern Appropriations and Counterappropriations," *South Atlantic Quarterly* 92/3.

——(1996) "Feminismo, experiencia y representación," *Revista Iberoamericana* 62/176–7.

Ross, Sir David (1938) *The Right and the Good*, Oxford: Clarendon Press.

Ross, James (1975) "Testimonial Evidence," in Keith Lehrer (ed.) *Analysis and Metaphysics: Essays in Honor of R. M. Chisholm*, Dordrecht: Reidel.

Sagar, Aparajita (1996) "Postcolonial Studies," in Michael Payne (ed.) *A Dictionary of Cultural and Critical Theory*, Cambridge, MA: Blackwell Publishers.

Said, Edward (1978) *Orientalism*, New York: Routledge.

Samsom, G. B. (1984) *The Western World and Japan*, Tokyo: Charles Tuttle Co.

Schmitt, Frederick (1994) *Socializing Epistemology: The Social Dimensions of Knowledge*, Lanham, MD: Rowman and Littlefield.

Schutte, Ofelia (1993) *Cultural Identity and Social Liberation in Latin American Thought*, Albany, NY: SUNY Press.

Shaftesbury, Lord (1969) "Selections," in D. D. Raphael (ed.) *The British Moralists: 1650–1800*, vol. 1, Oxford: Clarendon Press.

Shapin, Steven (1994) *A Social History of Truth: Civility and Science in Seventeenth Century England*, Chicago: University of Chicago Press.

Shrage, Laurie (1994) *Moral Dilemmas of Feminism: Prostitution, Adultery, and Abortion*, New York: Routledge.

Sosa, Ernest (1991) *Knowledge in Perspective: Selected Essays in Epistemology*, New York: Cambridge University Press.

South Atlantic Quarterly. 92/3 (1993).

Spivak, Gayatri Chakravorty (1990) *The Post-Colonial Critic*, ed. Sarah Harasym, New York: Routledge.

——(1993) *Outside in the Teaching Machine*, New York: Routledge.

Stebba, Gregor (1987) *The Dream of Descartes*, ed. Richard A. Watson, Carbondale and Edwardsville: Southern Illinois University Press.

Sugiyama Lebra, Takie (1984) *Japanese Women: Constraint and Fulfillment*, Honolulu: University of Hawaii Press.

Thornton, Russell (1987) *American Indian Holocaust and Survival: A Population History Since 1492*, Norman: University of Oklahoma Press.

Toulmin, Stephen and Goodfield, June (1982) *The Discovery of Time*, Chicago: University of Chicago Press.

Tuana, Nancy (1992) *Woman and the History of Philosophy*, New York: Paragon Issues in Philosophy.

Tuana, Nancy and Tong, Rosemary (eds) (1995) *Feminism and Philosophy: Essential Readings in Theory, Reinterpretation, and Application*, Boulder: Westview Press.

Tygiel, Jules (1983) *Baseball's Great Experiment: Jackie Robinson and his Legacy*, New York: Vintage Press.

Wellman, C. (1997) "Associative Allegiances an Political Obligations," *Social Theory and Practice* 23/2 (Summer).

West, Cornel (1993) *Race Matters*, Boston: Beacon Press.

Whorf, Benjamin Lee (1956) *Language, Thought, and Reality*, ed. John B. Carroll, Cambridge, MA: MIT Press.

Williams, Bernard (1978) *Descartes: The Project of Pure Inquiry*, New York: Penguin Books.

Williams, Patricia (1997) *Seeing a Color-Blind-Future: The Paradox of Race*, New York: Noonday Press.

Williams, Robert A., Jr. (1997) *Linking Arms Together: American Indian Treaty Visions of Law and Peace, 1600–1800*, New York: Oxford University Press.

Wittgenstein, Ludwig (1969) *On Certainty*, ed. G. E. M. Anscombe and G. H. von Wright, New York: Harper & Row.

——(1979) "Notes on Frazer's *Golden Bough*," in C. G. Luckhardt (ed.) *Wittgenstein: Sources and Perspectives*, Ithaca: Cornell University Press.

——(1989) *Philosophical Investigations*, ed. G. E. M. Anscombe, New York: Macmillan.

Wolf, Susan (1982) "Moral Saints," *Journal of Philosophy* 79/8.

Young, Iris (1990) *Throwing Like a Girl*, Bloomington: Indiana University Press.

Young, Iris (1990) *Justice and the Politics of Difference*, Princeton: Princeton University Press.

Zack, Naomi (1993) *Race and Mixed Race*, Philadelphia: Temple University Press.

——(1997) "Race and Philosophic Meaning," in Naomi Zack (ed.) *Race/Sex*, New York: Routledge.

——(1998) *Thinking About Race*, Belmont: Wadsworth.

Index

dualism between new and traditional
in west, 230 n. 27

earth as Mother, 88
East Asia, colonialism within, 219
education of black intellectuals, 25
ego in sleep, 296
elders
  in black literature, 35
  respect for in philosophy, 111
Ellison, Ralph, 256
empirical truth, 290–3
engagement, as not part of academic
  inclusion, 224
Epictetus, 92, 95, 114
epistemic assessment, 239
epistemic credibility and social identity,
  241
epistemic relevance of social identities,
  244
epistemological judgment, relevance of
  social identity to, 240
epistemologies, standpoint, 250–1
epistemologists, feminist, 236
epistemology, testimonial knowledge
  and, 236–8
equality in rational dialogue, 110–11
ethical rules for dialogue, 97
ethics
  taxonomy of, 131
  universal feminist, 62–3
ethnic group, history and identity of,
  177
ethnicity, 3–4
Eurocentrism, 217–18
  critique of, 222–4
European character, 70–1
European consciousness in nineteenth
  century, 217
evil, ideas of, 75, 77
exoticism as non-European, 217
experience, 255–6

Fairchild, Halford, 190
fallacies of informal logic, 155–65, 236
false analogy (fallacy), 158–9
false cause (fallacy), 157–8

false compositions and divisions
  (fallacy), 163–4
false dichotomy (fallacy), 164–5
Fanon, Frantz, 67 n. 16
fatalism, 81
FBI and criminal status of black
  women, 149–50
female body, 48
femininity and Asian category, 215–16
feminism(s)
  agency and, 62–4
  confrontational model in, 225
  of difference, 67–8 n. 19
  universal ethics and, 62–3
  western, 59–60, 64–5
feminist epistemologists, 236
feminist ethics, 51–2
  negotiations in, 63
feminist theory
  black, 145–6
  postcolonial, 47
fiction as culturally representational,
  29–30
first principles, 290–3, 297
Fish, Stanley, 213
Flanagan, Owen, 294–5
FLK ("funny looking kids"), 239
folk ethics, 17
  and black–white intermarriage,
  182–3
  philosophy and, 184–5, 196–8
foreknowledges, horizons of, 243–4
Foucault, Michel, 19, 253–5
Franti, Michael, 149
free will and God, 79–82
Frege, Gottlob, 113
friendship, demands of morality and,
  119
Fu-Kiau, Kika Bunseki, 30

Gadamer, Hans-Georg, 238, 255–6
García Canclini, Néstor, 50
gaze, the, as source of cognition, 254
gender
  identity construction and, 243
  and national identity, 61
  of philosophers, 4–6

internal restrictions of groups, 170
interpretation and perception, 249
interpretation of signs, 162
Interrace (magazine), 201 n. 4
intersectionality of race, gender, and
    employment, 6
intuitionism, 108, 118–19

James, Joy, 10–11, 145
Japan
    culture in, 218
    western philosophy in, 229 n. 32
Jaschok, Maria, 233 n. 47
Jesus, 75–6
Jewish people, history and identity of,
    177
Jewish–white intermarriage, 184
jobs in philosophy, 108–10
jury diversity and social identity,
    235–6, 258–9

Kant, Immanuel, 69, 90, 98, 126
    on "the dear self," 100
Kantian moral philosophy, 125
Keynes, John Maynard, 99–100
knowledge, 268
    intergenerational, 26
Kristeva, Julia, 47, 50
Kymlicka, Will, 170

labor, bonded, 62
Latin American identity, 44–5
Latina identity in US, 52–5
Latina women, race and, 3–4
Latinos in America, history and
    identity of, 177
laws and society, 76
Lee, Spike, 184
Lehrer, Keith, 237
Leibniz, G. W., 217
lesbian feminist writers, 51
Lewontin, Richard, 5
liberalism, communities and, 169–70
Lind, Michael, 199 n. 3
linguistic anthropology, 113
loans, consumption and, 62
logical positivism, 113

Loving v. *Virginia*, 16, 182–3, 186,
    198–9 n. 1
lucid dreaming, 282
Lyotard, Jean-François, 49

Madhyamika school, 222
magic, 28–9
mainstream philosophers, 1, 6–7
Marcuse, Herbert, 141, 143
marginality
    peripheral voices, 64
    in philosophy, 5–7
marginalization, triple, of Asian
    women, 225
Marxism, racism and, 138–9
materialism
    of west, 12
    western worldview and, 86–7
mathematical principles and awake–
    asleep distinction, 297
Mbiti, John, 28–9
McCarthy era, black activism and, 136
meaning, making and identity, 242
Melville, Herman, 39
memory, color and, 273–4
Merleau-Ponty, Maurice, 19, 251–5
mestiza self, 51
metaethics
    rationalism and, 121
    Socratic, 12–13, 116–21
metaphor, and racial identity, 3–4
metaphysics of science, 292
migration to and from the Americas,
    135
Million Man March, 146–7
Mills, Charles, 256–8
mind and soul, 72
Minh-ha, Trinh, 59
modern civilization as white, 218
Mohanty, Satya, 242, 255–6
Montaigne, Michel de, 85
Moore, G. E., 95, 99–100
moral communication, project of,
    117–18
moral obligations, 170–3
moral philosophers, Kantian, 125